Holy Wednesday

University of Pennsylvania Press
NEW CULTURAL STUDIES
Joan DeJean, Carroll Smith-Rosenberg,
Peter Stallybrass, and Gary Tomlinson,
Editors

The Spanish and Nahuatl texts translated in this volume
have been published in an electronic supplement.
Further information and an order form appear on p. 315.

Holy Wednesday

A Nahua Drama from Early Colonial Mexico

Louise M. Burkhart

PENN

University of Pennsylvania Press

Philadelphia

Library of Congress Cataloging-in-Publication Data
Burkhart, Louise M., 1958–
   Holy Wednesday : a Nahua drama from early colonial Mexico /
Louise M. Burkhart.
      p.   cm. — (New cultural studies)
   Includes bibliographical references and index.
   ISBN 0-8122-3342-5 (alk. paper). — ISBN 0-8122-1576-1 (pbk. :
alk. paper)
   1. Nahuatl drama—History and criticism.   2. Religious drama,
Nahuatl—History and criticism.   3. Christian drama, Mexican—
History and criticism.   4. Ash Wednesday—Mexico.   5. Holy
Week—Mexico.   I. Title.   II. Series.
PM4068.7.B87   1996
897'.45—dc20   95-53129
                                                       CIP

To Clare

noconetzin, nochpochtzin,
nocozqui, noquetzal

my child, my daughter,
my jewel, my quetzal plume

Contents

Illustrations

Acknowledgments

THIS BOOK WAS WRITTEN with the support of a grant from the Translations Program of the National Endowment for the Humanities, an independent federal agency. A New Faculty Development Grant and a grant from the Faculty Research Awards Program at the University at Albany, State University of New York, also assisted this project. Earlier research that contributed to this study was supported by a fellowship from Dumbarton Oaks, National Endowment for the Humanities-funded fellowships at the John Carter Brown Library and the Newberry Library, the Doherty Foundation, and the American Philosophical Society. I am grateful to all of these institutions for their assistance.

Many individuals have contributed to this project. I would first like to thank Alfred L. Bush, who arranged the Princeton University Library's acquisition of the Holy Wednesday manuscript and also invited me to work with the text. David Szewczyk's initial research on the manuscript established its significance, approximate date, and history; I thank him for sharing with me the results of his analysis. After I identified the play's Spanish source, Mr. Bush and Willard King of Bryn Mawr College tracked down the two earliest extant editions of that play.

In addition, I am grateful to the following persons, all of whom offered information, suggestions, and/or encouragement through discussions at various stages of the project: Monica Barnes, Margot Beyersdorff, John Bierhorst, Elizabeth Boone, Willard Gingerich, Gary Gossen, William Hanks, Doris Heyden, Frances Karttunen, Susan Kellogg, Jorge Klor de Alva, Tim Knab, Miguel León-Portilla, James Lockhart, Barbara Mundy, Wayne Ruwet, Susan Schroeder, Librado Silva Galeana, Donald Skemer, Dennis Tedlock, and Richard Trexler. I apologize to anyone whose contribution I have overlooked, and of course I take full responsibility for the final content of this book.

I thank the following libraries for providing me with access to their rare book and manuscript collections: the Fondo Reservado of the Biblioteca Nacional de México, the Biblioteca Nacional de Antropología e Historia, the Benson Latin American Collection at the University of Texas at Austin, the Latin American Library at Tulane University, the library of the Hispanic Society of America in New York City, the John Carter Brown Library at Brown University, and the Princeton University Libraries.

Thanks also to Maurice Westmoreland for his collaboration on the translation of the Spanish play and his linguistic insights. I am grateful to Jerome Singerman of the University of Pennsylvania Press for his enthusiastic support of this project and his suggestions for organizing the manuscript. I also thank Ridley Hammer and Alison Anderson at the Press for their efficient editorial work. Finally, I thank my husband, Brian Ladd, for his careful reading of the manuscript and for being *nonecehuiliznetlaçotlatzin* 'my repose and love' (line 4N:4).

Scenario

ABOUT SEVENTY YEARS after the Spanish invasion of Mexico, a native scholar translated a Spanish religious drama into his own language, Nahuatl. Spoken by the various local ethnic groups known collectively as the Nahuas, the Nahuatl language had been the lingua franca of the Aztec empire and was now the principal indigenous language of the colony called New Spain. The work was intended for public performance by native actors, but its actual performance history is unknown. This book is a study of this Nahuatl play.

The Spanish drama on which the Nahuatl play was based is called *Lucero de Nuestra Salvación*, or "Beacon of Our Salvation." *Lucero* may also be translated as "star" or "morning star." The term designates the dramatized events as chronological forerunners or initiators of salvation, comparable to the morning star's heralding of the coming day, and also as a guide or inspiration which may act, like a guiding star or a beacon, to lead one toward salvation.

Authored by a Valencian bookseller named Ausías Izquierdo Zebrero, the drama was probably first published in the early 1580s. Izquierdo dramatized Jesus Christ's conversation with the Virgin Mary prior to his arrest and crucifixion, a farewell scene called the *despedimiento*, or leave-taking, in Spanish art and literature of the Passion (the torment and execution of Christ). Izquierdo drew on the popular literary tradition of the *planctus*, or complaint, in which the Virgin suffers along with her son as he is tortured and killed. His work is rich in allusions to the events of the Passion and its redemptive purpose.

Izquierdo also incorporated the theme of the harrowing of hell, Christ's descent into the underworld—accomplished on Holy Saturday while his body lay in the sepulcher—to liberate from Limbo the souls of the dead who were to share in the salvation of humanity. These were the morally deserving figures of antiquity, those of Old Testament generations who despite assorted sins had been followers of God, with the addition of more recently deceased personages such as Saint Joseph and Saint John the Baptist. In the play, an angel interrupts the mother-son dialogue to bring letters from the Old Testament characters Adam, David, Moses, Jeremiah, and Abraham, inmates of Limbo who were anxiously awaiting Christ's arrival. Each of these correspondents presents Mary with one of the implements that will be used in the torture and death of her son: the cross, the crown of thorns, the three nails, the column and rope used in Christ's flagellation, and the lance that will pierce his side. The reading of these letters is followed by a second, shorter dialogue between mother and son.

The Nahua scholar adapted Izquierdo's work for performance in Nahuatl, making many additions and changes to the content of the Spanish original. To the material modeled on the Spanish source the scholar added four additional speeches at the end of his play, two for Mary and two for Christ. Someone then copied this Nahuatl text into a collection of miscellaneous preaching materials compiled by a Franciscan friar. This transcription dates to about the year 1591. Neither the scribe nor the friar left any clue as to the drama's author, source, or performance history, apart from the simple label *miercoles santo*, or "Holy Wednesday." This label refers to the setting of the drama's action on the Wednesday before Christ's crucifixion. It also indicates that the play was, or was intended to be, performed on Wednesday of Holy Week.

The manuscript was kept for a time at the Franciscan college in Tlatelolco, the northern sector of Mexico City, and bears a library brand from that establishment. It also bears an eighteenth-century brand from the Franciscan Convento de San Pedro y San Pablo de Santiago Calimaya, also in Mexico City.[1]

In 1869 the manuscript was sold by the London auctioneers Puttick & Simpson as part of the Fischer sale, an auction of nearly 3000 rare New World manuscripts and imprints, most of them from Mexico. Agustín Fischer (1825–1887) was a German Lutheran who moved to Mexico, converted to Catholicism, and was ordained as a priest. He became a confidante of the Emperor Maximilian, as well as a noted bibliophile. After Maximilian was deposed in 1867, Fischer engineered the exodus from Mexico not only of the items auctioned in London but of another large collection sold in Leipzig in 1869.[2]

After leaving Mexico, the manuscript spent more than a century in the collections of three European noblemen. The catalog of the Fischer sale lists the manuscript as item 1933, "An Anonymous Collection of Sermons in the Mexican Language." It was sold for 3 pounds, 10 shillings to a Mr. Cole, agent for the British collector Sir Thomas Phillipps. The catalog of Phillipps's massive collection lists the manuscript as item 21298, "Sermons in Spanish & Mexican." The manuscript was sold at Sotheby's in 1919 and entered Sir R. Leiester Harmsworth's collection, which in turn was sold at Sotheby's in 1948. It later belonged to Florencio Gavito, Spanish viscount of Alborada and Villarubio, whose bookplate remains in the manuscript.[3] Meanwhile, the drama within it lay unrecognized and uncatalogued as several generations of scholars searched out, studied, and published the few other early Nahuatl dramas that had come to light.

In 1986 the manuscript again went on the market. This time it came into the hands of a dealer with expertise in Nahuatl documents, David Szewczyk of the Philadelphia Rare Books and Manuscripts Company. Szewczyk recognized the drama for what it was and realized its significance as the only known sixteenth-century manuscript of a Nahuatl play. The Philadelphia Rare Books and Manuscripts Company teamed up with the William Reese Company of New Haven, Connecticut, to offer the text for sale. Alfred L. Bush, Curator of the Princeton Collections of Western Americana, became interested in acquiring the manuscript for that collection. With the generous assistance of Mrs. Charles W. Engelhard, the Princeton University Library was able to make this acquisition. The text is now safely ensconced among other rare texts in Native American languages in the Princeton Collections of Western Americana.

This Nahuatl drama is the earliest known extant script of a play in Nahuatl—or any other Native American language. It belongs to a genre of theatrical performances born of the encounter between the Nahuas of central Mexico and their Franciscan evangelizers. More specifically, the relevant encounter was between the friars and the young boys of the native nobility whom they took as students. The first three Franciscans to reach Mexico arrived in 1523; a party of twelve came in 1524 to set up the first official mission. By the early 1530s, Nahua neophytes were performing public dramas in Nahuatl on Christian themes.

Although drama came to be used widely in the emerging Nahua Church, no Nahuatl dramatic scripts issued from the colonial printing presses. Nor do the many manuscript compilations of sermons, orations, scripture readings, saints' lives, miracle narratives, and other devotional genres surviving from the sixteenth and early seventeenth centuries contain any hand-written scripts—with the exception of the manuscript now at Princeton. One early seventeenth-century script has been published; the original manuscript is lost. Five other scripts that may be copies—or at least versions—of sixteenth-century originals are known from manuscripts of the seventeenth and eighteenth centuries. A Nahuatl translation of three Spanish plays, made under Jesuit auspices around 1641, also survives, as do some later colonial compositions.

Apparently, play scripts were an ephemeral genre, passed from hand to hand, used and then lost or discarded, perhaps more likely to reside in the homes of native composers and performers than on the friars' library shelves. The serendipitous discovery of the Holy Wednesday drama is thus a major event in the recovery of early Native American written literature.

Written scripts may have been ephemeral, but theater was an important performance genre. It was indigenous people who performed the dramas, playing the parts of sacred beings and interpreting Christian narratives for their fellow Nahuas. This was a very different mode of behavior from passively listening to a priest's homilies or uttering prayers in home or chapel. Theater engages two realities simultaneously: the pretend world of the characters and script, which in religious theater mirrors a world of gods and saints who to the believers are very real, and the everyday world beyond the stage, from which actors and audience are partially and fleetingly removed. Juxtaposed in this way, these two realities cannot help but enter into a dialectical relationship: the world within the theatrical frame is seen in terms of the world outside, and vice versa. As Victor Turner states, ritual and theatrical performances "act as a reflexive metacommentary on the life of their times, feeding on it and assigning meaning to its decisive public and cumulative private events" (in Schechner 1985:xii). The audiences of colonial Nahuatl plays surely interpreted what they saw not only with respect to the imported Christian stories but also with respect to their own lives and the events of their time.

Imported into Mexico, Izquierdo's pious play became a colonial discourse: to its original functions in reference to Spanish religious practice was added the new function of furthering the Spanish domination of the Nahuas and their conversion into religious and moral actors in the friars' mode (Klor de Alva 1989:144; 1992:339). But once it was adapted by its native interpreter, it was rendered culturally ambivalent; its hybridized discourse carries multiple levels of meaning (Hanks 1986). It may be read as a colonial discourse or as a nativist one. It is both a translation of its source and a commentary on it, a rendering of Christian teachings into

Nahuatl and an adjustment of those teachings to the local situation. Its alterations and elaborations, by revealing what the Nahua author accepted and what he saw as inadequate or inappropriate for his purposes, constitute a cultural critique of the Spanish model, and through it of Spanish culture and Christianity more generally. He plays the role of critic as well as that of interpreter.

Situations of colonial rule call forth from the conquered many different responses. Simple formulas that contrast domination and absorption with resistance and survival hardly capture the complexities of the relationship between conqueror and conquered, which Comaroff and Comaroff (1992:236) characterize as an ongoing process of "challenge and riposte." Scott (1990) distinguishes between "public transcripts" and "hidden transcripts." Within a public context, subordinated people can voice protest only in a masked or otherwise indirect manner. Hidden transcripts, the private discourses and actions in which resistance is expressed more openly, only rarely find their way into the historical record. To recover the forms of "riposte" encoded within the public transcript, one must be sensitive to the presence of muted messages; one must also realize that these messages may be only the tip of a concealed iceberg of counter-hegemonic formulations.

Even when resistance speaks in a soft voice, hardly questioning the hegemony of the conqueror, it may yet foment modes of historical and cultural consciousness through which the conquered may invent new identities for themselves and even undermine dominant ideologies. Indigenous interpretations of Christian concepts subvert the Church's doctrinal authority: a refusal to practice Christianity quite in the European mode implies that there is something unsatisfactory, even inferior, about the European version.

At the same time, the adoption of Christian concepts, even in changed form, constitutes "an implicit, if muted, critique of native modes of explanation and ritual action" (Brown 1991:401). The task of reproducing native culture in a colonial situation sometimes demands the abandonment of precolonial cultural patterns in favor of new patterns based upon native constructions of the colonizers' culture. But these *are* native constructions, never precise reproductions of their foreign models. In such formulations, the boundaries between what is indigenous and what is European become, as Rabasa notes (1993:73), "difficult if not dangerous to draw," for they cannot be reduced to a syncretic blending of fundamentally and identifiably native and Christian elements.

There are many strategies through which the conquered may negotiate their relationship to the dominant culture. Clifford (1988:338) suggests "appropriation, compromise, subversion, masking, invention, and revival." Change need not result in assimilation, absorption, acculturation—provided the colonized continue to define themselves in opposition to the conqueror.

The Holy Wednesday drama is an appropriation of a Spanish Christian discourse into Nahua terms. Intended for public performance, its language accessible to many friars and other Nahuatl-speaking non-Nahuas, it is a public transcript; hence it could not openly challenge prevailing colonial discourses. In some respects it strikes a compromise with its source; in others it subverts its source's message and masks its own messages behind the façade of legitimacy furnished by the act of "translation." It puts forth a conception of history offered neither by the teachings of the evangelizing friars nor by "traditional" Nahua beliefs, but based on a creative fusion of both.

The author of the drama, whose precise identity remains unknown, was undoubtedly a pious Christian educated by Franciscan friars, reasonably literate in Spanish, and possessing considerable knowledge about things of the Church. He was someone the friars trusted to produce doctrinally sound transcriptions of Christian texts. He is hardly a person one could expect to formulate an anti-imperialist manifesto. And precisely for that reason, his work demands close scrutiny. His riposte to the challenge offered by his Spanish source is subtle and spoken in a soft voice. His recasting of a Spanish text reveals how distant from European conceptions and sensibilities even the most Christianizing[4] Nahua mind could be. It reveals that a Nahua author could produce Christian oratory—indeed, masterfully crafted oral poetry—that while in no way challenging Christ's supremacy nevertheless edits Christ's mission and message for presentation to a Nahua audience.

The present study is a close scrutiny of the Holy Wednesday drama. I examine its relationship to its Spanish source and to other Nahuatl texts. I also consider, as precisely and fully as possible in the scope of a single monograph, the historical moment from which the drama comes. This information and the comparative materials serve not simply as background or "context" for the "text" but must be considered an integral part of any reading of this document that, from a distance of four centuries and through the barriers of linguistic and cultural difference, I may presume to make.

Treating context as partially constitutive of the text itself, an interpretive strategy that Hanks (1989:106–7) calls "centering" the text, serves not only to compensate for the incompleteness and indeterminacy of any text considered in the abstract. To deal adequately in a work of cultural interpretation with issues of both poetics and power—and to reveal the capacity of poetry to empower, to alter, however subtly, the construction of power relations—demands just such close attention to a text's historical situation.

Ethnographic studies have shown that various indigenous peoples of Mesoamerica have appropriated the story of Christ's death and resurrection as a vehicle for conveying their own concerns (Reyes García 1960; Bricker 1981; Gossen 1986; Nash 1968). In Nash's words (1968:326), "In the Passion Play, the Indians have found a means of expressing what they want to say about their world in a form given to them by their conquerors." Ancient mythological themes are recreated in the identification of Christ with the sun and his enemies with the inhabitants of previous epochs of creation. At the same time, an appropriation of Christian moral dualism is evident in the association of the sun's enemies and the past ages with evil, sometimes personified as devils. And the native groups' status as besieged ethnic minorities within the larger mestizo or Ladino population is also represented: the Sun-Christ's enemies are given attributes of mestizos, foreign invaders, or other non-native personages. In the Tzotzil Maya community of Chamula, the annual Festival of Games is a version of the Passion in which Chamula itself, the center of the present moral order, is symbolically destroyed by forces from beyond its borders and before its time. It is then recreated and redeemed through the rebirth of the Sun-Christ (Gossen 1986).

The surviving indigenous peoples of Mesoamerica have had over four centuries in which to convert Christ into their defender and his enemies into their own oppressors. Alienated from the centers of power and often ignored even by the priests assigned to their communities, it is not surprising that they today possess such thoroughly indigenized understandings of Christianity's central narrative. They have fulfilled in their own terms the Passion story's universal potential for dramatizing a people's consciousness of powerlessness (Mitchell 1990:73–74).

But even in the Holy Wednesday play, a written text based directly on a Spanish source and produced under Franciscan supervision, may be found traces of some of the same themes that are salient for indigenous people today. The drama exemplifies an earlier phase of a process of accommodation and appropriation of Spanish Catholic cultural forms that continues into the present. The solutions worked out in the sixteenth century by those native people who were able to gain relatively free access to, and control over, Christian discourses established patterns to which their successors, who rarely had such direct access to the foreign materials, tended to adhere.

* * *

Chapter One discusses Izquierdo Zebrero's Spanish play and the literary and devotional traditions it represents. I do not venture to analyze in detail the social, ideological, or psychological correlates of any of these Old World developments. My purpose in this chapter is simply to provide the reader with a solid grasp of where the Spanish drama is "coming from" in terms of its religious content and literary form.

The second chapter introduces the Nahuatl play and examines questions of authorship, performance, and style. It also surveys the social and political situation of the native people in urban central Mexico at the time of the drama's redaction.

Chapter Three presents summary comments on some of the changes made by the Nahua playwright and their possible significance.

In Chapter Four the English translations of the two plays appear in facing-page format. The translation of the Spanish play was done with the collaboration of Maurice Westmoreland of the Department of Hispanic and Italian Studies, The University at Albany, State University of New York. Westmoreland is a specialist in Spanish historical linguistics and Spanish literature of the late Middle Ages and Golden Age.

The plays are followed by a stanza-by-stanza commentary comparing the two texts, tracing the development of the Nahua playwright's treatment of his source, and comparing the play to a number of other Nahuatl texts. Then, in the Appendix, translations of several longer text excerpts are presented. These comparative materials yield clues to the wider universe of Nahua-Christian discourse within which the Holy Wednesday drama was situated, showing what people were accustomed to hearing and saying about the Christian concepts and motifs that appear in the play.

Many of the illustrations in this book are drawn from sixteenth-century Nahuatl imprints and from works of art created by native artists for the adornment of churches, churchyards, and friaries. These relief sculptures and mural paintings were usually based on European woodcuts. Depictions such as these suggest how the playwright and his audience may have visualized persons and events that are represented or referred to in the play. They also would have provided models for the costuming of the drama's actors and the construction of props.

PART ONE

———

THE SETTING

I

Spain

Ausías Izquierdo Zebrero

LITTLE IS KNOWN ABOUT the author of the Spanish drama, except that he was a Valencian bookseller and a devotee of the Virgin Mary. Archival records in Valencia attest that Izquierdo was named a councilor of the parish of Santa Cruz in 1585. He dictated his last will and testament on September 20, 1596 (Martí Grajales 1927:281). An Izquierdo alluded to in a work by the great Spanish dramatist Lope de Vega may be this Valencian author (Barrera y Leirado 1860:196–97; Pérez Gómez 1976–77:505–6).

Izquierdo's earliest recorded publishing venture is a work of 1566 entitled *Relox de Namorados*, a collection of songs by diverse authors including some of his own works. After Izquierdo and a brother of his experienced what they believed was a miracle wrought by Our Lady of Puig, Valencia's principal Marian advocation, Izquierdo wrote a history of the Puig shrine, which was published in 1575. Bibliographers also list a *Quaderno espiritual* of 1577, containing eight poems about the Passion of Christ, and a 1589 play dramatizing a miracle of the Virgin of the Rosary. All these works were printed in Valencia (Ximeno 1747:I, 187; Barrera y Leirado 1860:196–97; Martí Grajales 1927:281).

The drama called *Lucero de Nuestra Salvación*, or "Beacon of Our Salvation," appears to be Izquierdo's only work to break out of the local Valencian press and to undergo several reprintings. Its publication record is somewhat confused and incomplete. The earliest edition may have been issued in Seville in 1582, but it seems that no one has laid eyes on this imprint for many years. In 1860, Barrera y Leirado catalogued an edition bearing the name of Sevillian printer Fernando Maldonado and the date 1532 (1860:197). This date must be incorrect, according to Escudero y Perosso (1894:272), because Maldonado did not begin publishing until 1582. It is also inconsistent with the dates of Izquierdo's other works. Escudero y Perosso hazards the guess that his predecessor misread or misprinted 1582 as 1532; other scholars have followed his lead in assuming a 1582 first edition (Crawford 1967:141; Pérez Gómez 1976–77:501–2; Rouanet 1979:IV, 281; Méndez Bejarano 1922:I, 126).

An imprint lacking any statement of date or publisher exists in the Houghton Library at Harvard University, where it is provisionally catalogued as a Valencian edition of 1590. Despite its uncertain status, this imprint appears to be the earliest available extant version of the drama, and it is the one that I use in this study.[1]

The Houghton Library imprint of Izquierdo's play bears this introductory statement:

Auto called Beacon of our Salvation, which treats of the farewell that our Lord Jesus Christ took of his blessed mother being in Bethany, to go to Jerusalem, in which are contained very devout passages, and contemplative thoughts about the Passion of Christ, and about his blessed mother. Composed by Auzias Yzquierdo bookseller, and examined by the Reverend father Fray Hieronymo Ferrer Prior. Printed with permission.[2]

Below this text are two small woodcuts. One shows Mary being crowned by the Trinity; the other depicts the crucified Christ flanked by Mary and Saint John the Evangelist. The script of the play begins immediately below the woodcuts and is printed in two columns (Figure 1). It is 495 lines in length and is composed in *quintillas*, or five-line stanzas of rhymed verse, most of which follow an ABABA rhyme scheme.[3] The language employed in the play is Castilian with some dialect features of eastern Spain, the region of Valencia.[4]

The Houghton Library imprint is bound in a volume with sixteen other Spanish devotional texts. Those that bear dates of publication range in date from 1588 to 1596. The volume, which bears the bookplate of the Marquis of Stafford, was deposited with the Houghton Library by Mrs. Imrie de Vegh of New York City in 1964.[5]

The later publishing history of Izquierdo's drama is better known, thanks mainly to the efforts of Antonio Pérez Gómez. The earliest edition surviving in Spain's National Library is one issued in Cuenca in 1603. Pérez Gómez (1976–77:495–500) reprints this edition. In size, format, and content it is nearly identical to the Houghton Library version. There are some minor variations in wording, a few of which indicate that the Houghton

2

¶ Auto llamado Luzero de nues-

tra Saluacion, que trata el despedimiento que hizo nuestro Señor
Iesu Christo de su bendita madre estando en Bethania, para yr a
Hierusalen, en que se contienen passos muy deuotos, y razonamien
tos contemplatiuos de la passion de Christo, y de su bendita madre. Compuesto por Auzias. Yzquierdo librero, y examinado por
el Reuerendo padre Fray·Hieronymo Ferrer·Prior.
Con licencia impresso.

Christo.

M Adre de gran dignidad
hija del Padre diuino
Virgen llena de humildad
yr vn poco de camino
tengo gran necessidad.
Y aunque soy Dios soberano
vengo a vos con obediencia
como hijo en quato humano
suplico os me deys licencia,
Virgen sagrada, y la mano.
Mar. ¶ O mi hijo y bien sin par
assentaos, q me days pena,

q os quiero vn poco hablar
delante la Magdalena.
xpo. Que me plaze de escuchar.
Mar. Hijo mio muy querido
mi bien, mi Dios y reposo,
donde vays tan affligido
y vuestro rostro glorioso
hijo tan descolorido?
¶ Vuestros discipulos veo
muchasvezes suspirando
los hijos del Zebedeo
veo yr tambien llorando
y es algun mal segun creo.

1. The first page of Ausías Izquierdo Zebrero's "Beacon of Our Salvation." By permission of the Houghton Library, Harvard University.

Library imprint is closer (if not identical) to the version used as a model
for the Nahuatl play. A 1620 edition from Seville, also printed on four
quarto leaves, is attested by Pérez Gómez (1976–77:502), Barrera y Leirado
(1860:197), Gallardo (1888:264–65), and Sánchez-Arjona (1898:213–14).
Pérez Gómez states that this edition varies only slightly from that of 1603.

After 1620 the drama became dissociated from its author and attributed variously to one Inocencio de Salceda and to a Doctor Ceballos,
Zevallos, or Zavallos of Seville. Its wording changed as it was reworked by
these later redactors. Pérez Gómez (1976–77:502–4) lists six editions since
that of 1620, the most recent one issued in Madrid in about 1915. An un-
dated eighteenth-century edition is reprinted in an anthology of Spanish
religious poetry (Sancha 1872:383–88).

In their catalog of sixteenth-century Spanish dramatic pieces, Díaz de
Escovar and Lasso de la Vega (1924:I, 88) find Izquierdo's play of so little
literary merit that they have no desire to learn anything about its author.
It is true that the play hardly exemplifies the cutting edge of Spanish theatrical art, which in Izquierdo's day was entering its most glorious era.
Nevertheless, its multiple reprintings attest to some degree of popularity.
It is firmly linked with Spanish devotional, literary, and theatrical traditions of the later sixteenth century, and may be considered less a work of
individual genius than a rather typical product of its times. The rest of this
chapter explores these links.

Religious Theater

Izquierdo called his play an *auto*. This was, in his time, a general term for
a one-act play, usually on a religious theme. Such plays were also variously termed *comedias*, *representaciones*, *farsas*, *églogas*, and *diálogos*, there
being as yet no standardized terminology for dramatic genres (McKendrick
1989:18; Shergold 1967:50–51). All such plays were written in rhymed
verse.

The history of Spanish theater has been extensively researched and
analyzed. In the following historical sketch I have included only those
points that I think are useful for understanding the origins and context of
Izquierdo's *auto* and the development of early Mexican theater.[6]

European drama has its roots in the Latin liturgy of the Middle Ages,
which came to include dramatizations of such events as the Nativity of
Christ, the visit of the Three Kings, and the Easter morning discovery

of Christ's empty sepulcher by the three Marys. Over time, this liturgical drama gave rise to performances conducted in vernacular languages and outside of the church building. For Spain, though, there is little evidence from the Middle Ages even for Latin liturgical drama apart from the French-influenced churches of Catalonia.

By the late fifteenth century, however, religious dramas in the vernacular were being performed in Castile both inside and outside of churches, especially in connection with Christmas and Holy Week. Some of these works were published. Juan del Encina's 1496 *Cancionero* contains two Easter plays set at the sepulcher (Shergold 1967:26–27). A Christmas play written by Gómez Manrique between 1467 and 1481 ends with a procession of martyrs who present the infant Christ with instruments of the Passion: the chalice, the column and rope, the scourge, the crown of thorns, the cross, the nails, and the lance (Shergold 1967:39–40). These include the five implements Izquierdo would later choose for his drama.

Three Holy Week dramas from the first half of the sixteenth century set other important precedents for Izquierdo's *auto*: they relate the Passion to Old Testament prophets, feature interchanges between Christ and his mother, display crosses and other Passion iconography, and act out Christ's descent into hell.

Lucas Fernández's *Auto de la Pasión* was written for performance in the cathedral of Salamanca in 1503, probably on Good Friday. The script was published in 1514. After Saints Peter, Dionysius, and Matthew lamentatiously recount the events of the Passion, they are accompanied by the three Marys in an interchange of mourning. The prophet Jeremiah, one of Izquierdo's Old Testament figures, joins the group. Stage directions call for an Ecce Homo, a painting showing Christ, tortured and bleeding, being displayed to the crowd by Pontius Pilate, to be revealed by drawing back a curtain. At the climax of the play a cross is uncovered, before which all kneel and worship (Shergold 1967:28–29; McKendrick 1989:17; Williams 1935:27–28).

In 1520 Alonso de Melgar, a printer in Burgos, published a Passion play consisting of three short scenes, each of which closes with a lament by the Virgin Mary, followed by a separate piece on Christ's resurrection (Gillet 1932; Shergold 1967:29–31; Williams 1935:69–70, 73). The drama begins with the Old Testament figures David, Solomon, Isaiah, and Jeremiah seated in a hall. After the Virgin Mary utters the opening lines, she and David converse. In spite of her pleas, each of the four prophets pronounces a death sentence on Christ. Christ comes and takes leave of his mother. He tells her that her suffering causes him no less distress than his own; she laments over his leaving, telling him that she bids farewell to her own soul.

In the second scene, an Ecce Homo is displayed and Saint John explains to Mary that this tormented individual is her son. She addresses her lament to the audience, stating that her suffering is worse than death. The third scene represents the crucifixion. Mary and John stand at the foot of the cross while Joseph of Arimathea and Nicodemus come to remove the body.

For the resurrection scene, the setting is hell, with Lucifer on his throne and the souls imprisoned in Limbo. David, Solomon, Isaiah, Hosea, Zachariah, and a sybil all sing prophecies of Christ's resurrection and their liberation. This motif derived from the Christmas Eve liturgy's *Ordo Prophetarum*, in which a series of prophets, sometimes impersonated in church by different individuals, foretell the birth of Christ (Shergold 1967:18). Mary then appears and prays for the resurrection of her son. The resurrected Christ appears and sends the archangel Gabriel to tell Mary that he has come back to life. Christ then enters Limbo and converses with Lucifer, who is frightened and flees.

Stage directions indicate that Christ now utters *Attollite portas*, or "Lift up your heads, oh ye gates," from Psalm 24. The last four verses of this psalm (vv. 7–10) describe a triumphal entry. In the King James English version they read:

7 Lift up your heads, O ye gates; and be ye lifted up, ye everlasting doors; and the King of glory shall come in.

8 Who is this King of glory? The Lord strong and mighty, the Lord mighty in battle.

9 Lift up your heads, O ye gates; even lift them up, ye everlasting doors; and the King of glory shall come in.

10 Who is this King of glory? The Lord of hosts, he is the King of glory.[7]

These verses were long used in the liturgy for Advent and Palm Sunday. But they were also interpreted as a prophecy of the harrowing of hell, constituting a dialogue between Christ or the angels who accompany him and the devils whose stronghold he breaches. The lines were eventually added to the Easter liturgy and incorporated into liturgical and vernacular drama (Young 1909:891–96). Izquierdo quotes from this psalm in his play.

Christ then leads the imprisoned souls out of Limbo and takes them to see Mary. Adam and Eve beg Mary's forgiveness for their sin, which she grants. David makes a long speech praising her on behalf of all the prophets; she gives the group her benediction. David closes the play with a song.

Even more elaborate is an Easter play by Juan de Pedraza, published in 1549 and probably intended for Easter morning performance (Gillet 1933; Shergold 1967:34–38; Williams 1935:93–94). Comic prologues and epilogue frame a series of twelve short scenes beginning with the harrowing of hell. Christ and accompanying angels command the gates of hell to open and Lucifer answers from within, their dialogue following and elaborating upon the Psalm 24 text. Christ orders Lucifer to release the prisoners, and Adam leads them forth. In the second scene, Judas appears alone and laments that, because he betrayed Christ, he must stay in hell while the others are permitted to leave.

The rest of the play is set in Jerusalem and centers on the resurrection of Christ. It includes the standard scene of the discovery of the empty sepulcher by the three Marys plus various interchanges involving the resurrected Christ, the apostles John and Peter, the Virgin Mary, and Mary Magdalene. In one scene Christ appears to his mother accompanied by the liberated patriarchs and prophets.

While Holy Week gave rise to such performances as these, the most important developments in Spanish religious theater were occurring in connection with the festival of Corpus Christi. A papal decree of 1317 ordered that, in observance of this day, the consecrated host (the communion wafer) was to be carried in a procession through the streets. This open-air religious service inspired processions with more and more elaborate pageantry: musicians, costumed marchers, riders on horseback, pantomime dragons and eagles, dances, and other entertainments.

In Spain, the dramatic potential of the festivities was first explored through the creation of tableaux made with wooden figures, representing scenes from Christian narratives. These were placed on carts and dragged or carried through the streets in the manner of parade floats. In the late fourteenth century, costumed people began replacing the statues on these carts.

In the fifteenth century, especially in eastern Spain—including Valencia—these elaborate tableaux evolved into a rudimentary form of theatrical presentation. Still primarily visual rather than dramatic in character, these were sometimes called, after French usage, "mysteries." This term survived in eastern Spain in reference to some religious dramas, such as the enactment of the Assumption of Mary still performed on that festival in the town of Elche.

By the early sixteenth century, Corpus Christi plays were an established institution in many Spanish towns and cities. At first the productions were sponsored and financed by guilds, but by the end of the sixteenth century it was usually the town or city council that controlled the proceedings. Typically, three or four *autos* were performed each year, first in the church building and then at a series of set locales within the city. The scenery, often involving elaborate architectural constructions, was placed on carts. At each performance setting, two carts would be wheeled up side by side and a wooden platform laid between them as a stage. The carts functioned as backdrop, wings, offstage dressing area, and an extension of the performance space.

The Corpus Christi procession, with its *autos*, became the highlight of the Church year. The popularity of the plays, with different towns vying for the most skilled and elaborate productions and with money for scenery and costumes flowing freely, was a powerful impetus for the professionalization of acting. The earliest known *autor de comedias*, or leader and manager of a company of professional actors, is a man named Lope de Rueda, who was running his own troupe by the 1540s (McKendrick 1989:43–46; Rennert 1963:9). The title *autor* does not indicate that these people actually authored the plays, though some of them did write plays as well as produce and perform them. The *autor* of a theatrical company would purchase finished scripts from writers. It was in this manner that playwrights profited from their efforts (Rennert 1963:174).

The companies included both men and women. Although there were occasional campaigns to ban women from the stage, in general Spanish theater followed the Italian model and had female roles filled by female actors, this being considered less offensive than cross-dressing by males. There were efforts to police the morals of these women, by insisting, for example, that they be chastely married and that they not cross-dress to play masculine roles (Shergold 1967:507–8; McKendrick 1989:49).

Companies of actors would contract with particular cities to produce their Corpus *autos*. In major cities—Madrid, Seville, and later Valencia—permanent public theaters first developed in the second half of the sixteenth century as companies of Corpus Christi performers sought to support themselves by their dramatic talents year-round.

These theaters—their name, *corrales*, aptly describing their rudimentary outdoor facilities—in turn provided a context for the further development of plays on secular themes, which until then were private entertainments staged at the courts of the nobility. However, religious plays remained standard parts of the repertory. Churchmen and other pious sorts were inclined to inveigh against the allegedly loose morals of professional players (Caro Baroja 1978:102; Rennert 1963:259–65). Therefore, maintaining a strong religious component was essential to the survival of the companies.

Even religious plays were subject to moral criticism, with charges that drunkards and promiscuous men and women were appearing on stage in the guise of Christ and the saints and that lewd songs and dances were performed along with the plays. McKendrick (1989:201) mentions an incident described in a Madrid document of 1598. An audience watching actors dramatize the Annunciation had been quite amused when the woman playing the Virgin Mary pronounced the lines in which she attests to never having known a man, for it was public knowledge that this woman and the actor playing Joseph were lovers. Later in the performance, "Joseph" stepped out of character and accused his girlfriend of flirting with another man. But criticisms of episodes such as this were countered by claims that playing religious roles led many actors to reform their ways, some even heading directly from stage to monastery (Rennert 1963:144).

The content of the Corpus Christi plays ran the gamut of Christian subject matter, including narratives from the Old and New Testaments and apocryphal gospels, the lives of saints and martyrs, stories of miracles, and morality plays about sinners punished or reformed. Stories connected with Christmas, Epiphany, Easter, and the Assumption of Mary could be included, even though those festivals were often celebrated with their own dramatizations. But the fact that the primary context for theatrical expression happened to coincide with a festival that honored the sacrament of the Eucharist gave rise to a new dramatic genre, the *auto sacramental*.

An *auto sacramental* differs from the broader category of *autos* in that it deals explicitly with the Eucharist, the sacrament of the consecrated or transubstantiated host. Typically, it is highly allegorical, with dramatis personae representing all sorts of abstract concepts from the Eucharist itself to Time, Virtue, the World, Penitence, and so forth. Its message is moralistic and dogmatic, urging reverence toward the sacrament and moral reform.

The earliest known eucharistic play from Spain is Fernán López de Yanguas's *Farsa sacramental* of 1520 or 1521. Arróniz (1977:13), noting that this was only four years after Martin Luther promulgated his heretical theses, emphasizes the link between the rise of Protestantism in Europe and the rise of eucharistic theater in Spain. Whether the consecrated host was indeed the body of Christ—the *corpus Christi*—was, of course, one of the principal points of contention between Catholic and Protestant. The elaboration of Corpus Christi celebrations in Spain was in essence a tactic of the Catholic Reformation, a way of directing intense popular devotion toward an aspect of Catholic dogma that was being undermined in other quarters. The development of Spain's professional theater, with the Church tolerating the notorious behavioral excesses of roving players, thus depended upon a "prudent pact between actors and authors and the Church Triumphant" (Arróniz 1977:13).

Spanish theater embarked upon its so-called Golden Age with the appearance of the poet and playwright Félix Lope de Vega Carpio (1562–1635). Lope de Vega and his "Lopista" followers converted the simple *autos* and *farsas* of the past into great literary and dramatic art, focusing on the genre of the *comedia*, which now came to mean a verse drama in three acts. The new *comedias* featured involuted plots and subplots with complicated intrigues and a lot of action and conflict. Casts were large and included many stock characters—shepherds and shepherdesses, clowning servants, marriageable maidens with their dashing suitors and autocratic fathers. Many *comedias* were secular in subject matter, but *comedias de santos* remained important, and even in secular stories the plot often hinged upon some point of religious doctrine.

Under the new playwrights, especially Pedro Calderón de la Barca (1600–1681), the one-act *auto sacramental* developed alongside the *comedia*. Elaborate eucharistic allegories came to dominate the Corpus Christi theatricals, pushing aside the simpler, narrative-based *autos* of earlier times. These allegories were simultaneously didactic works—Calderón called them "sermons in verse"—and devotional rituals, acts of faith that in themselves served to render homage unto God and confound the enemies of the faith.

Valencia had a public theater by 1583 or 1584, and as a theatrical center was surpassed only by Seville and Madrid. Lope de Vega spent two years in Valencia, beginning in 1588. It is likely that Ausías Izquierdo Zebrero attended performances at his city's *corral*; he may have met the great Castilian dramatist. However, Izquierdo's work pertains not to the Golden Age of *comedias* and *autos sacramentales* but to the simpler *autos* more typical of the second half of the sixteenth century. It is no wonder that historians of the Spanish stage, distracted by the glamor of the Lopistas, overlook the pious Valencian bookseller.

It is very likely that Izquierdo wrote his "Beacon of Our Salvation" for Corpus Christi. Although set during Holy Week, it is not, strictly speaking, a Passion or Easter play; the script is rich in allusions to the upcoming events but these are not staged. The play's action occurs prior to the Passion itself, which begins the evening of Holy Thursday with the Last Supper and Judas's betrayal. Its message, as reflected in the title, is salvational: the text emphasizes the redemptive power of Christ's self-sacrifice. Christ's death is represented as inevitable and essential, grounded in prophecy and in divine decree, and greatly to be desired by fallen and repentant humanity. Without ever referring directly to the sacrament of the Eucharist, the drama conveys the sacrament's essential meaning. Hence, though not actually an *auto sacramental*, it could easily have passed muster as an appropriate choice for performance on Corpus Christi.

The most important source of comparative material for Izquierdo's play is the manuscript known as the *Códice de autos viejos*. The manuscript, dating from the second half of the sixteenth century, is housed in Spain's Biblioteca Nacional and has been published by Léo Rouanet (1979). Shergold (1967:111) suggests that the codex may represent the repertoire of a theatrical troupe engaged in Corpus Christi performances. Its 96 pieces, all of them anonymous, include plays based on the lives of saints and martyrs, biblical subjects, and rudimentary *autos sacramentales*. Only one of the plays bears a date, a license for performance in a Madrid church at Easter, 1578. McKendrick's evaluation of the plays as "for the most part static discussion with little movement or conflict" (1989:38)—and hence of little relevance to the emergence of Golden Age drama—is equally apt as a description of Izquierdo's play. Various stanza structures are employed in the text, but the five-line *quintilla* is the most common (Rouanet 1979:I, xii).

Two plays in this corpus bear strong similarities to Izquierdo's *auto*, so much so that Crawford (1967:141) assumed Izquierdo must have been familiar with these works. One of the plays is, like Izquierdo's, an *auto del despedimiento* dramatizing Christ's farewell to his mother. In his notes on the play, Rouanet observes its resemblance to the Izquierdo drama (1979:II, 403–20; IV, 281–82).[8]

This *auto* begins with a conversation between Saints Peter and John. The Virgin Mary joins them, followed by Mary Magdalene and Martha. The five of them go to ask Christ where he will be spending Passover. He sends John and Peter on to Jerusalem and then, in the presence of Magdalene and Martha, engages in a lengthy dialogue with his mother. She attempts to dissuade him from his intended course of action. They converse without interruption for 188 continuous lines (out of the play's total of 559). The two other women then join their conversation, and John and Peter return. Christ bids farewell to his mother and pronounces his blessing upon her and the other women. He and his disciples then leave, and Mary utters a sad soliloquy. She is then joined by an angel and by Adam, who enters bearing a cross. He speaks to Mary of the necessity of her son's death, mentioning the imprisonment in Limbo of himself and others. Mary decides to leave matters in God's hands. The play concludes as Martha, Mary Magdalene, their brother Lazarus, and the Virgin prepare to follow the departed Christ.

The second *auto* is called "The Gifts That Adam Sent to Our Lady with Saint Lazarus" (Rouanet 1979:II, 388–402). It is set just after Christ has taken leave of Mary. Here the cast consists solely of Mary, Lazarus, and an allegorical figure representing Humanity. The drama builds on the Gospel text according to which Christ raised Lazarus from the dead after Lazarus had lain in the grave for four days (John 11). This story was conflated with a narrative that Luke (16:19–31) attributes to Christ, regarding a beggar named Lazarus who, after his death, was carried by angels to Limbo.

The *auto* has Lazarus bring back from Limbo a letter and a coffer of gifts, entrusted to him by Adam. In the presence of Humanity, Lazarus reads Mary the letter, which urges her compliance with Christ's imminent demise. The letter is sealed with an image of a cross. Four lines of this letter are identical to the opening of Adam's letter in Izquierdo's play.

The contents of the coffer, revealed one by one in the course of a conversation among the three dramatis personae, turn out to be ten instruments of the Passion. Some of these are masked as precious finery and are at first mistaken by Mary for bridal gifts. At the end of the play Mary entrusts these objects to Humanity, who tells her she will see them again on her son.

Spain's Biblioteca Nacional also contains a shorter manuscript collection of eleven *autos* dating between 1575 and 1590 (Kemp 1936; Buck 1937; Tyre 1938). One of these plays dramatizes the birth and life of Judas. It includes a 67-line *despedimiento* scene in which Christ and Mary appear onstage accompanied by two silent angels. This Mary does not attempt to dissuade her son from accepting his fate; his words are aimed at consolation rather than persuasion (Tyre 1938:83–84).

Dramatic renderings of the *despedimiento*, the harrowing of hell, and other deeds of Christ and his mother drew not only upon theatrical precedents but on a broader range of pious art and literature and devotional ritual. Some aspects of this wider context are explored in the following sections.

Imitatio Christi: Passion Literature

Anyone who is not familiar with the religious context of Izquierdo's play may be struck by the degree of influence and authority granted to the Virgin Mary. Her divine son must beg her leave before going to meet his fate; Old Testament prophets and patriarchs ply her with urgent missives. Her persona in this play is, however, not at all aberrant.

Over the course of the late Middle Ages, European Christians had turned increasingly toward the Passion of Christ as a vehicle for devotional expression. Gospel accounts of Christ's last days were insufficiently detailed to satisfy worshippers who wished to explore every excruciating detail of their savior's death. A new genre of literature, episodically structured biographies of Christ with extensive extra-Gospel narration, developed alongside a new type of private meditation, in which the individual events of Christ's life—and especially his death—were contemplated in chronological sequence (Marrow 1979:1–11).

The characterization of this devotional mode as "contemplative" does not imply an attitude of serene detachment. Concentration on the sacred subject matter was intended to induce profoundly felt emotional states. Ideally, the worshipper would so thoroughly empathize with the holy personages that she or he would feel transported beyond the boundaries of self and into a mystical union with God. Joyous events—the Annunciation, the Adoration of the Three Kings, the Resurrection—as well as sorrowful ones could inspire this transcendent experience. But the attention paid to Christ's Passion suggests that agony was found to be the surer avenue toward ecstasy.

To find a scriptural basis for the new narrative episodes and their iconographic correlates, scholars turned to the Old Testament. Passages in the Old Testament were interpreted metaphorically as prophetic allusions to Christ and his sufferings; these metaphors were then transposed into narrative form and added to the evolving story (Marrow 1979:5).

Members of the Franciscan order, which was established in the early thirteenth century, were especially devoted to these new modes of piety. They tended the shrine of the True Cross and other Holy Land loci associated with Christ's earthly life (Christian 1981a:221). Their founder, Saint Francis of Assisi, represented the fullest expression of personal identification with the Christ of the Passion: for the last two years of his life he bore the stigmata—the wounds on hands, feet, and side that mirrored Christ's own. The early Franciscan theologian Saint Bonaventure was particularly influential in systematizing and propagating contemplative devotion to Christ (Marrow 1979:9–11).

As Christians meditated on Christ's humanity and sought to identify with him, they also paid increasing attention to the woman who gave him his human form. The relationship between mother and child served as a crucial vector for this whole devotional movement. By conceptualizing the holy pair in terms of that most basic of human emotional bonds, one could try to imagine what they would have thought, to feel what they would have felt. As a result, Mary was elevated to a role in the Passion that rivaled Christ's own. Literature based on the contemplation of the Passion came to focus as much on the sufferings of Mary as on those of Christ.

Since Mary was fully human, one could more readily comprehend and identify with her suffering. She underwent what any loving mother would feel at seeing her only child tortured and murdered; it was easier for the worshipper to imagine these feelings than to put herself or himself into the place of a god—even a god who had taken human flesh. Mary's compassion for her son took her through a kind of co-Passion, with mother and son joined as one in a union both mystical and quasi-erotic (Mitchell 1990:166–69).

The chant *Stabat mater*, a standard of the Passion liturgy, describes the bereaved Mary standing at the foot of the cross. This piece provides liturgical authority for attending to Mary's role in the Passion, but it speaks in the third person without purporting to quote from the Virgin's mouth. However, influential writings on the Passion, such as the pseudo-Bernard's *Liber de Passione Christi et Doloribus et Planctibus Matris Eius* of 1133–42, written as a dialogue between Mary and Saint Bernard, came to feature direct discourse in the form of the *planctus* or "complaint" of the Virgin (Marx and Drennan 1987:32–33). In this genre of devotional text, the events of the Passion are recounted in a "play-by-play" manner, filtered through Mary's experience. News is brought to her of those of her son's torments that she does not herself witness, and those that she does observe she comments upon as they occur. Narrative descriptions—often quite graphic—are combined with emotional outpourings as the Virgin laments her son's fate and gives vent to her own pain.

The thirteenth-century Italian Franciscan Jacopone da Todi elevated the *planctus* from contemplative narrative to poetic drama in his *Donna del Paradiso*, a text Peck (1980:133) describes as the "prototype of the Passion play." The following excerpt from da Todi's poem was translated from the Italian original by Peck (1980:148):

Messenger: Lady, here is the cross which the people have brought, where the true light must be raised.
Mary: O cross, what can I do? Are you taking my son from me? For what can you condemn him, since he has no sin in him?
Messenger: Help, lady of sorrow! For they are undressing your little boy. It seems that the people want him to be nailed to the cross.
Mary: If you are undressing him, let me see how cruelly he has been wounded. He is all bloodied.
Messenger: Lady, they take his hand and stretch it on the cross. They fix it with a nail and hammer it right in. They take the other hand and fit it on the cross, and the pain lights up and is much increased. Lady, they take his feet and nail them to the wood. They take every joint and pull them apart.
Mary: And I begin my wailing: O my little son has been taken from me. O my son, my tender son, who has killed you? They would have done better to cut my heart out than for me to see you stretched on the cross.

This passage illustrates the emotional tone typical of the *planctus* genre as well as this text's potential for simple dramatization.

As medieval religious lore evolved, not only were the Gospel accounts of Christ's life and death embellished with many additional details but whole new episodes with no New Testament basis were added to the story. Some of these were derived from the apocryphal gospels. Such is the case for the harrowing of hell, which is based upon the apocryphal Gospel of Nicodemus. This text is comprised of two parts; the second, dating to the second or third century A.D., tells the story of Christ's descent into hell, quoting Psalm 24:7–8 for scriptural authority. In a version known as the *Sermo de Confusione Diaboli*, dating to around A.D. 900 or possibly much earlier, the story became widely known in Europe and inspired artistic and theatrical works (Verdier 1974; Young 1909; Rand 1904).

The parting dialogue between Christ and his mother lacks even this lengthy a pedigree. According to Peck (1980:140–41), the scene was invented in the thirteenth century by Giovanni da Cauli, a Franciscan of San Gimignano, Italy. Da Cauli wrote an influential work in Latin entitled *Meditationes vitae Christi*, or "Meditations on the Life of Christ" (Ragusa and Green 1961). This was one of the biographical treatments of Christ directed at providing textual fodder for private contemplation. Its frequent circulation under the name of Saint Bonaventure granted da Cauli's treatise considerable authority. It was translated into many languages and was an important source for pictorial art and for early dramatic works, including da Todi's *Donna del Paradiso* (Peck 1980:140–42).

Da Cauli's meditation 72, "How the Lord Jesus Predicted His Death to the Mother," is set on Holy Wednesday at the home of Mary Magdalene and her sister Martha (in Bethany, near Jerusalem). The Virgin Mary and Mary Magdalene strive to persuade Christ to remain there for Passover; he insists that it is his father's will that he go to Jerusalem, for the time of redemption is coming. Mary, realizing that her son is referring to his death, begs for a delay. She insists that God can provide for the redemption of humanity without Christ's death. As both women weep, Christ reminds them that he has no choice but to obey his father. He promises that he will soon return, since he is going to rise on the third day. Mary Magdalene decides that the women will spend Passover at her family's house in Jerusalem, and Christ assents to this (Ragusa and Green 1961:308–9).

Da Cauli dwells only briefly on Mary's sadness and Christ's imminent death. However, the incorporation of this farewell scene into the story of Holy Week provided space for further elaboration of the *planctus* genre. The conventional *planctus* narrates events that are occurring in the present or have just taken place. Mary could speak in similar fashion of events that lay yet in the future. Since the entire progress of the Passion was believed to be specified in prophecy, the events were knowable beforehand. Writers could subject the poor Virgin to a longer period of torment. She could be represented as alternately, and to varying degrees, protesting the upcoming events, consoling her son, and lamenting her own suffering. Such is the strategy followed in Izquierdo's play and other dramatizations of the Bethany farewell scene.

Although it never became obligatory to include this episode in narratives about Christ or Mary, it can be found in some sixteenth-century Spanish treatises. Miguel Pérez, a Valencian like Izquierdo, devoted two chapters of his biography of Mary to the leave-taking episode (Pérez 1549). The first of these tells how Christ got permission from Mary to go to his death and Passion. Pérez validates his imaginary dialogue by stating that the protagonists spoke words "similar" to those he presents.

In Pérez's version, Christ begins by asking his mother to accept the torment and sacrifice that his father demands of him, lest human nature remain forever in the infernal prison. Mary protests, asserting that her son need not die because any small labor or suffering that he has endured on earth should suffice to redeem humanity. He has the power to move heaven and earth, so why should he allow himself to be conquered by malicious people? Christ answers with a metaphor equating human nature to a fragile vessel on a tempestuous ocean. His death will be an example for martyrs who will navigate a sea of blood; Mary will guide sinners to the port of salvation. Mary then asks that she be allowed to die with him so that she need not witness his death. He explains that she must remain alive because of Solomon's prophecy in the Song of Songs 2:14; he interprets the line "O my dove, that art in the clefts in the rock" as referring to Mary's contemplation of his wounds, which will be as clefts in the foundation stone of the Church. He adds that he must die in order to disinter the precious gold of the saintly souls of deep Limbo and to begin the building of the Roman Church. He finishes by asking her to give him her benediction and to be content that he go to die. Her tears run down over the floor, but she accepts the divine will. After embracing him and receiving his blessing, she blesses him. He kisses her hands and departs, leaving her in the company of sad and painful thoughts (Pérez 1549:26r–v).

Pérez's subsequent chapter explores these thoughts of Mary's. At first she ponders whether there may yet be a way to prevent her son's death, but after reviewing all the ancient prophecies that refer to his Passion and death she concludes that it is inevitable. John then comes from Jerusalem to tell her, Mary Magdalene, and the other women that Christ is now on his way to Mount Calvary (Pérez 1549:27r–v).

Alonso de Villegas Selvago (lived 1534–1615) acknowledged the *despedimiento* episode's flimsy foundations, but nevertheless found it worthy of a brief treatment in his erudite treatise on Mary:

Some contemplatives feel that when the Savior was in Bethany, with his Most Holy Mother, at the time when he wanted to go to celebrate the Last Supper with the apostles, and to die, that he told her about everything, and he took leave of her, asking for her permission to perish, with so much sentiment of the two, such as was the love that they had for one another, and the business to which he was going being so very difficult and laborious. And the painters assist with this contemplation, painting Jesus Christ as if he were kneeling before the Virgin, asking her for this permission. This is not a certain thing. (Villegas Selvago 1760:90–91)

Villegas could probably speak for many Catholic churchmen evaluating the Bethany farewell episode three centuries after da Cauli proposed it: such a scene could have occurred, and if it inspired devout contemplation, there was nothing wrong with allowing people to assume that it had.

Prose narratives such as these were not the only non-dramatic devo-

tional texts circulating in Izquierdo's Spain. Religious poetry, a union of
the troubadour's art with contemplative and mystical trends in personal
devotion, was flourishing. Most of the poets were not theologians or even
priests but pious laymen like Izquierdo himself. Love songs to the Virgin
abounded, as did emotional treatments of the Passion (Castillo 1904; Wardropper 1954).

Christ's farewell to his mother is the theme of an 80-line poem by José
de Valdivielso, originally published in 1612. In this version Mary is silent.
Christ speaks to her and then the poet addresses his reader in a closing passage:

Man, if you are not made of stone,
show it on this occasion,
for the very stones turn soft
at the farewell of the two.
Go and accompany Christ
in his death and Passion;
your lord dies for you,
may you die for your lord.
Die courageous at his side,
consider that at the side of God
death will not be death,
nor will pain be pain.
And if you dare not go so far,
because fear freezes you,
it remains to you to console his mother
in such great affliction.
Weep and weep for your sins,
you will gladden the two of them,
because tears shed for sins
are their sweet consolations.
Weeping, even when God dies,
you can gladden God,
and console his mother
in her great solitude. (Valdivielso 1984:343)

Poetry such as this was meant to inspire cathartic identification with the
sufferings of the divine pair. Note that relating to Mary is treated as somewhat less of a challenge than to put oneself in Christ's place.

Poets did not neglect to write of the souls who awaited Christ's descent to Limbo. For example, there is the poem called *Triste estaba el Padre
Adan*, by Bartolomé Torres Naharro, an important early sixteenth-century
dramatist (in Scarpa 1938:99–100). It begins:

Father Adam was sad,
as he had been for five thousand years,
when he learned that in Bethlehem
Mary had given birth.
And in Limbo where he was
he could not contain his joy;
to some of them he walked,
to the rest of them he ran,
and to all the Holy Fathers
in a loud voice he proclaimed:
Congratulate me, my children,
for on this day is born
our blessing and Redeemer,
our pleasure and happiness,
to take us out of here,
where we are through fault of mine.

Adam goes on to describe the events unfolding on the earth's surface, as the shepherds and wise men come to visit Christ in his humble manger.

The setting of this poem at Christ's birth indicates that it was not only the events of the Passion upon which the souls in Limbo attended anxiously. Already in the twelfth century, Saint Bernard of Clairvaux had ascribed to the Old Testament patriarchs a role in Christ's very conception. In the fourth of his influential *Homilies* on the Virgin, he imagines the patriarchs—Adam, David, and Abraham are mentioned by name—imploring Mary to accept the role offered her by the angel Gabriel during the Annunciation (Bernard of Clairvaux and Amadeus of Lausanne 1979:53).

Religious *autos* like Izquierdo's are perhaps better understood in the context of contemplative devotional exercises than that of dramatic art. The *autos* move the subject matter for contemplation out of the private oratory and into a public space, where moving and speaking actors replace inert books and images. Shared with other spectators, the cathartic experience was perhaps rendered more intense. Rather than seeing all this as weak theater, one might choose to view it as a particularly powerful method of meditation.

Iconography

Devotional literature had its counterparts in religious art. Pictorial representations helped people to visualize the ancient events and also channeled these visualizations into certain conventional forms. Works of art provided models for costumes and stage sets when devotional narratives were dramatized.

Depictions of the Passion abound in late medieval and Renaissance art. Just as certain episodes were sure to be included in any meditational handbook, so were they the stock in trade of painters and engravers. Some of the most popular scenes were Christ's agony in the Garden of Gethsemane, his flagellation at the column, the placement of the crown of thorns on his head, the Ecce Homo scene, Christ carrying the cross en route to Calvary, and, most popular of all, the crucifixion.

Sometimes instruments of the Passion, which are also called the Arma Christi, or "arms of Christ," are shown in non-narrative scenes. Angels often carry them. Christ is sometimes depicted as the Man of Sorrows, wearing the crown of thorns and displaying his wounds while angels hover about bearing the cross, nails, scourge, column, or other implements of the Passion. A medieval legend about Saint Gregory claims that once when he was celebrating Mass, in place of the consecrated host there appeared Christ himself, in human form, bearing the wounds of his Passion. And ranged about the altar appeared all of the symbols and instruments of the Passion. A less commonly depicted scene associated Mary with the Arma Christi.[9]

The Bethany farewell and the harrowing of hell were less often subjected to pictorial treatment than the events of the Passion proper, but these scenes too had their conventionalized iconography.[10] In late medieval and fifteenth-century European art, hell was often depicted as the mouth of a monstrous beast or dragon; demons cavorted and condemned souls writhed, all within the beast's gaping maw. Correspondingly, the harrowing of hell was shown as the extraction of the redeemed souls from this mouth, beginning with Adam and Eve (Figure 2).

Alternatively, hell may be shown as a building, a cave, or a cave-like building (Figure 3). These more architectural interpretations predominate by the sixteenth century. The door having been cast down, Christ proceeds to extract the inhabitants. In some renderings, Adam and Eve, and sometimes others, have already exited and stand by while Christ assists the remaining souls. Adam or Eve may clasp the apple that started all of their troubles, as Eve does in Figure 3.[11]

Portrayals of the Christ-Mary farewell vary with respect to the number of people in the picture and their positioning in relation to one another. In eight Renaissance-period woodcuts and engravings that I have found of the scene, two of them by Albrecht Dürer, Mary is usually accompanied by

2. Christ's descent into Limbo. German, 1460/1480. Rosenwald Collection, Copyright ©Board of Trustees, National Gallery of Art, Washington, D.C.

3. Christ in Limbo, by Martin Shongauer, c. 1480. Rosenwald Collection, Copyright ©Board of Trustees, National Gallery of Art, Washington, D.C.

4. Correggio's *Christ Taking Leave of His Mother*, c. 1510. Reproduced by courtesy of the Trustees, The National Gallery, London.

Mary Magdalene, Martha, and sometimes one or more additional women. These women tend to crowd around her, such that Christ confronts a cluster of women. Some or all of the apostles may be shown waiting to accompany Christ to Jerusalem; they may form a cluster of men standing in opposition to the group of women. Most often, Mary is seated or kneeling before her son, who is standing. He may lean toward her and even take her hand, or he may already be heading toward the road, looking back at her over his shoulder. In one example, mother and son embrace standing while Mary Magdalene kneels with arms upraised. Architecture and landscape are rendered in detail.[12]

Some famous Renaissance painters committed the scene to canvas: Correggio, El Greco, Lucas Cranach, Lotto, Veronese.[13] Correggio's interpretation, which dates to 1510 or later, is shown in Figure 4. The Italian master placed Mary Magdalene standing beside and supporting Mary, as she does at the close of Izquierdo's *auto*. Christ kneels before his mother while Saint John the Evangelist stands beside him. Christ's positioning corresponds to Villegas's observation, quoted above, that artists paint the scene in this manner.

Cranach, Lotto, and Veronese all included Mary Magdalene and other figures in the scene. El Greco's *Despedida de Cristo de su madre*, executed in Spain in the 1580s or 1590s, is unique in that it portrays the mother and son alone, in a head-and-torso view with no extraneous features of landscape or architecture.[14] The two figures, approximately equal in size, look into one another's eyes as they engage in an intimate dialogue; Christ's face is turned toward his mother while his body begins to turn away in departure. Álvarez Lopera finds in the work "a psychological and spiritual profundity only rarely achieved in the history of painting" (1985:15). Although far less significant in aesthetic terms, Izquierdo's *auto*, with its limited cast of characters and its focus on the Christ-Mary dialogue, approaches the vision of his Cretan-born contemporary.

The Way of the Cross: Penitence and Public Life

Izquierdo wrote his play during the heyday of Spain's penitential brotherhoods. These were (and still are) voluntary organizations, usually called *cofradías*, or "confraternities," whose members held processions during Holy Week. Often associated with guilds or with certain neighborhoods, the *cofradías* also acted as mutual aid societies for their members and executed charitable works in their communities (Christian 1981b:51).

An older tradition of confraternities dedicated to saints had been outflanked by confraternities of the Passion organized around the cult of the crucified Christ (Christian 1981b:51; Mitchell 1990:42). The earliest Passion confraternities, many of them dedicated to the True Cross, were founded near the end of the fifteenth century. In Valencia, a brotherhood of the Blood of Christ was founded in 1535. By the 1520s some of these brotherhoods had begun routinely, and in imitation of Christ's Passion, to engage in their most distinctive activity, the practice of flagellation during their public processions (Christian 1981a:221, 1981b:185; Mitchell 1990:42).

By 1575 Spain's larger cities had flagellant brotherhoods whose members participated by the thousands in the processions of Holy Thursday and Good Friday and also ran hospitals, orphanages, and other social services. A single city could have a number of such brotherhoods. As an alternative to flagellation, some groups carried crosses in their processions. By 1580 flagellant brotherhoods could also be found throughout rural areas (Christian 1981b:185–87).

Not surprisingly, the Virgin Mary shared with Christ the adoration of confraternity members. Spaniards had until this time revered Mary mostly in representations that showed her as a young mother holding the infant Christ. But now a Passion-related interpretation was given to some Marian devotions that had had no direct links to the Passion. For example, certain images of Mary were seen to shed tears. And new devotions specifically directed to the Passion became popular. These showed Mary as the *mater dolorosa*, or sorrowing mother (Christian 1981a:221; Mitchell 1990:168).

Foremost among Mary's Passion-related personae was Nuestra Señora de la Soledad, Our Lady of Solitude, to whom a number of penitential confraternities were dedicated. The Soledad represented Mary in a bereaved state spanning the period of Christ's Passion and entombment. In Madrid in 1568, the brotherhood of the Soledad, founded only the previous year, contributed 2,000 flagellants and 400 candle bearers to the city's Holy Week processions (Christian 1981b:200).

By the late sixteenth century the processions of Holy Week had borrowed from Corpus Christi the use of processional floats bearing images carried either individually or arranged in tableaux representing scenes from the Passion. Images of the sorrowing Mary were always included in these processions. Some of the brotherhoods possessed life-sized crucifixes that the members carried in procession. As with Corpus Christi, stationary performances sometimes supplemented the processions, with various churches and convents staging simulations of the crucifixion (Christian 1981b:189–190).

There is one further tie between the Passion and the theater: Spain's first public theaters were sponsored by Passion confraternities. The authorities granted these brotherhoods a monopoly over the emerging professional theater in order to maintain some public control over the acting companies and to ensure that the community would benefit from the

potential profits of this new form of entertainment. The actors turned over
a portion of their proceeds to the confraternities, which in turn paid the
rent on the land used for the *corral* and devoted the rest of the money to
their hospitals for the poor. In Madrid, the confraternity of the Passion
and Blood of Jesus Christ, founded in 1565, was the first to run a theater,
beginning in 1568. The second was the confraternity of the Soledad, which
began to sponsor plays in 1574 (McKendrick 1989:47; Shergold 1967:177–
78). Thus, the dying Christ and the sorrowing mother not only starred
annually in their own drama but were also cast in the role of year-round
theatrical patrons.

2

Mexico

From Spain to Mexico

A COPY OF IZQUIERDO'S "Beacon of Our Salvation" traveled to New Spain via one of the biannual fleets that sailed to the Indies, either among the personal effects of an individual passenger or as part of a shipment of books and pamphlets sent from Seville to be sold in the colony. Arriving at the Gulf Coast port of Vera Cruz, it would have been transported inland to the city of Mexico.

The colonial book trade was a flourishing business: during just two months of 1585, 75 cases of books were conveyed by muleback into the capital city. Ecclesiastical and classical literature prevailed among the imported titles, but a fondness among the colonists for romances of chivalry and other light fare is betrayed by the registers of book shipments. Lists from the 1580s include various *farsas* and *diálogos* as well as works on the Passion, the life of Mary, and other devotional texts.[1]

Although no professional, public theater existed in New Spain until very near the end of the sixteenth century (Arróniz 1977:128), the colonists followed the custom of their homeland in celebrating Corpus Christi with the performance of *autos*. As early as 1565, the ecclesiastical chapter in the city of Mexico began to award a prize for the best play written or adapted for performance on that festival; the city council granted similar prizes (Castañeda 1936:7). In the last quarter of the sixteenth century, the colony was home to so many poets and dramatists of Spanish origin that the playwright Fernán González de Eslava gave these lines to one of his characters: "So you're becoming a writer of couplets! You'll not earn much as a poet, for they're more plentiful than manure here" (Leonard 1992:192).

With a religious theater in full swing, a colonial elite eager to fancy itself well read, and a local cohort of established and would-be literary artists, there was a market in the colony for works like Izquierdo's drama. It may originally have been imported for Spanish consumption, with no thought to its potential Nahua audience.

The city of Mexico was founded in the fourteenth century by the Mexica, a group of Nahuas, or speakers of the Nahuatl language. They gradually turned a couple of muddy islands into a great metropolis that was the center of a large tribute-paying empire. When Hernando Cortés first marched into this island capital in 1519, it was a thriving city of perhaps 200,000 or more people. With its whitewashed walls and green gardens rising from the surrounding lake, its busy markets and grand temples, its canals, roads, causeways, and aqueducts, it was at the time one of the world's greatest urban centers, comparable in size to London and Paris. In the course of the brutal siege of 1520–21, much of the city was destroyed and many thousands of people were killed or died of disease and starvation.

The colonial capital had been established on the ruins of the old city. Some of the canals had been filled in to form new streets, but one still could reach the mainland only by boat or along the old causeways. A cathedral stood beside the site of what had been the main temple; the central part of the city was dominated by administrative buildings and residences built in Spanish style. As the administrative center of New Spain, Mexico housed a Spanish viceroy, archbishop, the judges of the Real Audiencia (or supreme court), the officers of the Inquisition, and other officials, who presided over much of the city's public life.

In 1585 don Álvaro Manrique de Zúñiga, Marqués de Villamanrique, became New Spain's seventh viceroy. He was followed in 1589 by don Luis de Velasco, whose father of the same name had been the colony's second viceroy. Velasco the Younger held the post until 1595. Since 1574 the archbishop had been Doctor Pedro Moya de Contreras, a loyal ally of King Philip II and a champion of ecclesiastical power. Moya de Contreras sailed to Spain in 1586 to report to the king about dishonesty and corruption among colonial appointees. He never returned to the colony. His successor, appointed in 1592, died in 1600 without ever coming to New Spain.[2]

Repeatedly buffeted by epidemics of Old World infectious diseases, the native population level continued the downward plunge that would not end until early in the seventeenth century. The most devastating epidemic to date had hit in 1576–79, and there was another serious outbreak in 1587–88. The goal shared by all Spanish colonists, to live comfortably off the labor and tribute of the native people, was becoming increasingly unattainable; some feared that, as in the Caribbean islands, the indigenous inhabitants of New Spain would soon die out completely.

In the city, Spanish residents numbered somewhat above 10,000, and their numbers were steadily increasing. Africans both slave and free, though fewer here than in coastal regions, were present and, along with Spanish men, were contributing to a rapidly increasing population of mixed heritage: the mestizo offspring of Spaniards and natives, the mulatto offspring of Spaniards and Africans, the children of Africans and natives, and further combinations. There were several thousand such individuals living in the city by the late 1580s.

But Mexico was still predominantly an indigenous city. Most of the native people were Nahuatl-speakers, though other groups were present. With a population somewhere in the vicinity of 40,000, native people outnumbered all the other ethnic categories put together. About a third of them resided in Tlatelolco, the northern sector of the city renamed Santiago Tlatelolco after Saint James, the patron saint of Spain. The rest lived in Tenochtitlan, now San Juan Tenochtitlan, the larger, southern sector from which the Mexica kings had ruled their empire.[3]

Both Tlatelolco and Tenochtitlan had the status of *altepetl*; that is, each was a self-governing community with its own ruling dynasty. Mexico was thus two cities in one.[4] Its native residents could identify themselves in broader terms as Mexica or in narrower terms as Tlatelolca or Tenochca. They did not use the Spaniards' designation "Indian" or the linguistic-ethnographic category "Nahua" as terms of self-reference. To distinguish themselves from non-natives, they spoke of *nican titlacah* 'we people here' or, and increasingly, *timacehualtin* 'we commoners, we ordinary people.'[5]

Tlatelolco had been an independent Mexica polity until 1473, when it was conquered by Tenochtitlan. It remained a separate administrative unit under Tenochtitlan's and then Spain's rule. The colonial native community, like every Nahua *altepetl*, had its own *cabildo*, or governing council of elected officials holding jurisdiction over affairs internal to the community, including the planning and financing of religious ceremonies. These officials received salaries of up to a few hundred pesos per year (Gibson 1964:186–87). Tlatelolco's principal church was a Franciscan establishment facing the plaza where the district's main temple had stood, today called the Plaza of the Three Cultures. Relatively few non-natives lived in this sector.

Tenochtitlan was divided by major canals into four large quarters. Colonial rule perpetuated the quadripartite organization. These four areas comprised four administrative districts for the native populace, called Santa María Cuepopan, San Sebastián Atzacualco, San Pablo Teopan, and San Juan Moyotlan. The portion of each quarter that lay toward the city's center had been appropriated for the Spanish settlement. The outer areas ostensibly remained in native hands, but non-natives were increasingly interspersed.

The Nahuas of the four districts were represented on Tenochtitlan's native *cabildo* on a rotating basis. Each district had its own principal church. Originally, all four of these churches had been ministered to by the Franciscan friars based at San Francisco, their principal church and friary, located near the central plaza on what today is Madero Street. The friars at San Francisco also maintained a spacious, arcaded, mosque-like open-air chapel for the native people, San José de los Naturales. San José was situated adjacent to the church, with both buildings facing onto a large patio with a giant stone cross at the center. This chapel was a principal locus for indigenous religious events, including dramas, and for vocational and doctrinal education.[6]

In 1586 Viceroy Villamanrique granted the San Sebastián district church to newly-arrived Carmelite monks. Some years earlier, Augustinian friars had been given the church of San Pablo. The Dominicans and the Jesuits also had churches in Tenochtitlan, but did not directly oversee any indigenous parishes there.[7]

On the mainland all around the lake system were other Nahua communities where the Spanish occupation was less overt. These remained closely linked to the capital through regional economic networks. East of the Basin of Mexico, near the new Spanish city of Puebla, lay other large Nahua communities such as Tlaxcala, Cholula, and Huexotzingo. The Franciscan presence in this area was particularly strong. All these other Nahua communities were, like the capital, repeatedly ravaged by epidemics.

The vast majority of the Nahuas in the capital and adjacent regions spoke only Nahuatl, but only the very elderly among them retained memories of life before the Spanish invasion. Most had grown up as subjects of the Spanish Crown, baptized members of the Catholic Church, and objects of a system of economic exploitation that diverted their goods and labor to the profit of their Spanish overlords.

Despite the forces that obliged them to interact with one another, Nahuas and Spaniards inhabited separate realities. Nahuas imposed their own interpretations on the Hispanic world, as Spaniards did on the Nahua world. Such is, of course, inevitable in any situation of culture contact; it is what Clifford (1988) calls the "predicament of culture." One's perceptions and representations of a cultural other are colored by a whole range of contingencies arising from one's political and historical context as well as the conceptual and rhetorical conventions governing thought and expression.

In the case of Nahuas and Spaniards, these mutual mis-constructions of the other became institutionalized in a manner that perpetuated the cultural differences while promoting an illusion of sameness. Each side imagined the other to be more similar to itself than it actually was, and assumed that ideas that were in fact quite different bore analogous meanings in both cultures. Lockhart has called this process "Double Mistaken Identity," which he defines as a "partially unwitting truce . . . in which each side of the cultural exchange seemed satisfied that its own interpretation of a given cultural phenomenon was the prevailing, if not exclusive one" (1991:22; see also Lockhart 1985:447; 1992:445).

This ongoing gap between the cultures of conqueror and colonized may be a common characteristic of colonial situations. Zeitlin and Thomas (1992:287), analyzing a disjunction between Spanish and Zapotec political systems in colonial Tehuantepec, Mexico, compare that situation to the pattern of "working misunderstanding" delineated by Bohannan as a characteristic of colonial indirect rule in Africa (Bohannan and Curtin 1971:333). White (1991) describes the "middle ground" in relations between the French and native groups in North America; this locus of inter-cultural communication, constructed to facilitate trade, was fashioned in part out of mutual misunderstandings that worked to the advantage of both sides. Rafael, in a study of the early colonial Philippines, concludes:

Christian conversion and colonial rule emerged through what appeared to be a series of mistranslations. But in fact, . . . such mistranslations were ways to render the other understandable. Each group read into the other's language and behavior possibilities that the original speakers had not intended or foreseen. (1988:211)

These mutual misunderstandings allow conqueror and conquered to co-exist within a single, hierarchical order. Obviously, in order to justify and perpetuate their position the dominant must construct the conquered in their own terms, reduce them to their own categories. On the other hand, the dominated must construct the dominant in their own terms as a means of defense, survival, and challenge. As long as they keep one another at arm's length, pretending to communicate while each is actually missing much of the other's message, that hierarchy can be maintained while each group continues to reproduce itself with minimal interference from the other.

Having arrived in the city of Mexico, Izquierdo's play entered this world of conflicting realities. Somehow it found its way into the hands of its Nahua interpreter, probably because a Spaniard judged it an appropriate tool of evangelization. The Nahua interpreter would construct from it a different play, one that properly belonged to a Nahua reality.

Nahuatl Theater

Colonial Nahuatl theater was a literary and performance genre that developed separately from Spanish colonial drama. Plays were performed in the Nahuatl language, by Nahua actors, and for a principally Nahua audience. The subject matter was exclusively religious, usually biblical or hagiographic and bearing more resemblance to the earlier Spanish *autos* than to Golden Age *comedias* and *autos sacramentales*.

The performances occurred in conjunction with Church festivals or Sunday services; the festivals included Corpus Christi, but religious theater did not center around this event to the extent that it did in Spain. Performances were enacted in the open chapels and church patios that the native people used for their other public religious rites. Sometimes a platform was erected to serve as a temporary stage. All the actors were male, for the priests who oversaw this theater sought to maintain what they considered moral seemliness among the native people and to avoid raising any suspicions regarding their own celibacy. Efforts to police the content of plays included an edict, issued by Mexico's third ecclesiastical council in 1585, ordering that all scripts for religious dramas be submitted to the archbishop for approval a month before the planned performance (García Icazbalceta 1968:353).

Nahuatl theater has received considerable scholarly attention. I will not attempt here to reiterate the history of scholarship on the subject nor to inventory all of the available data.[8] At this point I offer only some general comments and interpretation. Comparisons between the Holy Wednesday script and other known Nahuatl dramas are made in the annotations on the plays.

The early Franciscan friars began staging Nahuatl plays as a strategy for evangelization. The first such performance on record is a dramatization of Judgment Day, with Christ meting out punishments on sinners who were unprepared for the world's end. Enacted at Tlatelolco in 1531 or 1533, this play so impressed the native audience that the event was recorded by Nahua chroniclers. The same or a similar play was performed in 1535 at San José de los Naturales in Tenochtitlan. The friars thought that the play led many people to accept Christianity. Drama became a standard tool of the missionary trade throughout the colony, with the other religious orders, even the Carmelite monks at San Sebastián, eventually following the Franciscans' example.[9]

The adoption of theater into the emerging Nahua Church was one example of a wider trend toward public and participatory modes of devotional expression. The early friars found that the most effective—indeed, the only—way to attract significant numbers of Nahua converts was through the use of song, dance, plays, processions, and their accompanying pageantry and paraphernalia: saints' images, crosses, costumes, banners, triumphal arches, musical instruments. The friars recognized the importance of public ritual in preconquest religious life and considered these activities acceptable for the Nahua Church, provided that they now be Christian in content and purpose.

Theater, in the sense of a prepared dialogue spoken by a group of role-playing individuals in front of an audience, did not exist among the Nahuas before the Spanish invasion. However, there were aspects of drama in Nahua ritual and social life that provided a basis for Nahua appropriation of the new genre.

In calendrical ritual, costumed individuals impersonated deities and interacted with priests according to standardized scenarios. Many if not all of these rituals were linked to sacred narratives referring to the mythological deeds of the deities and to the local ethnic group's own history, constructed according to mythic patterns. However, the existing descriptions suggest that these stories were represented more through details of costume and gesture than through speech. These rituals were acted out in the temple plazas, atop temple platforms, and within the temple buildings. These spaces were permanently set apart and sacred; they were not stages temporarily transformed in the immediate context of performance.

Performances, whether ritual or theatrical, place the performers in a liminal, "in-between" space where they are no longer quite themselves nor are they quite the character represented. As Schechner puts it, they are "not themselves" and "not not themselves." The actor brings something of his or her own personality to the character portrayed; conversely, even in

Western theater an actor's identity may be permanently altered by a role he or she plays (Schechner 1985:6, 126). In Mexica temple ritual, however, the identification between performer and character was particularly strong.

That Nahuas conceived of the human being not as a firmly individualized personality but as a rather unstable assemblage of parts affected their conceptions of impersonation. Putting on the costume of a deity made that being manifest in one's own person. The regalia represented the god via a metonymic substitution; the god's identity added itself to the aggregate of components that comprised the person. Both personae were fully present. This situation might be best expressed not as a state of being "not" and "not not" oneself, but rather as an equally liminal condition of being both oneself and another.

In the context of the ritual, one was treated as if one were indistinguishable from the divinity. This powerful divine presence could override and dissolve one's personal identity. It was not unusual for the "actor" to be killed as an offering to the deity he or she represented, the person's individuality being, thus, permanently eliminated.

Large numbers of people often participated in these rituals, at least to the extent of bringing offerings, engaging in penitential activities, or joining in songs and dances performed in the temple plazas. These songs and dances were themselves rather theatrical; the singers sometimes played roles, claiming for themselves the identity of deities, famous rulers or warriors of the past, other ethnic groups, or the opposite sex. Conversely, parts of the ritual were wholly or partially obscured from public view, atop pyramids or within temples. There was, thus, no sharp or consistent distinction between audience and actors, between the stage and the house, or between onstage and offstage spaces.[10]

Formal recitation of speeches occurred on certain social and ritual occasions. Some were prayers (*tetlatlauhtiliztli* 'asking someone for something') addressed to divinities; others were advice and admonitions (*tenonotzaliztli* 'advising someone') addressed to children or other family members, vassals, or other persons. These sometimes took the form of a dialogue, with the person of junior rank briefly responding to the words of his or her superior. Skilled orators employed a special genre of speaking style, which they called *huehuehtlahtolli* 'old speech' or 'words of the elders.'[11] The elite claimed particular mastery of this prestigious verbal art form. Speeches delivered in this style were part of day-to-day social relations; the speakers were not impersonating other characters or acting within the "make-believe" frame of the stage. Nevertheless, the formalized

and formulaic nature of these interactions lent them an aspect of theatri-
cality.

León-Portilla (1992) argues that ritualized discourses such as these
were passed along in a set form via pictographic manuscripts and memori-
zation. Although I agree that the Nahuas had the capability to pass along
such exact versions of their texts if and when they chose to do so, I doubt
that most ritual speeches were quite so standardized. Gruzinski (1991)
makes a valid point when he treats the expanding role of written expression
as an important aspect of colonization with profound, though difficult to
reconstruct, effects on the organization of thought. The fixed, written text
only gained primacy over the fluid, easily adapted oral versions as a result
of the friars' introduction of alphabetic writing. Although stylistic continuities were present and significant, text genres that in preconquest times
had been oral productions were now supplemented and in some cases
superseded by new kinds of texts that originated—like the Holy Wednesday play itself—as written products. However central the oral performance
remained as a part of native Christian worship, these performances were
colored by "the primacy, or at least the anteriority, of writing" (Gruzinski
1991:65). The dramatic script, even if written in Nahuatl by a native author, was a new form that challenged and replaced traditional modes of
generating discourse.

Thus, despite an affinity for costumes, impersonation, and recitation,
the Nahuas at the time of the conquest had no concepts of "theater,"
"stage," "actor," "script," "audience," or "play" as such. They did not distinguish between the dramatization of a sacred narrative and the performance
of a ritual in the way that, for example, a Spaniard would distinguish an
auto of the Last Supper from a priest's celebration of the Mass.

The religious theater introduced by the Franciscans was easily accommodated to native practice. The new plays were based on sacred narratives;
the new written scripts imitated *huehuehtlahtolli* style; the spaces employed
were the church patios and open chapels that had replaced the temples and
their plazas. Hymns were often sung during or after a performance, and
dances and processions were among the festival day's other activities.

It is very likely that Nahuas involved in these theatrical events did
not draw sharp distinctions between the play and the rituals, between the
actors and the audience, between space temporarily used as a stage and the
permanently sacred precinct of the church and its patio. Participation was
collective. In some plays, especially early ones, large numbers of people
were directly involved in the production as costumed "extras" on the set

or as dancers. Even in those performed by only a few actors, the people to whom they addressed their oratory were also on the scene and were engaged with them in a social interaction.

The Nahuatl term applied to the colonial theater indicates some differentiation from earlier ritual forms. The productions were often called *neixcuitilli* 'something that sets an example.' The term became so well established that in 1768 a Dominican priest, writing in Spanish, referred to Passion and other plays performed in Nahua communities as *Nixcuitiles*—the Nahuatl word had become a loanword in Mexican Spanish (Representaciones teatrales 1934:346, 351).

I suspect that the use of *neixcuitilli* for dramatic performances did not have preconquest precedents but was introduced to translate Spanish *ejemplo* and Latin *exemplum*, or "example" in the sense of an exemplary tale or anecdote such as priests employed as "real-life" models within their homiletic discourses. The term *neixcuitilli* could be applied to these stories. The friar who compiled the manuscript containing the Holy Wednesday play equates *exemplum* with *neixcuitilli* in this sense elsewhere in his text (159v). Conversely, the term *ejemplo* was sometimes applied to Nahuatl dramas. This usage appears, for example, in the chronicle of the Franciscan Juan de Torquemada. He describes dramas performed at San José de los Naturales in the late sixteenth century as "representations of *ejemplos*, in the manner of *comedias*, Sunday afternoons after there had been a sermon" (Torquemada 1975–83:VI, 395). A mid-sixteenth-century Nahuatl text quoted in Horcasitas (1974:73) pairs the words *neixcuitilli* and *ejemplo* in reference to a dramatic presentation.

Neixcuitilli was a convenient term for plays in general, whether or not they were based on the priests' stock of exemplary anecdotes, and could substitute for the Spanish terms *representación*, *auto*, and *comedia*. Its usage imparts to the plays a homiletic aspect that the temple rituals did not have. It also establishes a new category of performance within which such new introductions as the written script could be accommodated. However, this conception of theater is consistent with the advice-giving function of *huehuehtlahtolli*-style admonitions. Since the plays provided examples in the form of enacted narratives as well as verbal advice, the term for admonitive speeches, *tenonotzaliztli*, was not appropriate. The term *neixcuitilli* names a new performance genre, but one possessing continuities with earlier Nahua forms and not quite the equivalent of "drama" in the European sense.

Theater had different meanings in Nahua and Spanish worlds not only because of these differences in conceptual categories, this slippage in meaning between cultural systems. To the friars, this was a "theater of evangelization," as Arróniz entitles his book on the topic (1979). Its purpose was to spread the Word of God, to attract the Nahuas to the Holy Catholic Faith and inform them of their duties as Christians. The friars' attitude was, as Trexler (1987:575) puts it, "we think, they act."

The Nahuas' adoption of the term *neixcuitilli* shows that they acknowledged this didactic aspect of the theater. But this does not mean that many of them had much clue as to what the friars thought. What people in the audience saw was other Nahuas playing the roles of beings that they had come to recognize as sacred. Even when costumed like the images imported from Europe, these Christs and Marys, these angels and saints displayed the faces and hands of native people. Unlike the friars, they were fluent native speakers of Nahuatl. A written script lay behind the performance, but, in contrast to situations in which preachers read directly from prepared texts, it was not visible onstage; rather, the actors gave the appearance of generating their own discourse. Given the close identification the Nahuas had been accustomed to make between sacred beings and ritual impersonators, it may have seemed to the observers as though Christian personae had entered their presence and taken on Nahua identities.

The scripts imparted Christian messages, but when translated into Nahuatl these were never quite what the friars thought. Nahuas authored, co-authored, or at least edited the scripts, and thus had ample opportunity to reorient their content. The actors too, even if they followed the script word for word, could impart, through their gestures and tones of voice, different or additional messages as well as their own attitudes toward the words they were uttering. Much of performance consists of such metatextual aspects, the conventions for which are culturally transmitted and internalized. The friars would have been unable to recognize and understand, let alone control, the manner in which actors interpreted their roles.

Nahuatl theater was, then, not simply a theater of evangelization but also a theater of celebration, around which communities of people came together to observe religious holidays and express devotion to God and the saints.[12] Extra-community political alliances were eliminated under colonial rule, but identification with the local community or *altepetl* remained strong. Religious celebrations were important rituals of solidarity. Audiences for religious plays remained large, even after the people had suffered the worst of the epidemics. Participation in such events was a collective action on the part of community residents.

It was also a theater of self-legitimation, in which Nahuas represented themselves as pious Christians who understood Christian narratives, followed Christian teachings, and knew how to handle crosses, gifts of the Magi, and other props and costumes. Since members of the native nobility were more likely than commoners to plan, finance, and perform in these plays, theater was one means for nobles to establish and assert their claims to leadership.[13] They determined what discourses and practices would be authoritative within Nahua Christianity, thus mediating between Spanish overlords and Nahua commoners as well as controlling the form and extent of resistance. These representations of native Christianity were directed not only at other Nahuas but also at Spaniards. Torquemada describes the audiences at the San José plays as "innumerable" and including some Spanish observers (1975–83: VI, 395).

And it was a theater of transformation, in which Christian narratives were accommodated to the Nahuatl language and given local nuances via word, costume, and gesture. The sacred beings of Christianity appeared in Nahua guise and spoke to their fellow Nahuas. The local church patio, sacred heart of the community, became Bethlehem, Jerusalem, Assisi, Eden. Christianity slipped from the friars' controlling grasp; Nahuas negotiated directly with sacred forces that governed their conflicted, colonized reality.

The Holy Wednesday Drama:
Authorship, Date, Provenience

The Nahuatl version of Izquierdo's play lies near the end of a manuscript some 220 quarto leaves in length. The manuscript is bound in limp vellum and has fragments of ties once used to fasten it closed. The leaves are numbered by the original compiler, who also placed a partial table of contents at the beginning. His numbering begins on what is actually the sixth leaf of the surviving text, and occasional leaves elsewhere are misnumbered. The play, occupying leaves 207 through 215 according to his numbering, is the last substantial text inscribed within the manuscript.

The play is immediately preceded in the manuscript by a text in Spanish and Latin for the festival of the birth of Mary (204v–207r). This is preceded by entries, in Nahuatl with Latin citations, on the resurrection of Christ (202v–203r) and the triumph of the cross (203v–204r). These two entries bear a closer relationship to the subject matter of the play than any of the manuscript's other content. The resurrection text contains passages that appear to be influenced by the Easter songs of Sahagún's *Psalmodia christiana* (see Appendix, Text V). It also refers briefly to the harrowing of hell.

A few blank pages follow the play, then the verso of leaf 218 bears notes in Spanish regarding some medicinal remedies. A final two leaves were also left blank by the original compiler, but the verso of the last leaf was at some point inscribed, in a different hand from those within the text proper, with the names and titles (not signatures) of two Spanish officials of the General Indian Court: Juan Díaz de Agüero, *procurador general de los indios*, and *licenciado* Gaspar de Valdés, *letrado de los indios*.[14]

The document appears to be a kind of notebook in which miscellaneous entries were penned over a period of years. It comprises 19 signatures. Text is continuous across several of the boundaries between signatures, including one within the play itself (204v–205r). Discontinuities at other junctures indicate that the complete manuscript could have been written in sections that were later bound together.

Most of the manuscript is written in a single hand. Often difficult to read and full of flourishes and abbreviations, this is certainly the handwriting of a Spaniard. The exceptions are the play itself and leaves 44r through 55v. This section, written in the clear, even printing of an indigenous scribe, contains a series of sermons in Nahuatl, with some text in Latin and Spanish. The play is also written in a native hand, but one that differs sufficiently from the previous one that it must belong to a different individual.

The remaining content includes a variety of doctrinal materials written in Latin, Nahuatl, and Spanish, with the same entry often combining two or all three of these languages. Many of the Nahuatl texts are translations and elaborations upon Latin and/or Spanish passages that precede them. The bulk of the material consists of readings and sermons for various saints' festivals and Sundays of the Church calendar; or, more often, brief notes upon which a longer written text or an oral elaboration could have been based. Moralistic and theological discourses not connected with a particular occasion for preaching are interspersed among these calendrical entries. Entries not directed at Catholic preaching or moral guidance are limited to a few personal notes, Spanish discourses on salt and on the calendar, and the medicinal remedies on the last page. These refer to the use of chocolate, maize, vanilla, chile, achiote, and other native food products.

Who was the compiler? He had to be a Franciscan friar with some competence in Nahuatl. That he was a Franciscan is evident from the fact that he twice included materials for the festival of Saint Francis (110r–v, 190r–v) and once for the festival of that saint's stigmatization (199r–v); the festivals of saints associated with other religious orders are neglected. Furthermore, his personal notes document his presence in the towns of Tecali, Huexotzingo, and Tlaxcala. These three Nahua towns, located southeast of Mexico near the city of Puebla, were centers of Franciscan activity to the exclusion of the other religious orders. Finally, the native scribe whose pen filled pages 44r–55v states that he was working at Santiago Tlatelolco, another center of Franciscan activity.

Competence in Nahuatl is indicated by the Nahuatl passages written in the friar's own hand as well as his inclusion of the two sections transcribed by Nahuas. This does not necessarily show that he was truly fluent in the language, for he may have been copying from texts prepared by others or working directly with native speakers. Judging from the distribution of Spanish and Nahuatl notes for sermons, he seems to have preached in Nahuatl only on certain occasions, though perhaps in some cases for several weeks at a time.

These facts are not sufficient to identify this friar by name, for a substantial proportion of the Franciscans in Mexico preached in Nahuatl and had at least enough facility in that language to have produced this manuscript. In 1570, the Franciscan Gerónimo de Mendieta, a prolific chronicler and spokesman for the order, prepared a list of all the Franciscan priests in the province of Mexico, in which he noted their ages and their language abilities (Sempat Assadourian 1988:389–404).[15] Leaving out those men whom Mendieta says had arrived too recently to have learned any native language, there are a total of 148 priests, all but 38 of whom knew at least enough Nahuatl to hear confessions in it. Eight other Nahuatl-speaking Franciscans, including Mendieta himself, were currently in Spain.

By the late 1580s a number of the men on Mendieta's list were dead. Several of the most illustrious Franciscan figures in Nahuatl philology had passed away: Alonso de Molina, Andrés de Olmos, Pedro de Gante, Alonso de Escalona, Arnaldo de Basacio, Juan de Gaona, Miguel de Zárate. The great ethnographer Bernardino de Sahagún, frail and palsied, would live until 1590, but his distinctive, spidery hand does not appear on the manuscript.

However, the distinguished scholars Pedro Oroz and Mendieta himself were still active. Younger friars such as Juan Bautista, Francisco de Gamboa, and Juan de Torquemada had come on the scene. According to Torquemada (1975–83:VI, 395), all three of these men were involved in the production of Nahuatl plays; Bautista confirms his own participation (1606:prologue). Bautista, born in New Spain in 1555, joined the order in 1571 and began studying Nahuatl around 1578. As of 1591, he was lecturer in theology at San Francisco in Mexico (Zulaica y Gárate 1991:219). Gamboa had professed by 1580 and began preaching in Nahuatl as soon as he finished his studies (Torquemada 1975–83:VI, 394). Torquemada took the Franciscan habit in 1579 or 1580 and was ordained in 1587 or 1588. As of 1590–91 both he and Gamboa were posted at San Francisco; in 1592 Torquemada was at Tlatelolco.[16] I have, however, found no direct evidence linking any of these men to the Holy Wednesday drama.

At the beginning of the sermons written in the first native hand, the scribe left this note: *En Sanctiago delante de fray Jeronimo de Mendieta y otros p's.* Thus this part of the text was written in Santiago Tlatelolco "in front of" Mendieta and other *padres*, or priests. A similar statement appears in Nahuatl in one of the drafts of Sahagún's ethnographic work, stating that the text was made in front of Sahagún and at the college in Tlatelolco (Nicolau D'Olwer 1987:38). Mendieta's presence on this occasion, however, does not mean that it was he who compiled the manuscript. A document signed by him and apparently written in his hand does not match the handwriting of this text.[17]

As mentioned above, some of the manuscript's entries were penned in the towns of Tecali, Huexotzingo, and Tlaxcala. The friar may have been posted at each of these establishments for a time, since the personnel at any given friary were often rotated, or he may have been traveling for other reasons. On page 60r the friar recorded that he did not preach in Tecali on a particular Sunday because he went to preach in a nearby village. On page 90r he gives his first clue to the manuscript's date, stating: "I entered Huexotzingo on the eve of Saint Lawrence 88," that is, August 9, 1588. The name Huexotzingo also appears on pages 85v and 113r. The friar's whereabouts then remain undocumented until page 182r, where he wrote, "I entered Tlaxcala on the eve of Saint Bartholomew and I preached the following Sunday, the eleventh Sunday after Pentecost." Saint Bartholomew Eve is August 23. The Sunday following this date coincided with the eleventh Sunday after Pentecost in 1585 and in 1590; the latter date is most likely given that this part of the manuscript should postdate August of 1588. On page 194r the friar indicates that he was still (or again) in Tlaxcala. Another piece of evidence relevant to the dating of the manuscript is the watermarks in the paper, which were in use during the period 1550–1590.[18]

Given the drama's position within the manuscript, it must have been transcribed after August 23, 1590. It is possible that it was not transcribed until a later year, perhaps 1591 or 1592, and perhaps at a time when it was actually performed. This would place it, at the earliest, during Holy Week of 1591. However, the play could have been composed sometime prior to its inscription in this manuscript. If Izquierdo's play was indeed first published in 1582, it could have arrived in Mexico within months and been translated into Nahuatl anytime between then and the early 1590s. 1590 may be considered an approximate date for the play, but some leeway on either side of this date must be allowed.

I surmise that the compiler of the manuscript returned to Mexico from Tlaxcala between the time he penned his page 194r and the time, 13 leaves further on, that he engaged a native scribe to copy the Holy Wednesday play into his notebook. As evidence I cite the fact that the other section of the manuscript written in a native hand was produced in Mexico, specifically at the Franciscan establishment in Tlatelolco. On his travels through the Puebla region, the friar may have met Nahua scribes and scholars with the ability to copy or even to compose this text. However, the fact that over 150 continuous leaves are inscribed only with the friar's own hand would seem to indicate that he was not disposed to hand over his precious papers to local writers as he passed from town to town. His previous consultation with one or more Nahua scholars at Tlatelolco provided a precedent for this second occasion.

This evidence is, admittedly, circumstantial, but the role of Tlatelolco as a center of Nahua and Franciscan scholarship and text production—to be explored below—supports my contention that the Nahuatl drama is a product of the urban center. This particular friar's interest in the text suggests that he saw the play as potentially useful for his work in other regions. But since his manuscript effectively terminates with the inscription of the drama, and the manuscript itself ended up in the library at Tlatelolco, it is impossible to know whether he carried his copy of the play to other Nahua communities.

The Holy Wednesday script is written in a typical indigenous scribal hand and in an orthography that reflects Nahua pronunciations of Spanish loanwords (Figure 5). It also displays a sophisticated grasp of the oratorical genre *huehuehtlahtolli*, the "words of the elders" mentioned above. This genre is characterized above all by the use of parallel constructions, or strings of two or more phrases expressing the same or similar ideas and/or echoing one another phonologically. Points are stated and reiterated rather than being developed in a linear fashion leading to a conclusion. In 1606

5. The first page of the "Holy Wednesday" drama. Princeton Collections of Western Americana, Visual Materials Division, Department of Rare Books and Special Collections, Princeton University Libraries.

fray Juan Bautista alluded to this feature of Nahuatl expression as follows: "The Mexican language is in itself so elegant, copious, and abundant, that one can hardly translate a line of Castilian or Latin into it, that does not come out twice as long" (Bautista 1606:xi).

Gingerich aptly describes the *huehuehtlahtolli* style as

an elegantly evolved and polished example of the oral-formulaic style which characterizes pre- or semi-literate civilizations everywhere, [it] favors a highly repetitious, often circular, incremental, and subtly varying mode of expression which is long out of vogue in contemporary English. (1992:363)

A Nahuatl metaphor equated such speech with the scattering and spreading about of precious stones (Sahagún 1950–82:VI, 248–49). The figure is appropriate in that it conveys the idea of an assemblage or collection of polished and ornamental phrases, each valuable in its own right rather than as a component of a larger, linearly organized argument. Karttunen and Lockhart observe a similar structuring in Nahuatl songs: particular themes are explored through the reiteration of related points rather than through a linear development (1980:16–17).

This matter of style is vital to the issue of the Nahuatl drama's authorship, for it indicates that the author was a native speaker of Nahuatl. Friars skilled in Nahuatl could generate grammatically correct Nahuatl texts, but these tended nevertheless to follow non-native discursive models: linear, homiletic, their persuasiveness dependent on appeals to God and threats of hell rather than on the poetic power of the words themselves and the authority conveyed simply by speaking in this manner. Accommodation to indigenous style was accomplished through the employment of stock metaphorical phrases and the intrusion of formulaic couplets into prose text. The friars compiled transcriptions of traditional orations and catalogs of metaphorical phrases precisely for this purpose.

The Nahuatl play contains strikingly few such stock formulas. It is the work of someone who was not merely trying to mimic *huehuehtlahtolli* speech, but who knew how to construct good Nahuatl oratory. He adapts the traditional *huehuehtlahtolli* style to the practice of translation and to topics never discussed by his ancestors, while working within the somewhat limited and conventionalized vocabulary typical of Church-related texts.

The author also understood Christian teachings well and considered them worthy of being expressed in this oral-poetic format. He was also literate in Spanish, though not perfectly so—his misreadings of the Spanish text are further evidence of his indigenous identity. But he was competent enough in Spanish to comprehend most of Izquierdo's vocabulary and rather tortuous syntax. For a work of translation, however, the degree to which Nahua models of discourse and narrative structure intrude upon and compete with the style and organization of the Spanish source is striking.

It is very likely that he wrote his play at the behest and under the supervision of one or more Franciscan friars, who handed him Izquierdo's play and who would have been available to elucidate any points of language or doctrine that he failed to grasp. But his obligation to them would have been only to produce a translation, not the greatly expanded, masterfully crafted, significantly reworked, and stage-ready text that he did compose.

The Nahua playwright was almost surely an alumnus of the Franciscan college at Tlatelolco, and it is very likely that he wrote his play at that institution. The precise identity of this man cannot be pinned down; it is quite possible that two or more men worked together. But something can be said about his, or their, background, and some possible authors can even be identified by name.

The Colegio de Santa Cruz

The Colegio de Santa Cruz was founded in 1536 at the Franciscan church and friary in Tlatelolco[19] (Figure 6). Soon after their mission to New Spain was formally instituted in 1524, Franciscans had begun running informal boarding schools for sons of the indigenous nobility at their various establishments. Here they taught the boys to read and write in Nahuatl, Latin, and, to a lesser extent, Spanish. Thus the early friars introduced the convenience of alphabetic writing to a society that already had a tradition of pictographic writing and a great respect for books and scholars. No similar effort was made to educate native girls: what little European schooling was offered them focused on Spanish-style domestic arts and Christian devotional practices rather than reading and writing.

One goal of the friars' education program was to train assistants who would help the friars attain the language skills they needed to preach to the rest of the native population. A larger goal was to further the Christianization and pacification of the colony by raising young leaders whose loyalties would lie with their Franciscan teachers rather than with their own parents, who were as yet unbaptized or only nominally converted. In the early

6. The church and plaza at Tlatelolco, site of the Colegio de Santa Cruz. The extant church building dates to the early seventeenth century. Photograph by the author.

years, these boys served as "hostages for their unbelieving fathers, and an elite cadre for subsequent evangelization" (Trexler 1987:552).

Struck by the skill exhibited by many of these boys in the mastery of Latin grammar and other facets of European education, the Franciscans sought to provide the brightest of the boys with a secondary education. They would thus be better equipped to serve as administrators in the colonial government. Their knowledge of Christian theology and participation in pious practices would set positive examples for the people of their communities. The hope that some of them might prove capable of entering the priesthood was a further motivation, though the idea was later abandoned. The friars' plan won the approval and financial support of New Spain's first viceroy, don Antonio de Mendoza, who had a building constructed adjacent to the Tlatelolco friary and assigned to it the revenues from several properties he controlled.

The first institution of higher education founded in the colonial Americas, the College of the Holy Cross opened with great ceremony on January 6, 1536. This was the festival of Epiphany, which commemorated the three pagan kings who journeyed to Bethlehem to worship the infant Christ. Symbolizing the Christian conversion of all pagan peoples, the festival had local meaning in reference to the conversion of indigenous rulers. It was, thus, an appropriate starting date for a school intended to train Christian leaders for the native populace.

A few years later the original two-room adobe structure, consisting of dormitory room and study hall, was replaced by a two-story stone building with additional classroom and office space and a separate room for the library.

The guardian, or head friar, of the Franciscan friary at Tlatelolco was entrusted with supervision of the college. In deference to Franciscan vows of poverty, the college's financial affairs were placed in the hands of a Spanish steward appointed by the viceroy. This would prove a less than optimal arrangement, as this individual and his successors had no particular commitment to indigenous education.

Between 60 and 100 boys studied at the school, entering at age 10 to 12 and remaining for a three-year period before they returned to their home communities. Apart from an occasional commoner admitted on the basis of exceptional talent, these boys were the offspring of noble lineages from many different towns and cities. The plan was to take two or three boys from each principal town. The local friars selected the boys based on both their rank and their ability and persuaded—or compelled—their parents to let them go. The vast majority must have been Nahuas, but there may have been some boys from Otomi, Matlatzinca, and other non-Nahua groups among whom the Franciscans were active.

The students lived at the college and received their room, board, books, and classes at no charge. They were given a kind of cassock, or *hopa*, to wear. The boys all bunked together in one large room. Each boy slept on his own native-style bed, a wooden platform covered with a woven mat, and stored his books and clothing in his own small trunk. The dormitory was lit at night and the boys were watched to ensure that they maintained what Mendieta refers to as "honesty"—in other words, to prevent them from engaging in autoerotic or homosexual acts.

The boys ate with the friars in their refectory. They rarely ventured beyond the church patio, though they must have interacted with the Tlatelolcans who worshipped at the same church, especially the church officials. There were also the cooks, gardeners, and porters who were on the school's payroll. As of 1570, these employees included four women who prepared tortillas and other foods for the students' meals.

The educational program was modeled after the traditional liberal arts curriculum of European schools. The seven liberal arts were Latin grammar, rhetoric, logic, arithmetic, geometry, astronomy, and music. In addition, there was some instruction in theology and medicine. The teachers were highly qualified, for among the Franciscans were a number of notable scholars trained at such universities as Salamanca and Paris.

The daily round was structured and rigorous. The boys observed the canonical hours, going into the Tlatelolco church seven times daily to recite their prayers. The day began at dawn when the friars tolled the bell for the Office of Prime. Clad in their cassocks, the boys walked in procession to the church and joined the friars in the chants for Prime. One of the friars celebrated Mass, attended by student altar boys, and then the boys returned to the school to begin their lessons. These were interrupted for meals and for the other canonical hours. At midnight the boys rose from their beds to go one last time to the church for the Office of Matins.

Had they belonged to an earlier generation, these young nobles would have attended schools called *calmecac*, where they would have been trained in military, administrative, and religious duties. The lifestyle in these schools, as described in colonial texts, was more rigorous than that of the Colegio. Fasting, vigils, and other forms of self-mortification such as bloodletting were demanded constantly. The boys had to rise at midnight to offer incense to the deities, sweep the temples, and perform other rites.[20]

Although the *calmecac* provided an indigenous precedent for the Colegio, the latter institution represents a break with the past, a rupture between one generation and the next. The young men who emerged from its halls were a new breed, anomalies among their own people, fully literate and multi-lingual. Privy to the sacred knowledge of the conquerors, they were wise youths in a society that equated wisdom with old age. Interpreters between European and Nahua worlds, the young men became cultural brokers negotiating the exchange of symbols and meanings between conqueror and conquered.

For native boys to be cloistered away memorizing Latin declensions while their people suffered epidemics and exploitation may seem but one more cruel manifestation of conquest—ironic if not absurd; tragic, perhaps; irrelevant in any case to the larger scheme of imperial domination. Those who have taken the Franciscan education program seriously have tended to view it in terms of what Ricard called a "spiritual conquest"; Kobayashi entitled his 1974 book "education as conquest." The emphasis is on acculturation, assimilation. The students are seen as if through the friars' own eyes; the accomplishments of the graduates as scholars and statesmen reflect back upon the friars who trained them. If the Franciscan program was nothing but colonialism with a humanistic face, it may easily be dismissed as a hegemonic ploy.

But knowledge empowers, and so does language. The Nahuas who knew the most about the conquering culture were not thereby obliged slavishly to honor its tenets. Graduates left the Colegio conversant in two cultural traditions. They were able not only to speak Latin and Spanish in addition to Nahuatl, but had been taught to reason according to Western as well as Nahua logical principles and to construct arguments according to Western as well as Nahua rhetorical arts. Who could be better equipped to compare and evaluate both cultures, to challenge Spanish authority on its own grounds, to subvert its paradigms through subtle manipulations and restatements? Who could be better equipped to construct new ways of being Nahua, new models of the past and the present, suited to their people's current situation? The troubled history of the Colegio attests to the empowering character of the institution. Had it been harmless or irrelevant, had it churned out docile and obedient mouthpieces who furthered the cause of Spanish imperialism, it would not have met with such opposition and controversy.

Anomalies among the native people, the collegians were an affront to Spanish colonists aiming to make of the Nahuas a class of servile laborers.

Spaniards who could blithely dismiss all the accomplishments of native civilization as deviltry and nonsense were obliged to think again when confronted with boys who manifested their intelligence in a manner consistent with European values. Opponents of the school attempted to discredit it by asserting that the students were merely mimicking their teachers and in fact were no more intelligent than parrots.

Or, if persuaded of the students' capabilities, they claimed that free access to scripture would inspire heresies. The students would, for example, read of Old Testament figures who had multiple wives and take this as divine sanction to follow the polygynous custom of their own ancestors. Furthermore, reading Latin histories would teach them that Spain had once been a heathen land and had been conquered by the Romans. Seeing these parallels between their own and Spanish history, they might presume to question Spain's superiority. According to Mendieta, some priests opposed the school for fear that their own inadequate grasp of Latin would be exposed by these native scholars. In short, either the native pupils were stupid, or they were too clever for their own (or rather, the Spaniards') good; in either case, they ought to stay out of the classroom.

The Franciscans ardently defended their students against such charges, but they themselves were not entirely pleased with the youths' progress. Backing away from their plan to train indigenous priests, they declared the collegians unfit for the priesthood, not because they lacked intellectual ability but because they were over-endowed with sensuality. As Bishop Zumárraga phrased it in his oft-cited 1540 letter to Charles V, "they tend toward marriage rather than toward continence" (García Icazbalceta 1947:III, 204). In 1555, this exclusionary policy was formalized in the edicts of an ecclesiastical council meeting.[21]

The friars' reluctance to empower native men with the priesthood cannot really be blamed on the burgeoning hormones of adolescent boys. Discourse attributing excessive sensuality and carnality to colonized peoples was widely used as a mode of asserting and legitimizing European domination, including the friars' domination of the native Church. It was a way of reducing to a familiar and inferior category the ineffable otherness of native culture, of dismissing a moral and philosophical outlook that did not coincide with Christianity's uncompromising dualism of good and evil, spirit and flesh.

Enjoying in the native communities a degree of authority and influence far exceeding their initial expectations, perhaps the friars were reluctant to share their new-found power. For whatever reasons, their vision of a New World utopia came to feature no native priests. But they continued to support the separation of native and Spanish colonial societies, the formation of a kingdom of Christian Indians ruled by a viceroy only nominally subject to the Spanish king. In such a realm, educated men would have a place as leaders of a largely self-governing native population.

As for the collegians themselves, they may have had little motivation to become priests in the first place. Their education opened up to them employment opportunities within the colonial bureaucracy. As sons of noble dynasties, they had high status in their communities and, with their education, were strong candidates for political office. They also had an obligation to marry a girl of suitable rank and carry on the family line. Their relatives and neighbors at home contradicted the friars' teachings by condoning marriage and procreation. To renounce all worldly status and family ties may have been an unappealing, even unimaginable, alternative.

Particularly telling in this regard are three Latin letters that Pablo Nazareo, a Tlatelolco collegian and lord of the town of Xaltocan, wrote to the king and queen of Spain between 1556 and 1566 (in Osorio Romero 1990). Nazareo recounts his activities in support of the propagation of the faith: he has been instrumental in destroying idols, teaching doctrine, and translating Catholic texts into widely-used Nahuatl versions. Borrowing a figure from his Franciscan mentors, he represents himself and his fellow collegians as "new men" (*noui homines*) nurtured in Christian faith and customs and the knowledge of the liberal arts. However, the purpose of his letters is to petition the Crown for worldly possessions and privileges he claims are due him and his wife not only in return for his contributions to the faith but in respect to his status as a high-ranking nobleman and his wife's kinship with the former Mexica emperor Motecuhzoma. Each letter lists the towns for which his family had traditional tribute-collecting rights; the third letter lays out the genealogy of his own and his wife's families. For a "new man," he betrays a rather old-fashioned concern with dynastic lineage, wealth, and status.[22]

Friars adored the story of how Saint Francis renounced his birthright by stripping himself naked in front of his merchant father and striding out into the world with not a single trapping of his earlier life. Three years in Tlatelolco might not have been enough to convince a Nahua noble that his social identity was so readily expendable. The collegians' refusal to become celibate clones of the friars may be seen as an assertion of indigenous values, an act of resistance masked behind the friars' dismissive allusion to their sensual proclivities.

Sometime after the first decade of operation, the Franciscans withdrew from direct involvement in the Colegio and left it in the hands of a group of alumni. These men filled the roles of rector (a post filled for a time by Pablo Nazareo), counsellors, and teachers. The friars' dissociation from the Colegio suggests a declining interest in the institution and mixed feelings about its mission. The epidemic of 1545, which killed a number of the students and alumni, also contributed to this demoralization.

For over twenty years the school was run by its own graduates. According to Sahagún, they did not do a very good job; perhaps they did not run it as Sahagún thought they should. He does place part of the blame on a Spanish steward who mismanaged the school's endowment. In general, the school suffered declining financial fortunes beginning especially in 1564, when with the death of Viceroy Luis de Velasco the Elder it was deprived of any further viceregal and royal support. Thenceforward it was dependent on a small annuity and private donations, some of which came from Nahua property-owners. The building had fallen into disrepair and the dormitory was uninhabitable, reducing the college to a day school. As epidemics decreased the numbers of both current and potential students, more non-noble boys were admitted and younger students were brought in for elementary-level lessons.

In the early 1570s[23] the school was again brought under the supervision of the Tlatelolco friars, one of whom, Sahagún, had been present at its opening and had taught Latin there in the early years. The building was repaired. Some of the alumni continued to work there as teachers. In 1576 the worst epidemic yet to hit the native population left the school nearly empty. Sahagún, writing in that same year, predicted a continuing decline in the Colegio's fortunes: the natives were ill-disposed to learn, the friars were weary, external support was lacking.

In February 1586, a friar visiting Tlatelolco penned the following description of the Colegio:

Within the patio of this convent is built a college with the vocation of the Holy Cross, where they teach the Indian boys to read and write and parse grammar; the patron of this college is the king and a friar of that convent has charge of it and there the college receives rents with which the teachers who teach the children are paid. (Ciudad Real 1976:I, 144)

The salaried teachers must have been Nahua collegians, as friars would not have been paid for such work.

Mendieta, posted at Tlatelolco in the mid-1590s, describes the college as a day school where boys from Tlatelolco came to learn reading, writing, and "good customs." Latin was hardly taught any more. Higher education for Nahua men was by that time available only from the Jesuits, who founded their college for native scholars, San Gregorio, in 1586 (Jacobsen 1938:127). And few were able to take advantage of it. During the 1590s only seventeen native students were enrolled at San Gregorio, and some of them were forced to interrupt their studies in order to fulfill labor obligations on Spanish projects (Gibson 1964:383).

During the 1580s and 1590s, and even into the early years of the following century, the Franciscan establishment at Tlatelolco remained an intellectual center where Mendieta and fray Pedro Oroz penned their histories of the Franciscan mission; where Sahagún, defying efforts to suppress his work, produced his final ethnographic and historical writings; and where friars and former students worked together on Nahuatl catechistic and devotional texts.

Tlatelolco was also a bastion of the radical and millenarian crusade that had dominated the early years of the Franciscan mission, when friars dreamed of transforming the native people into a utopian society of perfect Christians. By this time the friars had become disillusioned due to persistent opposition from the ecclesiastical hierarchy, the Spanish colonists, and the Crown, as well as what they considered the recalcitrance of native people who refused to conform to Franciscan ideals.[24] But they continued to challenge the developing status quo of the colony, under which abuse and exploitation of the native populace was business as usual and the religious orders were losing influence within the colonial Church. As Poole astutely observes, the friars "were still trying to live the 1520s in the 1580s" (1987:213).

In the mid-1580s a number of the Franciscans in Mexico became embroiled in a political scandal surrounding the appointment of a Spanish friar named Alonso Ponce as Franciscan commissary general for New Spain. Ponce, who had yet to set foot in the colony, supported the colonialist policies that now prevailed in Spain, under which efforts to educate native people and study their culture were viewed with suspicion. Archbishop Moya de Contreras agreed with the king that there was no point in teaching the natives Latin, rhetoric, philosophy, or anything else except mechanical arts (Paso y Troncoso 1940:124). The vicar general of Mexico's archdiocese even thought that the Colegio de Santa Cruz should be converted to a center for Hispanicizing the Indians, where they would be taught to speak Spanish in place of their own languages (Poole 1987:141–42).

At the same time, the secularization of native parishes—the replacement of friars with diocesan clergy—was proceeding apace, despite opposition from the friars and from native leaders. In this climate the Franciscans in Mexico, anxious to continue their work with the native people, felt that Ponce was unlikely to prove the supportive spokesman that they needed.

On October 15, 1584, the newly-arrived Ponce visited Tlatelolco and was treated to a dramatization of the views on education that prevailed there. A native student greeted Ponce with a brief speech in Latin and in Spanish. Then a teacher—no doubt one of the Nahua collegians, although this is not specified—asked the commissary to pardon the boy, as the Indians only imitate what they are taught and do not truly understand it. Another student then responded in Latin and Spanish, with characteristically Nahua self-deprecation:

It is true, most reverend Father, that according to the opinion of many, we Indians of New Spain are like shrikes or magpies and parrots, which fowl can with some effort be taught to speak, yet quickly forget what they have been taught. And this is not said in vain, for in truth our ability is weak, and for that reason we have great need of help so that we can become complete men. (Nicolau D'Olwer 1987:100)

A Nahua dressed as a Spaniard then burst in and declared derisively in Spanish "that they well deserved to be helped so that they could become as worthless and drunken as the rest." To this the teacher replied:

The scoundrel lies, for they are good sons, careful of their virtue and of their studies; it is just that you never open your mouths without speaking ill of them, and whatever benefits them bothers you. You would like them to be laden down, busy in your service. But behold that God is just, when he says, *"Beatus qui intelligit egenum et pauperum."*[25]

The skit makes clever use of irony to criticize those who hold low opinions of the native people. Nahuas voice these viewpoints themselves, while their eloquence and language skills serve to refute what they are saying.

The pro-native faction's opposition to Ponce's appointment soon erupted into open conflict. Viceroy Villamanrique and his wife sided with the radical Franciscans, while Archbishop Moya de Contreras and the officers of the Mexican Inquisition supported Ponce's appointment. The Franciscans managed to prevent Ponce from ever actually taking up his post; the standoff finally ended when Ponce's term expired in 1589 and he returned to Spain.[26]

Two of the friars most active in the Ponce dispute were Pedro Oroz, then guardian at Tlatelolco and in charge of the Colegio, and Bernardino de Sahagún, who, now in his late 80s, still resided at Tlatelolco. Thus, even as the Colegio declined into a grammar school for local boys, Franciscans connected with the institution remained politically active in defense of their work with the native people. The nature and capabilities of the native people, as well as their treatment by colonists, were still issues contested openly in public fora. Although the Colegio alumni were not directly involved in the Ponce affair, they surely observed the goings-on and were aware of the implications, as were other educated Nahuas such as the chronicler Chimalpahin, who mentions the affair in his writings (Reyes García 1971:343). The Franciscan stance was what validated their own status as educated native leaders; those who opposed the friars were likely to insist that the collegians were irrelevant curiosities—the trained parrots referred to in the student play.

The Nahua Scholars

In 1576 Sahagún wrote the following testament to the collegians' vital and continuing role in the Franciscan mission:

This college has persisted for over forty years and its collegians have transgressed in nothing, neither against God, nor the Church, nor the king, nor against his state. Rather they have helped and still help in many things in the implanting and maintaining of our Holy Catholic Faith, for if sermons, *Apostillas* and catechisms have been produced in the Indian language, which can appear and may be free of all heresy, they are those which were written with them. And they, being knowledgeable in the Latin language, inform us as to the properties of the words, the properties of their manner of speech. And they correct for us the incongruities we express in the sermons we write in the catechisms. And whatever is to be tendered in their language, if it is not examined by them, if it is not written congruently in the Latin language, in Spanish, and in their language, cannot be free of defect. With regard to orthography, to good handwriting, there are none who write it other than those reared here. (1950–82:introductory volume, 83–84)

The students and alumni of the Colegio were, thus, instrumental in interpreting Christianity for their fellow Nahuas. Even while working closely with friars, they exercised considerable control over what actually got said in Nahuatl in the friars' preaching and in the prayers and songs that the Nahuas learned to intone on their own. The corpus of published and unpublished Christian writings in Nahuatl from the sixteenth and early seventeenth centuries, as yet only partially studied, is vast and includes works in a variety of genres.[27]

Collegians also participated in the documentation of indigenous culture. One such project paired a Nahua doctor from Xochimilco, Martín de la Cruz, with a collegian named Juan Badiano, also from Xochimilco, in the production of a beautifully illustrated Latin herbal, sent off for presentation to Charles V in 1552 (Cruz 1964). Several other collegians collaborated on the massive ethnographic research project carried out by fray Bernardino de Sahagún between 1547 and 1577. Sahagún's studies resulted in the encyclopedic twelve-book *General History of the Things of New Spain*, the only complete copy of which, housed in the Laurentian Library in Florence, Italy, is called the *Florentine Codex*.[28]

In his prologue to Book Two of his treatise, Sahagún mentions by name some of the collegians who participated in the project (Sahagún 1950–82:introductory volume, 54–55). He states that they had been his students when he taught Latin at the Colegio; this indicates that they matriculated before the school was turned over to the group of alumni. Four to five men at a time worked with the friar, even moving along with him from Tlatelolco to the town of Tepeapulco, northeast of Mexico, where he was posted from 1558 to 1561.[29]

The men whom he names as having assisted most in his research are Antonio Valeriano of Azcapotzalco, Martín Jacobita of Tlatelolco, who was rector of the Colegio during the 1560s and early 1570s, Alonso Vegerano of Cuauhtitlan, Latin teacher at the Colegio as of 1574, and Pedro de San Buenaventura, also from Cuauhtitlan.[30] All four were expert in Latin and Spanish. In addition, Mateo Severino of Xochimilco and the Tlatelolcans Diego de Grado and Bonifacio Maximiliano were engaged as scribes.

The research assistants, scribes, and unnamed artists who participated in Sahagún's project were immersed in the study of Nahua beliefs and practices. They collected information on ceremonies that had been suppressed under Spanish rule and on many other customs that the friars were seeking to obliterate and replace with Christian ways. Some of these traditions were already in the process of reinterpretation in response to the Spanish and Christian presence.

The researchers also documented styles of speech and lexical usages with which, Sahagún hoped, the friars might improve their rhetorical and communicative skills in Nahuatl. Book Six of the treatise contains a series of Nahuatl orations of the *huehuehtlahtolli* style, which Sahagún recorded as early as 1547.

Thus Nahuas who were among the most knowledgeable about the culture of the conquerors became also among the most expert of their generation regarding the ways of their ancestors. They helped the friars to render Christian teachings intelligible—or as intelligible as possible—in Nahuatl. They also sought to represent Nahua culture in a manner intelligible to non-Nahuas, to reduce an entire civilization, with all of its ongoing changes and variability, to a compilation of pictures and written text.

That from this standpoint as interpreters on both sides the collegians should arrive at not only a somewhat Europeanized version of native culture but also a "Nahuatized" version of Christianity is hardly surprising. This process of bringing the two cultural traditions together should not be seen, however, simply as mixing or blending: a culture is not a milkshake. It was not that European elements were added to Nahua ones, or vice versa. Rather, the Nahua scholars constructed their own models of both, based on their upbringing, education, and experiences. And the two models were accommodated to one another in a manner that provided, taken as a whole, at least some degree of coherence. They understood their past in light of their present and they understood their present in light of their past.

Among Sahagún's Christian doctrinal texts, two stand out for their indigenous style and nativist content: the *Colloquios* and the *Psalmodia christiana*. Although Sahagún claims authorship of these texts, crediting the collegians with editorial responsibilities, the content and style of at least large portions of both works suggest that the Nahua scholars played a large, perhaps the larger, authorial role.

The *Psalmodia* is a book of songs for Church festivals (Sahagún 1583, 1993). The songs were composed during Sahagún's stint at Tepeapulco, circulated in manuscript beginning in 1564, and published in Mexico in 1583 (Sahagún 1583:prologue; 1950–82:introductory volume, 54). The Nahua collaborators were probably the four trilingual men mentioned above.

Sahagún states that he "dictated" these songs and the collegians "wrote" them (1950–82:introductory volume, 54). Such a statement may easily conceal a much more complex process of text production. That it indeed does is shown not only by the Nahuatl poetic style of many passages but also by the indigenous slant the authors take on portions of the subject matter. Sahagún's assistants here go beyond the level of accommodation with Nahua sensibilities that the friar permitted in his other catechistic texts. Passages that purport to be translations of Latin liturgical materials can diverge rather markedly from their models. The text in no way challenges Christianity as such but it does present an indigenized version of that faith.[31]

The *Colloquios*, written in 1564, is a fictionalized and idealized dialogue between the first Franciscan evangelizers and Nahua nobles and priests (Sahagún 1986). These representatives of Nahua civilization are portrayed in reverential and heroic tones; after an eloquent defense of their own customs, they are persuaded of Christianity's higher authority. Only the first fourteen of the *Colloquios'* thirty chapters survive, although a table of contents in Spanish outlines the missing material. In his prologue to the work Sahagún names the collegians involved: they are Valeriano, Jacobita, Vegerano, and Andrés Leonardo, a Tlatelolcan whom the friar does not mention elsewhere. He also states that they consulted with elderly men regarding the accuracy of the content.

Although Sahagún originally intended the *Colloquios* for the printing press, submitting it along with the *Psalmodia*, the work was withdrawn from the publication process between 1578 and 1583. Klor de Alva (1988b) suggests that Sahagún himself suppressed the text because he had ceased to believe that the Nahuas had so easily and sincerely converted to the Catholic faith. It is also possible that the friar disapproved of the respectful, even nostalgic manner in which the Nahua co-authors, in league, perhaps, with the elderly consultants, had chosen to represent indigenous society and religion.

The most important source on the scholars of the Colegio is the prologue to fray Juan Bautista's 1606 *Sermonario*. By the beginning of the seventeenth century, Bautista was the most prolific Franciscan scholar of Nahuatl. He served as guardian at Tlatelolco from 1598 to 1603, and between 1599 and 1606 he published several Nahuatl books in collaboration with scholars from the Colegio.[32]

Bautista pays tribute in his prologue to the Nahua scholars who had helped him with his work. It is very likely that one or more of these men— all of whom, with one possible exception, were alive in 1590—is the author of the Holy Wednesday drama. The information on these scholars being otherwise so scanty, I am including here much of what Bautista says.[33]

Hernando de Ribas, from Texcoco, was one of the first alumni of the Colegio. A devout Christian who helped the friars to learn Nahuatl, he could easily translate anything from Latin or Spanish into Nahuatl. Bautista describes his translation style as "attending more to the meaning than to the letter." He assisted with fray Alonso de Molina's Nahuatl dictionary and fray Juan de Gaona's *Coloquios de la paz y tranquilidad christiana* (Gaona 1582). Before his death in 1597 Ribas had provided Bautista with over 700 sheets of Nahuatl materials.

Don Juan Berardo—the Spanish title "don" indicating high rank in the Nahua nobility—was born in Huexotzingo and later lived in Cuauhnahuac (Cuernavaca). He wrote letters in Latin which, though plain in style, were pleasing and fluent. A great choir leader and devout churchgoer, he died in 1594.

Diego Adriano, from Tlatelolco, was a skilled Latinist and an expert typesetter in any language. He could translate anything from Latin to Nahuatl "with great propriety." Bautista speaks of him as though he were deceased but does not give his date of death.

Don Francisco Bautista de Contreras was born in Cuauhnahuac and as of 1606 was serving as the native governor of Xochimilco. He wrote excellent letters in Spanish and had helped Bautista with his Nahuatl version of the *Contemptus mundi*.

Esteban Bravo came from a small town near Texcoco. He had helped Bautista with the *Sermonario*. Bravo could translate any text from Latin or Spanish into Nahuatl "with such an abundance and multitude of words as to cause astonishment." Bravo too is described as if already dead, though he must have lived into the 1590s in order to have worked on the *Sermonario*.

Don Antonio Valeriano is the only scholar named in Sahagún's work who also appears in Bautista's list. It is possible that his former colleagues in the sahaguntine project were by this time deceased. Valeriano himself had died the year before Bautista's writing, in 1605. The most distinguished Latinist the Colegio produced, Valeriano could speak Latin spontaneously with, in Bautista's opinion, the eloquence of the classical rhetoricians Cicero and Quintilian.

Thanks to the Nahua historian Fernando Alvarado Tezozomoc, some details of Valeriano's personal history are known, including the fact that he was not of noble birth. Alvarado Tezozomoc describes Valeriano as "not a noble, just a great scholar, a collegian, he knew the Latin language." He also calls Valeriano a *tlamatini* 'one who knows things,' a sage or wise man (Alvarado Tezozomoc 1975:171, 176). Admitted to the Colegio on the basis of aptitude rather than rank, Valeriano's education and alliance with the Franciscans gave him sufficient credentials to marry into the high nobility of Tenochtitlan. His wife, doña Isabel, was the daughter of don Diego

Huanitzin, a nephew of Motecuhzoma and dynastic ruler, or *tlahtoani*, of Tenochtitlan from 1539 until his death in 1542 (Alvarado Tezozomoc 1975:168–71).

Valeriano's fortunate marriage enabled him to pursue a distinguished political career, earning for himself, in spite of his humble origins, the noble title "don." In 1565 he was elected governor of his hometown, Azcapotzalco. The top post in the colonial town council, or *cabildo*, the governorship had by now superseded the old dynastic rulership as the most important political office for native men. By this time Valeriano, probably in his mid-thirties, may have completed his contributions to Sahagún's opus but he maintained his involvement with the Colegio intermittently after his election. In 1567 he received a salary as a Latin teacher. The college's 1570 records describe him as a former teacher; the 31 pesos paid to him that year were, presumably, back wages.

After eight years as Azcapotzalco's governor, Valeriano became the governor of Tenochtitlan. This was the most influential post that any native man could hold in the colonial administration. He still found some time to teach Latin, for he appears on the Colegio's payroll for 1577. Valeriano held Tenochtitlan's governorship for 23 years, retiring only when he was in his mid-sixties and his health began to fail.[34]

Pedro de Gante was from Tlatelolco. He was named after a famous Franciscan friar from Ghent, a lay brother who for several decades taught reading, writing, and vocational arts to young Nahuas at San José de los Naturales. Fray Pedro de Gante was a great favorite among the native people; it is no surprise that a Nahua man should bear his name. The Nahua Pedro de Gante was a longtime teacher at the Colegio. He translated many texts for Bautista, especially saints' lives. Like Valeriano, Gante died in 1605.

Agustín de la Fuente, still living in 1606, was Bautista's principal assistant. Like Gante, de la Fuente was from Tlatelolco and was a teacher at the Colegio. According to Bautista, de la Fuente had spent his whole life writing texts for Franciscans, first for Sahagún, then for Oroz, and, since Oroz's death in 1596,[35] for Bautista. De la Fuente presumably remained in Tlatelolco teaching at the Colegio while also working with these friars. Sahagún spent most of his career at Tlatelolco and Oroz, a scholar of Nahuatl and Otomi, was there from 1587 until his death.

Bautista states that everything he had so far published, plus a backlog of texts for future publication, had been written by de la Fuente's hand.[36] The allusion is to the mechanical act of writing. Bautista's words pass through de la Fuente's hands; the engagement of de la Fuente's mind in this process is left unacknowledged, its significance thereby elided. Like Sahagún's assertion that he dictated texts for the collegians to write, Bautista's statement reflects the ambiguous role of the native scholars: are they just scribes, or are they co-authors? This authorial sleight-of-hand obviously slights their role.

There were, however, two compelling reasons for representing the collegians' participation in this manner, neither of which is to attribute to the friars a selfish desire to claim all the credit. First, the friars really did think that their words, and the words of holy writ in general, could pass into Nahuatl translation without being significantly altered. Sacred words had universal meanings, and all human symbolic systems were thought to be essentially cognate. Not only did texts have unambiguous meanings residing in the words themselves, independent of how individual receivers constructed their messages, but these meanings carried over directly into other languages and cultures. Translations were mirror images of the original text. The mediating and creative role of the translator's mentality, deciphering one text and constructing another, was not recognized.[37]

Second, the enterprise of circulating native-language manuscripts and publishing native-language books faced obstacles enough, given growing opposition to the friars' program plus the prevailing opinion that translating anything from the Bible was a Lutheran heresy. Friars depended on their own prestige as both men of God and speakers of the native languages in order to gain legitimacy for such writings and permission to publish some of them. To attribute authorship to native men would have undermined this legitimacy; there was no way that a religious book in Nahuatl could have been printed with a Nahua man listed as the author. Anonymity shielded the Nahua scholars from ecclesiastical and civil authorities who might have challenged their participation.

Of Agustín de la Fuente, Bautista also states:

With his help the author has made the three books of *comedias* that he has ready to publish. The first, of Penitence, and its components. The second, of the principal Articles of our Holy Faith, and Parables of the Gospels. The third, of the lives of the Saints. (1606:prologue)

These collections of plays were never published; or if they were, they have left no trace. Bautista's statement makes de la Fuente the only Nahua scholar to whom dramatic compositions are directly attributed, though he surely was not the only one to lend his pen to such works. The Holy

Wednesday play predates de la Fuente's collaboration with Bautista by several years at least, but de la Fuente may be considered a likely candidate for its authorship.[38]

One known Nahuatl play does bear an explicit connection to Bautista—an Epiphany play that probably dates from 1607. According to Paso y Troncoso, who published this now-lost manuscript in 1902, the text was titled *Comedia de los Reyes conpoesto a noestro Padre fray Ioan Vauhtista*. A drama of the (Three) Kings composed "to" fray Juan Bautista, the play was presumably written by one or more collegians for that friar. Based on Bautista's attribution of plays to Agustín de la Fuente, Paso y Troncoso (1902:79–80) and Garibay K. (1971:II, 149) assume that de la Fuente was the author of this Epiphany play. Both scholars were engaging in unwarranted speculation. De la Fuente may be considered a possible author of the *Comedia de los Reyes*, and of the Holy Wednesday drama as well, but no more secure attribution can be made.[39]

Agustín de la Fuente does make one other documented appearance. In 1607 the Augustinian friar Juan de Mijangos published a Nahuatl devotional treatise entitled *Espejo divino*, or "Divine Mirror." Instructions for the spiritual education of children, it is written in the form of a dialogue between a father and son, named Augustín and Juan. On the book's colophon is printed:

The corrector of the language was Agustín de la Fuente, a native of Santiago Tlatelolco, very knowledgeable (who in this work, and in all those others[40] that father fray Juan Bautista, of the order of the seraphic father Saint Francis, made, has helped greatly, and served our Lord) may the Lord reward him, and keep him for many years. (Mijangos 1607)

How many more years de la Fuente survived is unknown.[41]

After the fruitful collaboration of fray Juan Bautista with his sundry Nahua partners, Franciscan scholarship in Nahuatl declined. The Franciscan enterprise in New Spain was itself in decline, what with the secularization of native parishes and the gradual passing away of the older, European-born friars who had set the enthusiastic and humanistic tone of the sixteenth-century mission. The passing away also of the cohort of collegians, the skilled Latinists of whom Agustín de la Fuente may have been the last survivor, helped to bring to a close this chapter in Nahua history.

During the seventeenth century the Jesuits emerged as the principal linguists of Nahuatl and redactors of Nahuatl religious texts. In this enterprise they drew on their own indigenous students from San Gregorio in Mexico and their school at Tepotzotlan, northwest of the capital in Otomi territory.

But Nahuatl literacy in broader terms—that is, literacy of Nahuas in their own language—was already a well-established tradition. Its survival no longer depended on intervention by priests of any stripe. With the knowledge transmitted from Nahuas to Nahuas, though always restricted to a minority of elite rank, Nahua writing flourished through the rest of the colonial period. A vast corpus of historical annals and chronicles, wills and land documents, town council records, letters, and legal testimony attests to the practical uses the Nahuas made of the alphabetic writing introduced to them by their first Franciscan teachers.[42]

Nahuas in the Colonial City: Political and Spiritual Economy

At the time the Holy Wednesday play was written, the scholarly don Antonio Valeriano presided over the Tenochtitlan *cabildo*. In Tlatelolco the governorship had apparently been rotating, since at least 1583, among different sons (or other male kin) of don Diego de Mendoza, who had been Tlatelolco's dynastic ruler from 1549 to 1562. Don Juan de Mendoza was governor in 1588; don Gaspar de Mendoza took over in 1590 (Barlow 1989:147–48, 364–66).

The Nahuas of the city of Mexico were spared two of the most onerous burdens inflicted under Spanish colonial rule. They lived far enough from the mining centers to avoid the often deadly forced labor in the silver mines. And since they already lived in nucleated settlements they were not subjected to the policy of *congregación* or *reducción*, the forced resettlement of rural dwellers into larger communities. However, they bore a heavy load of tribute and labor obligations.

Tribute payments were assessed on the basis of a head count. Each married male counted as a full tributary. Widowed men and women, bachelors, and single women living apart from their families paid half the full amount, with exemptions for elderly or disabled individuals. *Cabildo* officials were encharged with collecting the payments. In the city, tribute was collected separately in Tlatelolco and in each of the four Tenochtitlan wards. A small portion of the total tribute payment—one quarter or less— went to the local *cabildo* to pay the officials' salaries, maintain public buildings, and support community projects. The bulk of the payment, however, was passed along to the Spanish administration.

Typically, the basic tribute payment going to the colonial authorities was about one peso plus a half-*fanega*, or about three-fourths of a bushel, of maize per year for each tributary. At the prevailing wage rate an unskilled Nahua laborer earned one *real*, or one eighth of a peso, per day. An additional half-*real* per tributary went to a fund for the construction of the metropolitan cathedral.

In 1592 the king began to charge all tributaries an additional half peso per year to subsidize the royal fleet. In the same year Viceroy Velasco tried to increase chicken production by instituting a chicken tax, under which each tributary had to provide one chicken in place of one *real*'s worth of monetary tribute. Franciscans protested on behalf of the Nahuas of the city, who lacked the facilities for raising chickens. They were unsuccessful, and until the tax was revoked in 1600–1601 the urban dwellers had to purchase chickens at the market price of one and one-half to three *reales* in order to pay this tax.

A sales tax was levied on all commercial transactions with non-natives. Sales involving only native persons were exempt from this tax provided the goods involved were grown or manufactured by native hands. Non-natives were supposed to steer clear of the indigenous people's markets. Many communities near the capital were required to provide building stone, hay, and other goods needed by Spaniards in the city. They were paid for these products, but at less than market value.[43]

Nahuas living in the city itself did not have to supply these extra material goods, but like all native people they were subject to the exploitative and controversial program of compulsory labor drafts known as *repartimiento*. At the time of the Holy Wednesday drama, the legitimacy of this institution was one of the most hotly contested issues concerning the Nahua population.

Instituted in 1549, the *repartimiento* was intended to siphon native labor toward useful public works. Native communities were required to provide a certain number of men to labor on these projects. The drafts were imposed twice yearly and for periods of four to ten weeks. Spaniards desiring to engage these workers would apply to a special official in charge of assigning the work crews. The laborers were to be paid a fair wage and the projects were to be such as would, at least by Spanish estimations, benefit the common good: roads, bridges, canals, agricultural production, churches, hospitals, and other public buildings.

In practice, the men were often underpaid or not paid at all, and were provided with inadequate meals and housing. Many of the projects were private enterprises that benefited only their Spanish owners. Thus for the unscrupulous colonist *repartimiento* provided convenient access to what was in effect slave labor. A further problem was that, unlike tribute payments, the *repartimiento* drafts were not directly linked to population levels and productive capacity. At first, the quota of workers corresponded to 1 or 2 percent of the tributaries at a time. But after the epidemic of 1576–79 the decreasing number of available workers led to drafts of 5 and 10 percent of tributaries and a tendency toward longer periods of employment. *Repartimiento* officials sometimes exceeded even the 10 percent legal limit. Since the *cabildos* were responsible for providing the work crews, native governors could be jailed if the quotas were not met. Spaniards, forced to compete for a diminishing number of laborers, resorted to beating their workers, imprisoning them, or confiscating their food and clothing to prevent them from leaving.[44]

As the *repartimiento* system grew more exploitative, the native people found more and more supporters among the Spanish. Franciscans could generally be counted on to speak out on behalf of the natives, and as early as 1575 Mendieta sent the king a lengthy accounting of *repartimiento* abuses. Most churchmen, however, supported the institution at least in principle. The Church benefited economically from the system, and many believed that the native people should work for the colonists and would only do so under coercion.

But when Archbishop Moya de Contreras convened the colony's bishops for New Spain's third ecclesiastical council in 1585, *repartimiento* was one of the principal issues discussed. The bishops were at first inclined to agree that the institution was necessary and would be acceptable if abuses were eliminated through legislation and careful oversight. But the Franciscan position, presented by Mendieta, that the system was intrinsically abusive now carried enough weight to reframe the debate and move the consensus closer to an outright denunciation. The bishops, skirting the issue of *repartimiento*'s intrinsic legitimacy, condemned the system in its current form and denounced *repartimiento* mine labor altogether. Moya de Contreras stopped short of promulgating a public decree to this effect, which would have incited the ire of powerful colonists without being enforceable. He chose instead to refer the matter to the king and the Council of the Indies.[45]

A decade after Moya de Contreras's council, Mendieta was still denouncing the injustices caused by *repartimiento*. He devoted two chapters of his historical chronicle to the institution, calling it "the greatest and most harmful pestilence of the Indians" and the greatest impediment to their Christianity. For him, it was a form of slavery. Being forced to labor for Spaniards led the native people to despise the colonists and their Christian law and lifestyle as well (Mendieta 1980:519–20).

Decisive royal action on *repartimiento* would not be taken until 1601, when an overhaul of the system removed some of the more coercive aspects. The institution survived until the 1630s, by which time changes in New Spain's demographic and economic situation had in any case rendered it obsolete (Gibson 1964:233–36; Poole 1987:179).

Another problem that had assumed crisis proportions by the late 1580s was the Nahuas' by now notorious litigiousness. Nahuas appeared before the Real Audiencia to pursue lawsuits against one another and against non-natives. Suits even against Spaniards were successful often enough to encourage Nahuas with a grievance of any kind to take their opponents to court. The plaintiffs were often women, acting independently or on behalf of their families. Kellogg (1984, 1992, 1995, in press) concludes that Nahua women manipulated the early colonial legal system in order to maintain and even enhance their authority within Nahua society; however, a gradual erosion of their social position led in the seventeenth century to a decline in their legal activity.

Spanish policy had been respectful of indigenous customs for resolving conflicts, but those traditions had been disrupted and in any case were insufficient to deal with the many new situations in which Nahuas were finding themselves. As Nahuas turned increasingly to the court to seek definitive resolutions to their problems, the judicial docket became clogged with cases that often seemed, to Spaniards, trivial. The participation of women struck some as unseemly. In 1599 one Spanish observer commented on women's outspokenness in the courtroom and concluded that the native men must be submissive to the will of their women (Gómez de Cervantes 1944:135).

But those who claimed to be sympathetic to the native people emphasized the costliness of these legal actions, especially for people who had to come from far away, and the unscrupulous behavior of lawyers who encouraged native people to pursue cases with no legal merit. Such was the argument of Viceroy Velasco, who in 1590 petitioned the king to appoint a salaried official as *defensor general*, a kind of public defender for the native people. This official would review all cases that native parties sought to bring before the Audiencia, pursuing those that were worthy and rejecting those that he judged groundless or futile; it was better that such people be denied a hearing than be allowed to waste their meager resources on useless litigation (Paso y Troncoso 1940:174–75).

Legal reform came the following year. The king went further than Velasco's recommendations, appointing what amounted to an entirely new court with sole jurisdiction over all cases involving native parties except for the relatively rare lawsuits in which Spaniards sued natives, which would come under the viceroy's jurisdiction. Indigenous plaintiffs were to be exempt from any legal fees unless the suit was brought by native rulers or by whole towns, in which case the plaintiffs would pay half the amount the Audiencia charged Spaniards.

The new court, which became known as the General Indian Court, became fully functional early in 1592. Later that year a method of financing this court was instituted. For each tributary, half of a *real*'s worth of tribute was to go to the court; in return, the native people were assured of free legal service as needed. It was Viceroy Velasco's intention that this payment would be deducted from existing contributions; in practice, however, it tended to be added to all the other tribute requirements. The new legal system would remain in operation until 1820.[46]

The creation of a separate judicial structure for the native people is one manifestation of a tendency toward the institutional segregation of native and non-native societies. The sales tax exemption segregated native from non-native commerce. Native people had their own churches and their own governing councils, even in the capital city. Communal land tenure was permitted for native communities. The Inquisition, established in Mexico in 1571, formally exempted indigenous persons from prosecution on the grounds that they were too new in the faith to be held to the same standards as everyone else, although persons of African descent were subject to investigation.

In part, the special treatment of the indigenous residents derived from a recognition that, as the original inhabitants of the land, and as civilized folk with hereditary rulers, they had a right to go about their business with some degree of self-determination, provided that activities the Catholic Church regarded as religious or moral offenses were prohibited. But also, and increasingly so as the sixteenth century wore on, Spaniards believed that native people needed special consideration because of inherent physical and mental weaknesses and because of their susceptibility to Spanish exploitation. The devastation wrought upon indigenous society by Spanish rule was by now obvious; at the same time, the humanistic outlook of the Renaissance was giving way to the more puritanical and legalistic attitudes of the Catholic Reformation, which fostered a negative view of human nature and human potential in general (Poole 1989:16). In juridical terms, the native people came to be seen as *miserabiles*, poor and wretched individuals who had rights to special legal assistance (Borah 1983:80–83). In theological terms they were seen as *rudes*, persons who, like the crudest of Europe's peasants, were incapable of understanding more than the rudiments of the faith (Poole 1987:153, 1989:15).

The native people benefited from these special protections and lowered expectations (that the Inquisition could not prosecute them for heresy was certainly a blessing) but for these advantages they paid a price, enduring the prejudices of Spaniards who assigned to them such limited capacities and among whom even the best intentioned seldom avoided a condescending attitude. All segregated societies institutionalize prejudice; for many colonists their native neighbors were no more than brute animals. Spaniards who sought to provide safety nets for the poor and exploited posed no real challenge to the overall structure of the colonial occupation.

The political economy within which the colonial Nahuas struggled to subsist cannot be neatly separated from their religious life. Debates over indigenous rights were always phrased in religious terms; the status of the Nahuas and other native peoples as Christians was as hotly contested as any economic or juridical issue. Every time Nahuas participated publicly in Christian ritual they were not only rendering homage to the sacred but also making a political statement about who and what they were.

The Christianization of the colonized peoples served Spain as the moral justification for the conquest. It was therefore necessary to pay at least lip service to the evangelization program. That is why the religious orders were permitted the latitude that they had so long enjoyed (Poole 1987:68). But if the native people were indeed to achieve equal religious status with Spaniards, then the colonial power structure would be undermined. Colonists could justify living off native land and labor only if they continued to define those natives as their inferiors. One's status as a Christian was a vital component of personal identity as Spaniards constructed it. How easy it was to belittle the native people's Christianity, to dismiss them as *rudes* who would never progress very far in the faith, to assume that they were still half-enamored of their pagan demons.

But the Franciscans colluded in this hegemonic endeavor, for they too considered the native people's Christianity to be different from and inferior to their own. They had a vested interest in doing so. On the one hand, they had sought all along to keep indigenous society separated from Spanish and culturally distinct from it. Given that the Nahuas preferred distinctive devotional patterns, the friars found it expedient to condone and even encourage these activities. The Nahua Church developed as a separate religious tradition rather than an extension of the Spanish Church.

On the other hand, the friars needed to justify the continuation of their program and stall the secularization of their indigenous parishes. At the outset of their mission the religious orders had been authorized to evangelize heathens, not to minister to established Christian communities. If the friars were to allow that their Nahua charges were fully Christianized, they would be declaring themselves obsolete. Instead, they emphasized the Nahuas' potential to become good Christians, were it not for all the obstacles that colonists, Crown, and administrators placed in the friars' way.

Future progress was limited, however, by the nature of the native people. The friars' construction of the native person was an effort to come to terms with cultural otherness by reducing it to familiar categories. These categories validated the friars' position as perpetual caretakers and, in a larger frame, Spanish imperialism itself. Too sensual to become priests, the native people were weak and carnal beings who lacked spiritual depth. They were easily distracted by the external appearances of things in the world, failing to see beyond the surfaces to perceive higher, spiritual truths. Their fondness for pageantry and performance, which stemmed from this aspect of their character, was to be permitted and encouraged because it was the only way to keep their attention focused on sacred things (Burkhart 1996).

Thus, while non-natives put forth different and competing constructions of Nahua Christianity, all agreed that the Nahuas had not come very far in the faith. The fact that all parties had political reasons for taking this view does not mean that they were wrong—Nahuas had indeed undergone nothing like the "spiritual conquest" of early Franciscan fantasies. But neither were they the pagan devil-worshippers, ignorant children, or spiritually deficient sensualists that their critics imagined.

In a colonial situation, customary symbolic orders are disrupted; the world is turned upside down and its interpretation is up for grabs. The colonized people rethink and reorganize their own received ways of constructing reality. They also take over complexes of symbols from the culture of the conquerors, dissociating them from their former contexts and recombining them with their own symbols, thereby transforming the meanings of both sets. These reformulated symbols may then be manipulated in rituals through which the colonized people seek to redefine and thereby regain control over their changing material circumstances (Comaroff 1985:119–20).

The Nahuas of Mexico and nearby settlements had adopted a considerable amount of Christian symbolism. They had, however, interpreted Christianity according to their own understandings and their own circumstances. They took what appealed to them, what made sense, what they could use. Even that was not taken directly, for symbols do not pass across cultural and linguistic boundaries like molecules through membranes. Nahuas constructed their own interpretations of Christianity based upon what they saw and what the friars told them.

What the friars told them, in Nahuatl, was already half-transformed by being translated into a language ill-equipped to convey the meanings of many Christian concepts. As Nahuas took what they understood of these concepts and worked them in with their reformulations of traditional symbolic patterns, new constructions emerged. These Nahua interpretations of Christianity resembled Spanish Catholicism, yet in both conceptual and experiential terms—modes of thought and modes of behaving and feeling—they now belonged to a Nahua reality.[47]

Observers were thus correct in sensing that there was something different about Nahua usages of Christianity, that the Nahuas had somehow failed to get the message straight. What they were not willing or able to acknowledge was that the Nahuas could integrate Christian symbols into a separate spirituality that was neither a relapse into paganism nor a childish, rudimentary form of their own purportedly universal faith. And that the Nahuas should be satisfied with Christianity as they practiced it could only mean that they were stubborn and obtuse, not that they found spiritual fulfillment in the religious life they were leading.

Nahua Devotional Practice

As it had before the Spanish invasion, Nahua religious life centered around public ritual: processions, song and dance and the playing of musical instruments, theatrical performances. As decreed in a papal bull of 1537, native people were required to observe twelve annual Church festivals, fasting on the preceding day and attending services on the festival itself. These festivals included six related to the life of Christ (Christmas, the Circumcision, Epiphany, Easter, the Ascension, and Corpus Christi), four devoted to the Virgin Mary (the Nativity of Mary, the Annunciation, the Purification, and the Assumption), plus Pentecost and the festival of Peter and Paul (Mendieta 1980:272). Indigenous people also celebrated the festival of their community patron saint. This amounted to fewer feast days than Spaniards were obligated to observe, but the native people celebrated their holidays with such elaborate preparations and ceremonies that they tended to outdo their Spanish neighbors in public displays of piety.

Such rituals were part of the colony's political discourse, the negotiation of power relations between conqueror and conquered. The Nahua participants were representing themselves as devout Christians practicing their own varieties of religious worship. They were declaring the world to be a place where Nahuas worshipped God and the saints and received their blessings in return. They were borrowing the conquerors' symbols of martyrdom and redemption to comment upon their own experience under colonial rule. They were also representing and negotiating relations among themselves, for as Lockhart observes (1992:206–10), rival communities, and rival neighborhoods within the city, competed with one another in the construction of church buildings and the acquisition of elaborate ritual paraphernalia.

That Nahua rituals had a political dimension does not mean that the Nahua celebrants were insincere in their devotion to Christian sacra. All ritual has an instrumental as well as an expressive aspect; it does not merely seek to represent reality but actively to create it, to impose a preferred interpretation upon it (Comaroff 1985:125). By acting as Christians, Nahuas became Christians; they declared themselves to be Christians and Christianity to be what they did.

Though barred from the priesthood, Nahuas held other religious offices through which they exercised considerable control over community religious life, often mediating between the priests and the community at large. Each town, and each district in the city, had a hierarchy of officials attached to the local church. The principal religious official was the *fiscal*, a general steward who acted as an assistant to the priest, handled some of the religious instruction, managed the church's financial affairs, and often acted as the executor of wills. Another official was in charge of the choir and prepared music for Church services and festivals. Lesser officials, known collectively in Nahuatl as *teopan tlacah* 'church people,' served in a variety of roles as sacristans, constables, notaries, and custodians. The only office for women was that of *cihuatepixqui* 'keeper of women,' who was charged with seeing that girls and women attended religious services.[48]

Religious confraternities, modeled on those of Spain, played a large role in Nahua devotional life. They organized festivals, sometimes staging dramas, and sponsored charitable works, including hospitals. Nahua confraternities were not associated with occupational specialties, as in Spain, but instead were foci of community and neighborhood groupings. These religious sodalities appealed to Nahuas because of their collective and voluntary nature. Their members enjoyed some measure of control over local affairs, with the prestige that accrued to such leadership, and also benefited from a network of mutual support. The confraternities were especially important as a source of religious participation and community prestige for Nahua women, to whom few formal leadership roles were available under colonial rule (Mendieta 1980:420–21; Lockhart 1992:220).

The Franciscan historian Augustín de Vetancurt credits fray Pedro de Gante with the founding of the first Nahua confraternities, including a confraternity of the Holy Sacrament that was still operating—along with seven other confraternities—at San José de los Naturales at the end of the seventeenth century, when Vetancurt wrote (Vetancurt 1971:part 4, 35 and *Menologio*, 67). Motolinia mentions a confraternity devoted to Our Lady of the Incarnation operating in Tlaxcala in 1539, when it put on a play about Adam and Eve and also donated clothing and food to the poor (1979:65).

Relatively few confraternities were founded among the Nahuas before the latter decades of the sixteenth century, with the institutions becoming a standard feature of Nahua life during the following two centuries (Lockhart 1992:218–19). In 1569 the author of the *Códice franciscano*, probably Mendieta, reported that some friars had founded confraternities to the Holy Sacrament in some locations, and in other places confraternities with one or another Marian advocation. Some towns had both, and also one to the True Cross, which practiced flagellation on Holy Thursday (García Icazbalceta 1971:76–77, 103).

By the mid-1590s, when Mendieta wrote his historical chronicle, confraternities to the Holy Sacrament and the Virgin were to be found not just in certain towns but throughout the Franciscan province. Larger towns also had the True Cross confraternity plus those of the Name of Jesus and Our Lady of Solitude (Mendieta 1980:420–21). The other religious orders had followed suit, the Dominicans sponsoring confraternities of the Virgin of the Rosary and the Augustinians devoting theirs to the Souls in Purgatory and to the Virgin (Dávila Padilla 1955:355–60; Grijalva 1624:72v).

According to the Nahua historian Chimalpahin, a Nahuas-only confraternity of Our Lady of Solitude was formally instituted at San José de los Naturales in 1591. The new confraternity was authorized by the vicar general of the archdiocese at the request of Governor Valeriano and the nobles and commoners of Mexico. The venture was supported by the Franciscan officials and the local friars, especially Francisco de Gamboa, then the vicar at San José, Gerónimo de Zárate, and Juan de Torquemada (Chimalpahin Cuauhtlehuanitzin 1965a:33–34, 38; Torquemada 1975–83:VI, 395).

In preparation for the formal opening, members had begun enrolling in the confraternity on the first day of Lent. The founding members included Governor Valeriano and the *fiscal* of San José, Miguel de los Angeles. The opening ceremony took place on the evening of Good Friday, April 12, 1591. The new Mexican *cofrades* of "our precious mother of the Solitude" marched in procession with a crucifix and an image of Saint Clare. Apparently they had not yet acquired an image of the Sorrowing Mother and had to make do with an available female image.[49]

It may be only a coincidence that the Holy Wednesday drama's probable date corresponds so closely to this event. The play would have been a very suitable choice for enactment during the same Holy Week that the new confraternity began operating, but this can only be a matter of speculation. However, the founding of the confraternity does indicate that Nahuas in Mexico were at this time aware of and interested in the Virgin Mary's role in the Passion.

Franciscan chroniclers give more information regarding Nahua observations of the Easter season. Motolinia's report, dating to 1541, describes how on Palm Sunday they decorated the churches and the processional route with an abundance of flowers, branches, and floral ornaments. Children climbed trees and threw branches down as the procession passed.

All the people, men and women alike, were "*cofrades de la cruz*"; I assume that Motolinia is referring to membership in a confraternity of the True Cross. All through Lent they would flog themselves in church three days a week, the men in one part and the women in another. On Holy Thursday in Mexico the Spaniards and the native people held separate processions, the native one with ten or twelve thousand participants. Many of the native marchers flogged themselves; the others carried torches. All sang prayers from the catechism: the Our Father, Hail Mary, Credo, and Salve Regina. Afterward they washed their lacerated skin with hot water and chile pepper (Motolinia 1979:55–56).

The fact that Spaniards and Nahuas held similar processions did not make for an atmosphere of harmony. In 1572 Viceroy Enríquez informed the king that every year, for at least the last thirty years, unfounded rumors circulated among the Spanish colonists that the native people were planning to rebel during the Holy Thursday procession. Therefore, a party of armed guards on horseback took to the streets before and during the processions in order to secure the city against the feared attack (*Cartas de Indias* 1970:I, 283–84).

The Augustinian chronicler Juan de Grijalva confirms that it was a native custom to practice flagellation on Fridays during Lent, as well as to stage very elaborate Holy Week processions (1624:72v, 74r). Mendieta repeats the information in Motolinia's account but adds many details based on his own observations. His description of the Holy Week activities at San Francisco and San José de los Naturales is especially valuable.

On Holy Thursday the people gathered at the church of San Francisco and the friars entered in procession. The guardian and two other priests then washed the feet of twelve very poor natives—all of them blind, lame, or paralyzed—who had been selected for the purpose. Then Nahua nobles dressed the twelve in new garments and fed them a meal. This was an Old World custom, commemorating Christ's washing the feet of his disciples and sharing with them his Last Supper. The nobles also provided a big dinner for one or two hundred other needy people, who gathered outside in the patio and received alms from the people going into the church (Mendieta 1980:435–36).

Mendieta goes on to describe the processions as they were performed in 1595. The new confraternity of Our Lady of Solitude was in full swing, along with one devoted to the True Cross. Mendieta writes as follows:

On Holy Thursday the procession of the True Cross went out with more than 20,000 Indians, and more than three thousand penitents, with 219 insignias of Christ and insignias of his Passion. On Friday more than 7,700 flagellants went out in the procession of the Solitude, with insignias of [Our Lady of] Solitude. Easter morning the procession went out from San José with 230 images of Our Lord and Our Lady and other saints on platforms, all gilded and very attractive. All the members of both the above-mentioned confraternities of the True Cross and the Solitude marched in it (which is a great number) with much order and with wax candles in their hands, and in addition to them there went alongside innumerable men and women, almost all of whom also had wax candles. They went arranged according to their neighborhoods, according to the superiority or inferiority that they recognize among one another, in conformity with their ancient customs. The wax is all as white as paper, and since men and women also go dressed in white and very clean, and this is at dawn or a little before, it is one of the loveliest and most solemn processions in Christendom. And so said Viceroy don Martín Enríquez, that it was one of the things most worth seeing that he had ever seen in his life. (1980:436–37)

Mendieta states that all the major towns of New Spain had similar processions. Chimalpahin notes that on Good Friday, 1587, the town of Coyoacan, on the lakeshore just south of Mexico, staged its first dramatization of the Passion (1965b:291).

Although Mendieta is describing events of 1595, apart from the addition of the new confraternity much of what he says applies, at least in general terms, to earlier years. Since Viceroy Enríquez left New Spain in 1580, the Easter morning procession must date back at least that far. Sahagún's Easter sermon of c. 1540 mentions the morning's procession (1563:54r).

Torquemada, in his biography of his colleague fray Francisco de Gamboa, states that during Gamboa's second stint at San José—which would have been at least a few years after he participated in the Solitude confraternity founding—Gamboa "instituted the Friday stations among the natives, putting on a representation of a scene from the Passion of Christ Our Lord, in the course of the sermon that was preached" (Torquemada 1975–83:VI, 395). Performed on Fridays during Lent, these probably were not full-fledged plays but were pantomimed while the preacher spoke. Vetancurt describes such performances occurring at San José at the end of the seventeenth century (1971: part 4, p. 42).

Torquemada also comments on the Holy Week processions. He borrows Mendieta's account, changing the date to 1609 and adding a few details, such as that most of the Passion insignias were crucifixes and that Nahuas from all four of the native districts—including those no longer under Franciscan tutelage—participated in the event (V, 340).

Separate Holy Thursday and Easter morning processions were held in Tlatelolco, at least in the early seventeenth century. According to Torquemada, the Tlatelolco processions featured as many or more crucifixes and holy images as those of Tenochtitlan. For Corpus Christi, the two sectors combined forces in a single procession with all of their images (Torquemada 1975–83:V, 340–41). In Tlatelolco the foot-washing ceremony for the poor was sponsored by a single person, with a new volunteer taking on the duty each year (V, 337).

The numbers Mendieta gives, most of which Torquemada repeats exactly, may well be inflated. Even so, they suggest a very high level of Holy Week participation among the urban Nahuas near the close of the sixteenth century, when they only totaled about 40,000 people. In a time of ongoing demographic and economic crisis, Nahuas were asserting their presence and their piety by coming out in force to participate in a collective imitation of Christ and Mary. The Holy Wednesday drama had a large potential audience among these confraternity members and their fellow citizens.

Notes on Later History and Ethnography

As of 1655, a confraternity specifically devoted to the *Santo Despedimiento*—the Christ-Mary farewell—was operating at San Francisco in Mexico (Gardel 1959; Vetancurt 1971:part 4, 35). Although this sodality was sponsored by the Franciscan church rather than the Nahuas' chapel of San José, its existence nevertheless suggests an ongoing interest in a Holy Week event perhaps first introduced into Mexico's ceremonial life via the debut performance, several decades earlier, of the Holy Wednesday play. Torquemada, in fact, mentions that confraternities of the *despedimiento* were already common in the larger native communities in his time. To the list of typical confraternities given by Mendieta (see above), he adds this one and *Nazareos*, or Nazarenes, another Passion advocation (Torquemada 1975–83:V, 173). Thus, some confraternities of the *despedimiento*, perhaps including the one at San Francisco, were operating in the first decade of the seventeenth century.

Passion processions and reenactments persisted as established devotional practices within many Nahua communities. In 1768 officers of the Mexican Inquisition considered extirpating all such performances. Significantly, the impetus for this campaign came in response not to native practice but to the burlesque imitations that some Spanish-speaking residents in Nahua areas were staging. Native behavior tended to be ignored unless it somehow intruded into Spanish colonial reality. An edict was issued ordering the confiscation of all written scripts for such plays, whether in Nahuatl or Spanish. However, the Dominican priest Francisco Larrea testified in support of the general practice of Passion reenactments and the specific customs of Tepoztlan and other Nahua towns, which he characterized as devout and free of heresy. Based on Larrea's arguments, the Inquisition modified its position, banning not the performances but only such abuses and errors as might be associated with them (see documentation in *Representaciones teatrales* 1934).

More recent Nahua Passion devotions are described in ethnographic studies of Nahuatl speakers in the Sierra Norte of the state of Puebla (Montoya Briones 1964:138–141) and the Gulf Coast lowland town of Ichcate-

7. Good Friday procession, Iztapalapa, Mexico City, 1984. Photograph by the author.

pec (Reyes García 1960:75–85). In Ichcatepec, the story of Christ's Passion is also, according to Reyes García, the story of the sun's struggle against the forces of darkness. The Sun-Christ's enemies represent, simultaneously, Jews, devils, and ancestors—the people of a previous mythological age of darkness now superseded by the victorious solar entity. Some participants personify these forces of darkness and disorder. Playing these roles is seen as inherently bad and dangerous, and those who do so must participate in a collective rite of purification via the Holy Saturday burning of a human effigy made of trash (a local variation of the widespread custom of burning an image of Judas). Other ritual impersonators perform a comic caricature of the dress and behavior of mestizos, specifically, officials of the Catholic Church. The celebration thus operates, much like the Chamula carnival rites discussed by Gossen (1986), to define the people's relationship to sacred powers, mythological epochs, moral rectitude, and the surrounding national culture.

Passion drama remains a part of Mexico City's public life. Iztapalapa, formerly a Nahua town of the old lakeshore and now a working-class neighborhood within the huge urban sprawl, hosts elaborate Passion devotions annually on Good Friday. Processions from the Iztapalapa church, with participants carrying crosses and bearing images of Christ and his sorrowing mother, surely retain some of the flavor of colonial Mexico's Passion processions (Figure 7). These penitential processions are followed by a reenactment of the crucifixion. A young man chosen for his exemplary moral character imitates Christ. Bearing a cross, he is accompanied by other actors dressed as Roman soldiers on horseback, the Virgin Mary, Mary Magdalene, the two thieves, and other personages.

Iztapalapa's Calvary is the Hill of the Star. Here the preconquest Mexica performed their world-renewing New Fire Ceremony every 52 years, testing to see whether the sun would retain its sovereignty over the forces of darkness and chaos. Ruins of the Mexica temple still stand on the hill. During the Good Friday rites, thousands watch from the hillsides below as Christ and his companion thieves are raised up on their crosses, silhouetted against the smoggy sky. Perhaps it is a mere juxtaposition of ancient ritual site and modern rite, or perhaps one may sense, on the Hill of the Star, a continuing presence of the early accommodations between native and Catholic cultural worlds that were worked out by the first generations of Christianizing Nahuas.

3

Interpreting "Holy Wednesday"

THE FOLLOWING ARE SUMMARY COMMENTS based on my comparison of the two plays. The development of these interpretations and their expression in the texts may be traced in more detail in the commentary on the scripts.

Mother and Child

For Izquierdo, as for other authors of contemplative Passion literature, the relationship between Mary and Christ is the nexus through which the devout person achieves an empathetic understanding of Christianity's principal sacred narrative. The portrayal of that relationship acts as a potent model both of and for inter-gender and inter-generational communication and conflict. Mary is the ultimate mother, Christ the supreme son; their interaction elevates human family ties to a cosmic level. The nature of those ties impinges, thus, not only upon religious practice but also upon broader constructions of kin relations, authority patterns, and personhood.

The Nahua playwright's treatment of Mary and Christ differs significantly from Izquierdo's. The Nahuatl Mary is invested with more authority and more knowledge than her Spanish counterpart. Her son is less inclined to contradict her and treats her with more deference. Mother and son engage in displays of agreement and solidarity that are lacking in the Spanish source. Given the Nahua elite's sophisticated codes of polite conversation, plus the fact that sixteenth-century Nahua women had more authority within the family than their Spanish contemporaries, these alterations are not surprising. Nor do they overtly contradict the friars' Christian doctrines; the Franciscans were great devotees of Mary and would not have taken offense at this depiction of her character. However, the changes do, in two subtle ways, affect the play's overall message.

First, because the Nahuatl Mary fails consistently to oppose her son's plans and accepts his fate before the angel arrives, the letters from Limbo are left with no obvious function. If they are not required to mediate the dispute and persuade Mary, then what purpose do they serve? The significance of these ancestral voices is explored in the following section.

Second, Christ is represented as a dutiful and obedient Nahua son. He is less responsible for his own actions than is his Spanish model. The Nahua Christ seems to lack any will to disobey his mother and does so only because his father and the ancient prophecies demand it. He does not even entertain the possibility of doing otherwise, as does his Spanish counterpart. In presenting a Christ who allows his behavior to be wholly determined by the demands of his parents and ancestors, the Nahua playwright contradicts Christian docrine in a manner that may be seen as an assertion of Nahua moral values.

For the friars, to be a moral actor is to have free will, to be a responsible, autonomous individual who knowingly chooses the proper course of action. Nahuatl confession manuals propagated this insistence on personal moral responsibility, encouraging the native penitent, in Gruzinski's words:

to put aside his surroundings, his social group, the weight of his tradition, and the external forces that used to influence his behavior, such as the power of a god's ire. . . . In other words, by centering on the "subject"—in the Western meaning of the word—the interrogation of the confession breaks down the ancient solidarity and social networks, as well as the physical and supernatural ties. (1989:98)

Nahuas, however, whose moral philosophy was aimed more at harmonizing human behavior with cosmic forces than at struggling against evil, appeared to the friars little disposed to take this sort of individualized responsibility for their own acts. Consequently, they were rarely able to generate, for ritual confession, autobiographical narratives of their individual moral histories (Gruzinski 1989; Klor de Alva 1988a; Burkhart 1989).

By stripping his Christ of even the small degree of willfulness and rebelliousness exhibited by the Spanish Christ in his cavalier treatment of Mary, while at the same time placing more emphasis than Izquierdo on the inviolable nature of the ancient prophecies, the Nahua playwright endows his Christ with characteristics that the friars sought to eradicate in their Nahua charges. Christ tries his best to do as he is bidden by a hierarchy of authorities external to himself: an angry paternal God who must be appeased, ancestral prophets whose words must be fulfilled, a mother whom he strives not to offend.

The Nahuatl Christ has no choice; his actions are determined by a pre-established pattern from which he feels no temptation to diverge. He does not freely sacrifice himself but, like many Nahuas at the hands of their Spanish overlords, is a victim of forces he does not control. He and his mother act as a unit not only out of their mutual love and understanding. They are equally subject to those exterior forces. And as close kin, they are part of a social collective whose cohesion takes precedence over the individual personality differences, including moral choices, that might otherwise result in conflict. The respect the Nahuatl Christ shows his earthly mother may also mirror a Nahua scholar's attitude toward his own family members, with whom he strives to maintain harmony while simultaneously serving his fatherly Franciscan mentors. Like Christ, he must tread delicately between conflicting authorities.

The Past Recovered

In its treatment of the past, the Nahuatl play differs from its Spanish source in three principal ways. First, it places additional emphasis on ancient prophecies about Christ, referring to them more frequently and at greater length than does Izquierdo's play. In addition to highlighting the predetermined nature of Christ's actions, this strategy calls attention to the ongoing significance, in the present time, of past events, and to the compelling authority of utterances and writings generated in ancient times. It also legitimates the playwright's own authorial voice, as that of a literate and educated man himself capable of reading and understanding those writings.

Second, the Old Testament personages who send the letters to Mary are treated differently. Their suffering is emphasized and is designated with the same vocabulary as Christ's torments, as if they too were undergoing a Passion; they are cast as penitent wrongdoers who seek Mary's pardon; they are described as Mary's fathers; David predicts the return of former glories.

Third, by disrupting, with redundancies and with his premature mother-child agreement, the Spanish play's linear dramatic structure of conflict, mediation, and resolution, the playwright also disrupts the teleological thrust of Christianity's construction of history. For Christianity, the Old Testament past is relevant only as a prelude to, and prefiguration of, the Christian present. Time is oriented forward, out of the Old Testament toward the coming of Christ and the redemption, and beyond that to the approaching apocalypse and millennium. The purpose of the letters from Limbo is to push that chronology forward.

According to native Mesoamerican views of time, the present is influenced by and repeats, with slight variations, patterns laid down in the past. Time proceeds not as an unbroken sequence but in a periodic fashion, intermittently interrupted by non-chronological intervals. The past leaves traces in the present, remnants that leap across the temporal gaps to be integrated into new orders. In this non-linear, non-absolute view of time, the present incorporates past phenomena that have accumulated over the ages and continue to set the pattern for ongoing events (B. Tedlock 1982:177; D. Tedlock 1985:64).

The Nahuatl play, if viewed from this perspective rather than through the lens of the Christian telos, may be seen to fit these native conceptions to some extent. The letters from Limbo interrupt the flow of the present events rather than helping them forward. The past erupts into the present, intruding a non-chronological gap between the first dialogue and the second. Mary and Christ fall silent and listen to voices that speak from the place and time of darkness. Christ's imminent actions will fulfill a pattern established by these ancient authorities. In addition to suffering themselves, such that Christ in his Passion imitates them, the Old Testament figures predict Christ's torments and present the actual implements that will be used to afflict him. They may thus be seen to play a decisive role in determining the course of Christ's Passion. It is they who give meaning and form to his present actions; he does not confer retroactive significance upon their ancient deeds. His descent to Limbo will have the effect of incorporating these representatives of the past into the present order.

The friars, when they spoke of the ancient prophets and patriarchs, sought to replace the Nahuas' own past with a Christian one, to eradicate the memories of ancient rulers and former deities and replace them with the characters and stories of the Old Testament. Christianizing Nahuas could lay claim to these stories of the ancient Hebrews, just as Europeans had done before them. But even if old ancestors were replaced by such new ones, old attitudes toward the past could serve as points of reference for life in the present. Traditional ideas would now be seen in juxtaposition to Spanish culture, such that their assertion would serve to contradict Spanish-Christian discourses.

For the Nahuas, the location of present events in the prophetic patterns of the past was a key strategy for coping with change. They made sense of the Spanish invasion by inventing an array of omens and prophecies that they asserted had preceded Cortés's arrival. The grounding of Christ's story in ancient prophecies filled the same function: it rendered Christianity not something new and unprecedented but expected and predictable. If these prophecies had to be borrowed from Old Testament prophets rather than historical Nahua ancestors, it hardly mattered; these foreign ancestors could be appropriated and treated as the Nahuas' own. The Holy Fathers in Limbo are *totahhuan* 'our fathers.'

In a Nahuatl prayer from 1574, the speaker takes as his or her ancestors the Three Kings or Magi, the wise pagan rulers who were prototypes for the conversion of Mexico's native elite:

They who are our grandfathers, the three sovereigns, they became our forebears, our progenitors through belief, us idolaters. They went to take on our behalf the believing in you [God] and the knowing of your precious child. (Sahagún 1574:16r)

Membership in the Church allows one to claim direct descent from these illustrious figures.

This borrowing of ancestors, this conflation of indigenous and Christian pasts, is a strategy pursued also by other Native Americans seeking legitimation for their cultural patterns. The early seventeenth-century native Andean historian Guaman Poma drew analogies between Old Testament personages and the ancient Andeans (Adorno 1986:60, 63, 100). In North America, contemporary Tlingit elders describe the old-time shamans as having professed elements of biblical teachings. According to Kan (1991:373), the Bible provides "a rich source of images in which to couch an 'old-fashioned' phenomenon like shamanism and make it more palatable to themselves and their younger native and non-native audiences."

A particularly compelling expression of this ancestor substitution comes from the autobiography of Nobel peace prize laureate Rigoberta Menchú. Describing how people in her Guatemalan Maya community approached their study of the Bible, she states:

. . . there is a lot that is similar. For example, we believe that there existed ancestors; and our ancestors are important because they are good people, because they obeyed the laws of our ancestors. The Bible also tells of some ancestors. Thus, it is not something strange. We accommodate the ancestors of the Bible as if they were our ancestors, following our own culture and our own customs. (Menchú 1987:107)

Having ancestors, and being able to point to them as models for one's actions—Menchú cites Moses, Judith, and David as models for Maya militants (1987:156–57)—is what counts. For Nahuas, the Old Testament (in its Christian exegesis) provided models of wise and just leaders who predicted Christ's coming and willingly embraced his worship.

In the *Colloquios*, the Franciscan-Nahua dialogues written by four Nahua scholars, the spokesman for the native side defends the ancestors for establishing the people's customs, in particular the worship of the deities (Sahagún 1986:148–51). This worship is justified because the deities did penance for people when it was still the time of darkness—that is, the time before the creation of the present solar age. This alludes to myths such as that of the creation of the sun and moon at Teotihuacan, recorded in Sahagún's ethnographic encyclopedia, according to which one particularly penitent god becomes the sun and the others sacrifice themselves in an attempt to set it in motion (Sahagún 1950–82:VII, 3–8). When recorded, these myths were immersed in a process of revaluation in response to Christian evangelization and colonial experience; the image of the penitent deity and of the prophetic ancestor were both engaged in the ongoing negotiation of what constituted Nahua cultural identity in the colonial context.

This primordial function of the native deities, the carrying out of penitential acts in order to establish the conditions for human existence, is also performed by Christ in his self-sacrifice. The application to Christ of solar metaphors, a liturgical tradition carried over into Nahuatl texts, furthered this parallelism with native myths of cosmogenesis (Burkhart 1988b). The Nahua playwright's representation of the Holy Fathers as also doing penance in a time and place of darkness acts as both a substitution for the ancient actions of native deities (as constructed after the conquest) and as a prophetic prototype for Christ's Passion. That is, like the old deities, the Limbo inmates carry out penances for the benefit of humanity, and Christ in his own torments partially reiterates that pattern.

Simultaneously, in their penances the play's Old Testament figures act to atone for the misdeeds they committed in their ignorance of Christian law. The friars consigned all the Nahuas' ancestors to the flames of eternal damnation; there was no way that those who died without Christian baptism could be redeemed. Yet the story of the harrowing of hell tells of ancestral figures liberated from the underworld and incorporated into the new Christian order. If those figures may act as generic ancestors, and one may speak, as the Nahuatl Christ does in the play, of a "great many others" who are to be redeemed, perhaps the pre-Christian ancestors may attain pardon for their errors and merit an escape from their torments.

Ambiguity regarding the fate of the ancestors is evident in the *Cantares mexicanos* song texts (Bierhorst 1985). Some of these songs are colonial compositions; others are traditional orally transmitted texts that, even if passed down from before the Spanish invasion, have been modified to reflect colonial experiences. Many of these songs cite the splendid achievements of past rulers and ancestors. Various songs lament that these glories have passed away and comment wistfully upon the transience of earthly life. Some songs consign the heroes to the underworld (e.g., Bierhorst 1985:239). But others show less resignation. One song regrets that those old heroes died before having come to know Tloque Nahuaque, an epithet for an omnipresent deity that came to be applied to the Christian god (145). Another, having earlier spoken of Christ's crucifixion, goes on to ponder whether Motecuhzoma, Nezahualcoyotl, and other old rulers will return (231). Some songs place old heroes into the Christian heaven and associate them with God, Christ, or Mary (e.g., 141, 188–89, 340–41). These varied treatments suggest a lack of consensus and a willingness to improvise solutions to the problem of the past, including solutions that would not have met with the approval of friars.

A similar desire for accommodation between the old myths and the new affected the story of Quetzalcoatl's descent to the underworld and transformation into the morning star. According to the *Anales de Cuauhtitlan* version, redacted by a Christian Nahua in 1570, the god is disgraced and obliged to flee from his realm of Tollan. But before departing he lies in a stone coffer for four days. Only after that does he instruct his pages to hide his riches and flee with him. He then immolates himself and rises into the sky in the form of a quetzal bird's heart, accompanied by other precious birds. The text goes on to explain that on his death he spent four days in the underworld (Bierhorst 1992a:12, 1992b:36). The eight-day total corresponds to the inferior conjunction of Venus, its apparent disappearance beneath the earth between its stint as evening star and its first rising as morning star.

The story of Christ's three-day entombment in a stone coffer has intruded itself into this myth. The term *tepetlacalli* 'stone mat-house,' used throughout the Nahua-Christian corpus for Christ's sepulcher, is here applied to Quetzalcoatl's temporary residence; the Christian sacred number three is changed to the Nahua sacred number four. I can think of no reason why Quetzalcoatl should take such a strange course of action except in imitation of Christ.

Quetzalcoatl's entombment, like Christ's, is associated with both a descent into the underworld and an ascent, accompanied by birds/angels, into the heavens. In the 1558 *Leyenda de los Soles* version of Quetzalcoatl's descent, the god harrows the place of the dead, stealing from the underworld lord the bones of dead humans. From these purloined fossils, mixed with his own blood, he and a female creator deity fashion a new group of humans to populate the new (fifth) solar age. As in the *Florentine Codex* story of the creation of the sun, all the gods do penance, now in order to help the human beings come to life (Bierhorst 1992a:88–89, 1992b: 145–46).

Quetzalcoatl thus incorporates ancestral remains into the present order while also revitalizing human existence. Christ's penitential bloodletting and underworld descent accomplished the same ends. Nahua scholars familiar with both the old myths and Christian narratives could hardly be unaware of these relationships, and may have reworked the old myths just as they reinterpreted the new. Even if not explicitly realized, a concern with the place of the past in the present order may have informed their thinking and affected their treatment of these topics. In the playwright's interpretation, Christ goes to the underworld to rescue his precious ones—and "a great many others"—from their miserable imprisonment by the demons who rule that place, a category of beings synonymous with non-Christian deities.

This is, I suggest, the Nahua playwright's solution to the problem of the past. The redemption of the Limbo inmates symbolically incorporates the ancestral age into the colonial and Christian order while casting the coming of Christ as an event that not only was prophesied in ancient times but recapitulates ancestral patterns of penance and world renewal.

This construction fits a broader pattern of native response to Spanish domination, one that Klor de Alva (1992:341) has called a "counter-narrative of continuity." Spanish and Catholic hegemonic discourse insisted upon a violent and irrevocable rupture with the past and its replacement by a new order, a new law, indeed "new men." Nahuas responded by finding precedents in their past for all of this newness. Spaniards viewed the objects of their colonial enterprise as weak, childish, perhaps demonic, perhaps angelic, but in any case ineluctably different from themselves. Nahuas, rather than rejecting the invaders as an alien form of life, accommodated them within their own reality (see also Lockhart 1982; Wood 1991).

Klor de Alva describes the Nahua attitude in the following way:

. . . the Other is always latent in Ourselves, and is revealed as something already known and expected, predicted by the ancestors, by the governors of the past and by the diviners of the present. (1992:345–46)

The ancestors, who wait in the underworld for Christ to come and free them, know in advance that the Catholic faith will come to Mexico. They too will be a part of this "new" order, which they foresaw and which is, after all, but another of the periodic realignments to which the Nahua cosmos was subject.

Passion and Redemption

The torments of Christ, so lovingly documented in European Passion tracts, take on new resonances in the Mexican context. On the one hand, bloodletting, fasting, and other penitential practices were so much a part of indigenous religiosity that Christ's participation in such acts helped native people accept him as their own. On the other hand, his unjust arrest, sentencing, torture, and execution, carried out at the hands of colonial Roman officials and soldiers, was a potential vector for symbolizing the Nahuas' own oppression. They were overtaxed, weakened by disease, and subject to an alien judicial system that was failing to meet their needs. In the closing years of the sixteenth century, as their population level approached its nadir, they faced the possibility of ethnic extinction. Their words for the Passion connoted overwork, fatigue, exhaustion—unhealthful conditions now often brought on by forced labor under the *repartimiento* program. If the play's "great city of Jerusalem" stands for the great city of Mexico, when Christ falls into the hands of abusive strangers these are Spanish hands.

To what extent did early colonial Nahuas realize the Passion's potential to dramatize their own status as victims of oppression? This question is difficult to answer, but a collective identification with Christ and Mary was surely operative in the context of Holy Week observations. With their own processions and confraternities segregated from those of non-natives, and with the Spaniards' procession marching under armed guard, ethnic as well as community differences were highlighted. Even though Nahuas easily embraced ideas, behaviors, and technologies introduced by their colonial overlords, their accommodation of otherness did not erase the boundary between Spanish and Nahua persons. Spaniards and their creole offspring remained foreigners, *castillan tlacah* 'people of Castile'; meanwhile, such cultural imports as the Church and its saints were divorced from them and could even be treated as though they had arrived in Mexico without Spanish military assistance (Burkhart 1992b). Hence, the historical accident that the Church had come as a by-product of conquest did not preclude the appropriation of its symbols and texts for nativistic and even anti-Spanish purposes. When Christ and Mary were played by Nahua actors, spoke proper Nahuatl, and behaved toward one another according to Nahua codes of politesse, their non-Spanish-ness in itself added a subtext to their script. If they are Nahuas, then they are not Spaniards. And if they are Nahuas, they may represent any given Nahua community as a collective body, as set apart not only from other Nahua or non-Nahua native communities but also, and perhaps most saliently, from Spaniards.

Christ's coming to Mexico was treated as an act of redemption. Freed from the tyranny of their demon gods, the native people now had access to Christ's mercy and to heavenly reward. There is, in such texts as the *Colloquios*, the *Psalmodia christiana*, and the Holy Wednesday drama, a sense of a permanent transformation of cosmic proportions. Christ, the new solar deity, drives away the forces of darkness, even liberating "our fathers" from them. Radiance shines down upon the redeemed and they are showered with riches. Redemption is collective and irreversible.

The problem with this construction is that, even though it has native people recognize their past errors and accept Christ, it finesses the issue of individual moral struggle. From the friars' point of view, Christ may have come to Mexico but the individual Nahua had still to make constant moral choices, fleeing the Devil's temptations and holding to the path of righteousness. To construe the redemption as world renewal, as collective experience, as victory of light over darkness, is to overlook the shadows that friars saw still lurking in even the most avid convert's soul.

Friars labored, largely in vain, to impress their notions of the moral self on their Nahua charges; meanwhile, the most effectively evangelized Nahuas—the scholars of Tlatelolco—wrote texts that celebrate collective redemption and even suggest its extension to non-Christian ancestors. Nowhere in the Nahua playwright's elaborations upon his source does he attempt to give moral guidance to his audience, to define for them thoughts or deeds in which they should or should not engage. The Old Testament figures have erred, it is true, but they are about to be rescued from the consequences of those errors. It is difficult to imagine a friar producing such a lengthy adaptation of an Old World text without adding even one moralistic aside directed at reforming the audience. The Nahua playwright was concerned with cosmic events, not individual consciences.

Turning Words

Given the striking differences between Izquierdo's *auto* and the Holy Wednesday drama, I need hardly point out that the Nahua playwright viewed translation as a process as much of invention and adaptation as of a quest for linguistic equivalence. He ascribes authority to the written word, as represented by the prophecies of Christ's death, yet takes great liberties with the interpretation of his own source. Written texts have authority, but their meanings are unstable.

If the adaptations were directed at simplifying the play for an audience of poorly educated quasi-Christians, at bringing it down to the level of the *rudes* that some presumed the Nahuas to be, the alterations would be less significant. Some of the playwright's elaborations do impart knowledge that Izquierdo may have taken for granted in his Spanish audience. However, the Nahuatl play cannot be viewed as a simplification of its source. Far from being an abridgement, it is much longer than its model and it introduces ideas and images not found in Izquierdo's text.

In some cases the playwright seems to have avoided translating Izquierdo's statements because he failed to understand, or find a convenient Nahuatl parallel for, the Spaniard's choice of wording. Or, in other cases, he has chosen to pursue his own images and metaphors instead. Rarely, if ever, does he omit theological or devotional content simply because it might prove too subtle for his audience; possible omissions are more than balanced by new material that he introduces. Nor does he treat his audience as if it were composed of children who needed to have everything spelled out for them. Nothing in the play conveys any sense that it has been written for people who are inferior in their mentality, their religiosity, or their morality to Izquierdo's Spanish Christian audience. Indeed, by recasting the character's interactions according to Nahua behavioral codes and rewriting their terse speeches as formal Nahuatl oratory, the playwright indicates that the original characters lacked the decorum and speaking skills that the subject matter demanded. The task of translation is to bring the text across the cultural divide and also to raise it up to the level of Nahuatl discourse.

The friars considered drama to be an effective evangelical tool because the Nahuas and other native people were attracted to elaborate pageantry, ornaments, and costumes, as well as to the songs and dances that often accompanied dramatic performances. Native people, they believed, understood what they saw with their eyes, not what they heard with their ears. The Nahua playwright does add six costumed boys to the play's cast, and it is clear that he intended for them to carry mock-ups of the Passion insignia. However, his other additions and changes involve no further comings and goings, no additional props, no singing and dancing—practices that would, in any case, have been inappropriate during Holy Week. Instead, he adds words, and many of them. He must have believed that his audience would attend to these words and find them persuasive. Perhaps it was the friars' didactic, moralizing, linguistically unpolished preaching that failed to hold the native people's attention, not any inherent inattentiveness in respect to the spoken word. Give them good Nahuatl oratory delivered by skilled actors and perhaps they would gladly listen to lengthy Christian discourses even without the musical interludes, multi-level stages, and elaborate stage settings that accompanied some Nahuatl dramas.

The comparison of Spanish and Nahuatl scripts makes visible the gap between these cultures that persisted seventy years into the colonial occupation, even in those contexts where persons and discourses from both sides were brought into closest contact. If for a trusted scholar and interpreter the gap is so wide, the slippages in form and meaning—both intentional and inadvertent—so evident as a text is transported across it, how separate must the worlds of Spaniard and Nahua have been. And how deluded were the friars to think that their discourses could cross that divide unaltered, and to label the native people obtuse and incalcitrant for failing to respond in the expected fashions.

If this Nahua playwright's approach to translation was at all representative of the interpreter's art, one must wonder how many other Spanish discourses were similarly transformed as they passed, orally or in writing, into Nahuatl. Spanish texts that purport to translate utterances originally rendered in Nahuatl must also be questioned—can these actually represent what native people really said? No translation is ever a completely faithful and transparent reproduction of its source, but if the interpreter does not even attempt accurately to convey the content and meaning of the original message, the result is something other than what is conventionally termed a translation.

In Nahuatl, the art of translation was designated the "turning of words," *tlahtolcuepaliztli*. The verb *cuepa* refers to acts of turning around or inside out, of returning, of responding, and of changing (Molina 1970: 114v; Campbell 1985:85–86). The English "translate" and Spanish *traduzir* derive, respectively, from the Latin verbs *transferre* 'to carry across' and *traducere* 'to lead across.' Translation, construed as such, carries meanings across boundaries. Nahuas could have used verbs referring to crossing or carrying rather than returning or changing. But by treating translation as a turning about, a response, or a change, they avoid the fallacious assumption that translation can be a mere conveyance. And they leave space within the practice of translation for the translator to respond to the text, to change it, to turn it to his or her own ends, to return it to earlier discourses that inform its interpretation. Such is how the Nahua playwright approached his work.

The irony is apparent, and the lesson a humbling one for any translator. I would like to imagine that I have "carried across" these two plays into English; at the same time what I most want to convey, to transmit, to get across—the metaphor of transfer seems inescapable—is the extent to which the Nahua playwright avoided doing this in his own work of text production. Can I claim mastery of the technique he eschews? If I have failed to "translate" these eighteen pages of Nahuatl script, this remnant of the Nahua past that has intruded into my own time and space, may it be that I have at least managed to turn some words of merit, to scatter a few precious stones.

PART TWO

———

THE PLAYS

Prologue to the Translations

TO FACILITATE COMPARISON of the two dramas, I have paired the five-line stanzas of the Spanish text with the corresponding segments of the Nahuatl script, numbering them accordingly. Each segment of the Nahuatl play includes all the text that is modeled on the corresponding Spanish stanza plus any additional content without a basis in the Spanish, up to where text based on the following Spanish stanza begins. Since the stanza boundaries in the Spanish nearly always coincide with discursive breaks in the Nahuatl, the pairing of the texts in this manner presents few problems; it is clear that the Nahua author, despite his many changes and digressions, was keeping a close eye on the structure of the Spanish text as he composed his own. In the manuscript, seven of these boundaries are marked visibly by extending the last letter of the last word into a short horizontal line (this is also done, where space permitted, at the end of each turn at speech), by skipping to the next line on the page, or both.

The scribe who recorded the Nahuatl drama placed it on the page in a format that resembles prose literature, with the characters' speeches written in paragraphs. As noted in Chapter Two, the Nahua playwright composed his text in the oral-poetic style of Nahuatl oratory. This non-linear, indirect, formal, and repetitive style lends itself poorly to prose translation. I have therefore chosen to translate the play in the form of lines rather than continuous prose. In this I am following the conventions for "ethnopoetic" translations of Native American oral literature that have been developed over the past two decades by Dell Hymes, Dennis Tedlock, and others.[1]

The advantages of translating in lines are well stated by Bright:

First, it represents an effort to present the elements of phonological, grammatical, and semantic *parallelism* that exist in the originals and that are basic to their effectiveness. Second, it represents a typographic attempt to focus the attention of readers: to encourage the type of close reading that we might not accord to a page of run-on, wall-to-wall prose. (1993:xiv; emphasis in original)

Arrangement in lines reveals the poetic devices employed in Native American—including Nahua—verbal art, which are often obscured when texts are forced into prose.

One drawback of this method is that the line divisions I impose on the text are inevitably somewhat arbitrary. The sixteenth-century Nahuas seemingly did not possess a concept of "a line of poetry" as such, in respect to either spoken oratory or songs.[2] However, phrasal units of varying length can be identified in Nahuatl oratory based on syntactic, semantic, and occasionally orthographic criteria. Representing such units of phrasing spatially as lines on the printed page has been done to good effect by translators such as Sullivan (1965, 1966, 1980), León-Portilla (Sahagún 1986), and Klor de Alva (1980).

In setting line divisions, I have been guided by the use of particles (*auh*, *ca*, *ma*, *tla*, and others) in the Nahuatl, by semantic parallelism (couplets, triplets), by forms of vocative address, and in some cases by the scribe's use of capital letters, colons, and periods. I have also considered the coherence and aesthetic appeal of the English translation. Lines that turned out too short and choppy in English would not convey the elevated formality of the Nahuatl. In short, the line structure is very much my own interpretation of the text and is based on many arbitrary decisions. Text that I place in a single line could sometimes be divided into two or more; conversely, I place divisions between phrases that another translator might join in the same line.

The language employed in the Nahuatl text is canonical Classical Nahuatl of the variety typical of Church literature. Though composed by a native speaker, the text should have been comprehensible to those friars who had a good mastery of the language and I presume it was intended to be so. In some cases where the Nahuatl text seemed ambiguous, I chose the translation that more closely corresponded to the Spanish text. Clear digressions from that text are translated as such.

The reverential or honorific system of Classical Nahuatl is used throughout the play. Mary never addresses Christ without using reverential inflections, nor do Christ, the angel, or the Holy Fathers ever address her except in tones of respect. To speak reverentially, Nahuas added the honorific suffix *-tzin* to any nouns referring to the revered person ("his book" becoming "his honored book" or, better, "the book of him, who is honored"). They also added an extra layer of prefixes and suffixes to every verb addressed directly to that individual or referring to him or her in third person. Transitive verbs took the form of reflexive causative verbs ("you eat beans" becoming "you cause yourself to eat beans"); intransitive verbs became reflexive applicatives ("she sleeps" becoming "she sleeps in respect to herself").

To translate these constructions literally into English makes an extremely formal and elegant speech style sound absurd; to insert the parenthetical asides (rev.) or (hon.) destroys the flow of the text. One can try to attach a reverential sense to the translation, but one may end up with constructions like "you who are an honored person respectfully eat your revered beans." Not only would no one ever say this in English, but it does not even convey the sense of the Nahuatl, which has to do not with table manners but with the social relationship between the speaker and the addressee. Gingerich comments:

No one . . . has found a way to naturally and consistently translate the honorific and reverential inflections attached frequently to Nahuatl verbs, but that is certainly because no one now, if they ever did, naturally adopts in English the social relationships that these inflections require. (1992:365)

I do not translate the reverential inflections. However, I do aim to impart a certain formality through the wording of my English text, in the hope that giving a slightly stilted, indirect air to the English may compensate to some degree for the loss of the reverential mode of address. My unwillingness to employ a more colloquial, chatty tone is, thus, calculated. The characters should not sound quite like they are putting on airs, but they should sound like they are speaking in a formal manner while also laying on the mutual admiration rather thickly.

The final four speeches of the Nahuatl text, which have no basis in the surviving editions of Izquierdo's text, are treated as four additional Nahuatl segments (100N–103N). There are two possible explanations for the existence of these final speeches. The Nahua playwright may have added his own coda to his adaptation of Izquierdo, perhaps drawing upon some other text. Or, a Spanish version of those four speeches may have existed in some earlier, now unknown edition of Izquierdo, which was truncated prior to the printing of the extant imprints. The motivation for so amputating the ending might have been to force the text to fit onto eight printed pages (four leaves), as the extant versions do. It could then be printed on a single sheet of paper folded into quarto size. That such truncating was not unusual is attested by a statement made by the playwright Montalvan in a volume of his plays printed in Madrid in 1635. He complains of how the booksellers of Seville routinely cut plays down to four sheets, even if eight are necessary (Rennert 1963:174).

I originally hypothesized that the four final Nahuatl speeches did have a model in Izquierdo.[3] However, after closer study of the Spanish text I have changed that evaluation. Izquierdo's drama comes to a logical close at the end of the extant editions; additional material would have been superfluous. In the appended section Christ blesses Mary, even though he has already done so in the parallel texts. The style of Christ's second blessing is quite different from that of his first, just as a long speech by Mary in the appended section differs stylistically from her previous speeches. She also requests a favor that, in effect, she was already denied earlier in the play. The Nahua playwright delays the characters' embrace until his closing stage directions, even though it was referred to in the dialogue at the close of the parallel segments. In light of these factors, I think it most likely that these final speeches were added by the Nahua playwright, probably based on some other Nahuatl source. Further comment on these added passages may be found in the annotations.

Stage directions and speakers' names or titles are printed in boldface and reproduce, as closely as possible, the wording of the original texts. Transcriptions of the Spanish and Nahuatl texts can be found on the diskette that is available as a supplement to this book.

The Translations

Beacon of Our Salvation

Christ:

1S:1   Mother with great dignity,

  2   Daughter of the divine Father,

  3   Virgin full of humility,

  4   I have a great need

  5   to take a short trip.

2S:1   And although I am the sovereign God

  2   I come to you obediently,

  3   as son in a human sense,

  4   I ask that you give me permission,

  5   and your hand, sacred Virgin.

Mary:

3S:1   Oh my Son and blessing without equal,

  2   seat yourself, as you give me concern.

  3   I would like to speak with you a while

  4   in front of Magdalene.

Holy Wednesday

Christim:

1N:1 You who are the supreme noblewoman,

2 you who are my precious mother,

3 you who are the daughter of the one who lives forever, God the father,

4 May you know that today,

5 oh my precious mother,

6 you who are a very humble one,

7 it is now the hour, it is now the moment,

8 it is now that the time has arrived

9 for the people to be rescued.

10 And this:

11 I wish to set off for Jerusalem.

2N:1 And well do you understand,

2 oh my precious mother,

3 that I am a divinity, I am God, I am sovereign,

4 along with my precious father and the Holy Spirit.

5 However, it was in your pure womb

6 that I came to become a man, I came to assume flesh.

7 Hence, now I am your precious child,

8 in the sense that I am a man.

9 And in the sense that I am a man,

10 I will be made to suffer great fatigue,

11 because of the misdeeds of the people of the world.

12 Thus, because of them I now beseech you:

13 may you give me your command, your send-off,

14 so that I may go to Jerusalem,

15 oh my precious mother.

Mary:

3N:1 Oh, you who are my consolation and precious child,

2 you who emerged from my womb,

3 in the sense that you are a man,

4 what is this that you are saying?

Christ:

3S:5   I am pleased to listen.

Mary:

4S:1   Beloved son of mine,

2   my blessing, my God, and my repose,

3   where are you going, so upset

4   and with your glorious face,

5   son, so pale?

5S:1   I often see your disciples

2   sighing,

3   I also see the sons of Zebedee

4   come crying,

5   and I believe it's something bad.

6S:1   Son, my God and Lord,

2   give me the answer to this

3   and do me this favor,

4   that you remain here for this festival.

5   I ask you this out of my love for you.

7S:1   Have pity on me,

2   do not give me such suffering,

5 You are making me very anxious.

6 Do sit down.

7 I want to say a few words to you here,

8 in front of Magdalene, who is standing here.

Christ:

3N:9 Oh my precious mother,

10 what is it that you want to say?

11 May it be that I hear it!

Mary:

4N:1 My precious child,

2 my sweet goodness and consolation,

3 my lord, God, sovereign,

4 my repose and love,

5 what is this that you are saying?

6 That you want to go where?

7 From what I see of you,

8 you must be greatly afflicted,

9 because your face of utter goodness

10 has become quite pale, has become quite white,

11 with anxiety, with sadness.

5N:1 May you know,

2 my precious child,

3 how I see your students:

4 all the time, because of you

5 they go about sad, they go about distressed,

6 the children of Zebedee.

7 And this:

8 it is true.

9 Something very frightful will happen to you,

10 torment, death.

6N:1 My precious child, my sovereign, my lord,

2 may you oblige me, may your heart be compassionate!

3 For I beseech you

4 that the great pascua may occur while you are right here.

5 Fervently I beseech you.

6 May it be just because you love me very much,

7 since I am your mother in the fleshly sense.

7N:1 My precious child,

2 be compassionate!

3   because I tell you truly
4   I think you are going to your death
5   when you go away to the city.

Christ:

8S:1   My Lady, and mother of mine,
2   great blessing of all the world,
3   because of a great mystery it falls to me
4   that I go to Jerusalem.
5   My father orders, and commands.

9S:1   And my going is something very necessary
2   for the whole world,
3   and thus, prudent mother,
4   do not impede my leaving,
5   I beseech you humbly.

Mary:

10S:1   Do not order me, my life,
2   that I consent in your leaving,
3   God, true Messiah,
4   and as I am not happy,
5   do not wish it, my joy.

3 May you have pity on me,
4 so that you will not go to Jerusalem,
5 and so that my spirit will not hurt, will not ache because of you!
6 Quite truly do I say to you,
7 for it is true,
8 that as soon as you go you will fall into the hands of others,
9 thus you will die,
10 in the great city of Jerusalem.

Christ:
8N:1 Oh my precious mother, oh noblewoman,
2 may you know,
3 that the people of the world are to be greatly favored.
4 They are to be rescued.
5 Thus, it is essential that I go to Jerusalem.
6 My precious father, God, desires it to be so.
7 It is he who set it down in this way,
8 so that I came here on earth
9 so that I would die
10 because of the misdeeds in the world.

9N:1 It is true,
2 oh my precious mother,
3 that it is very necessary for the people of the world
4 that I go, that I go up to Jerusalem.
5 And this:
6 you will not be able to hinder me,
7 you will not forestall me,
8 with your sadness, your weeping.
9 Fervently I beseech you,
10 oh my mother,
11 for it is true, for I will go!

Mary:
10N:1 Oh, you who are my life, you who are my consolation,
2 may your soul not reflect upon such a thing,
3 that you will go away!
4 Because I know very well
5 that it is true that you are God, your power is total,
6 and that you are a human being, you are a man.
7 May you desire not that you will go away,
8 my precious consolation and joy!

11S:1   And although it might be disobedience
    2   to give you, Lord, such a response,
    3   may your mightiness forgive.
    4   At least on this festival
    5   you will not go with my permission.

12S:1   Other sons exiled,
    2   while their parents are at home,
    3   on such notable days
    4   they rush home
    5   to relax with their mothers.

13S:1   As these do very well,
    2   and it's good that they do this,
    3   say, Jesus the Nazarene,
    4   why are you leaving me
    5   on this solemn festival?

Christ:
14S:1   The ancient prophecies,
    2   Mother, cannot lie,
    3   that truly I need to go,
    4   and I need to fulfill
    5   those old designs.

11N:1 And although it may seem
2 as though I hold you in low esteem,
3 you who are my precious child,
4 the way I keep responding to your words,
5 may it be that you pardon me,
6 by means of your total power.
7 For I do not wish
8 that I myself should give you my send-off,
9 so that the great festival should befall you there in Jerusalem.
10 And this:
11 may I be right here near you, next to you
12 on the pascua.
12N:1 May you know
2 that some children, who are living on the run,
3 or who live elsewhere,
4 when it is the pascua,
5 they all come back.
6 They are consoled beside their mothers,
7 thus together they console one another on the pascua.
13N:1 This, my precious child,
2 it is good, what they do,
3 and it is necessary that they act in this way.
4 So I just beseech you,
5 my precious child,
6 do tell me,
7 you who are Jesus the Nazarene,
8 why are you abandoning me
9 on the very great pascua?
10 That which is about to happen,
11 it will not happen to you here.
Christ:
14N:1 Oh noblewoman, oh my precious mother,
2 may you know
3 that everything the prophets of old left foretold,
4 it is really the truth,
5 it is not false words.
6 And all that happened a long time ago,
7 that still is only signs,
8 it will all come true now.

15S:1 How much easier it would be
  2 for the high starry Heaven to buckle
  3 and for the earth to be destroyed,
  4 than it would be for what is prophesied
  5 for me not to be carried out.

Mary:
16S:1 Very sad consolation
  2 you give me, my true God.
  3 Why do you give me so much suffering?
  4 Whom do you love more than me?
  5 Say, my heart.

Christ:
17S:1 Mother with great dignity,
  2 through whom I came from Heaven,
  3 what I tell you is true,
  4 that I came to earth to die.
  5 For that reason, mother, make an effort.

9 And this:

10 I will go, I will go cause to come true

11 all the prophecies

12 that lie written in the sacred book.

15N:1 Oh my precious mother, know

2 that the sky

3 and all the stars

4 and the earth,

5 their strength is nothing whatsoever,

6 they are not strong.

7 They will crumble, they will be scattered.

8 But the sacred words that lie written in the sacred book,

9 which is quite strong with sacred words,

10 they are really the truth.

11 And this:

12 oh my precious mother,

13 I will cause them to come true.

Mary:

16N:1 Oh, how my heart is torn open to its very bottom!

2 It as if you plunged a knife into it

3 by answering me in this way,

4 you who are truly God and sovereign.

5 My precious child,

6 why do you afflict me so with sadness?

7 Do tell me.

8 Why do you afflict my spirit, my soul,

9 I who am your mother in the fleshly sense?

Christ:

17N:1 Oh, you who are filled with goodness, with propriety,

2 you who are my precious mother,

3 I speak truthfully to you!

4 As to how I came down here upon the earth,

5 it was for this reason:

6 that I should be made to suffer fatigue, I should be made to hurt,

7 that upon the cross I should be stretched by my hands.

8 In the sense that I am a man, I will die there.

9 And this:

10 oh my precious mother,

11 may you exert all your effort!

12 May you be strong,

18S:1 You know well that I have come,
   2 being God and sovereign,
   3 to make right what was lost
   4 by all the human lineage,
   5 which was conquered by Lucifer.

19S:1 And as I came, mother of mine,
   2 to redeem the world,
   3 the day is already very near
   4 on which I must die,
   5 so consider what I am to tell you.

20S:1 Put aside the excessive crying,
   2 because I tell you for certain
   3 that it will be much more terrible for you,
   4 because soon I will be dead,
   5 although now you see me alive.

Mary:
21S:1 Oh painful response
   2 for me, and cruel suffering,
   3 oh harsh response
   4 more bitter than bile,
   5 oh grave and maddening pain.

22S:1 Oh my God, highest truth,
   2 son of the celestial father,
   3 tell me, your divinity,
   4 why you show such cruelty
   5 to your sad mother.

13   may your heart not be very sad!

18N:1 Well do you know,

2   oh my precious mother,

3   that I am God, I am sovereign,

4   none soever is as great as I, as awe-inspiring as I!

5   However, this is the reason for my being a man,

6   this is the reason why I came:

7   I came to heal, I came to rescue the human being,

8   whom the great demon, Lucifer, had made his slave.

19N:1 Oh, oh my precious mother,

2   by this may you be consoled.

3   And this:

4   it is already here, it is already beside me,

5   the time when I will die

6   so that I may cause to come true, I may confirm the predictions

7   that the prophets left uttered in regard to me.

20N:1 So now I beseech you,

2   may your heart, your soul be not distraught!

3   For it is true, I tell you with certainty

4   that it is great, that it is extreme,

5   the way your precious soul will ache, will hurt,

6   when you see me with my hands tied.

7   And this:

8   oh my precious mother,

9   soon I will die,

10   although now you still see me standing alive.

Mary:

21N:1 Oh, it is very lamentable, it is very saddening,

2   the way you answer me,

3   you who are my precious child!

4   It is true that it is extreme,

5   the way my heart is afflicted, the way it hurts.

6   There is no bitter medicine so hurtful to the heart

7   as the way you answer me.

22N:1 Oh, you who are the utterly truthful divinity,

2   you who are the sovereign,

3   you who are the precious child of eternally living God the father,

4   I beseech you,

5   do tell me,

23S:1 Why don't you show pity for me,
  2 tell me, my son, the reason?
  3 Remember, God, that I gave you birth,
  4 and remember when I raised you,
  5 that milk that I gave you.

24S:1 Why, my God, are you leaving me,
  2 to die, being infinite?
  3 how and in this way are you leaving me?
  4 And the flight with you to Egypt
  5 so little do you hold it in regard?

25S:1 Fleeing through the mountains
  2 I carried you, my son, in my arms.
  3 Remember my insides,
  4 that I was being broken into a thousand pieces
  5 by very odd departures.

26S:1 Remember what I suffered,
  2 my son, whom I contemplate,
  3 Remember, sorrow of mine,
  4 when I lost you in the temple
  5 the great sorrow I felt.

27S:1 Why do you forget
  2 these things, my God?

6	for what reason do you so greatly sadden your mother with anxiety of the heart,
7	by wanting to go to Jerusalem?
23N:1	Why is your heart not compassionate, not pitying,
2	my precious child?
3	For what reason?
4	Do tell me.
5	Perhaps you do not remember how I gave birth to you
6	there in the eating-place of the deer?
7	Perhaps you do not remember my milk,
8	with which I nurtured you?
24N:1	Oh, you who live forever, you who are God,
2	why, for what reason,
3	will you die, in the sense that you are a man?
4	And I, I who am your mother,
5	you are going to leave me!
6	And with whom will I console myself,
7	how will my heart be joyful,
8	when I do not look to you for my measure?
9	Perhaps you do not remember
10	all the exhaustion, heat, wind, ravines, and hills
11	we passed through as we went to hide you there in Egypt
12	when Herod wanted to kill you?
25N:1	You do remember what I endured,
2	how I went just carrying you in my arms,
3	just in my hands you traveled,
4	when we went to Egypt.
5	And there were not just a few times when, by stumbling, I might have let go of you.
6	And there were not just a few other things I endured for your sake.
26N:1	And I remember
2	how I used to worry about you night and day.
3	Perhaps you do not remember
4	how I was afflicted,
5	the anxiety, the affliction,
6	when I lost you there in Jerusalem,
7	where you want to go now?
27N:1	Why do you just forget,
2	my precious child?

3   Do not die, son, I beseech you,
4   let me obtain this from you,
5   my son, much beloved.

Christ:

28S:1   Oh you have wounded me,
2   mother, with your reasonings.
3   Oh mother, it is all right,
4   although in your requests
5   you have importuned me much.

29S:1   The sin committed
2   by Adam was of such a sort,
3   that God being infinite,
4   unless it be with my death,
5   it cannot be redeemed.

3   May you thus have pity on me, favor me.

4   Fervently I beseech you

5   that you not wish that you will die,

6   you who are my utterly precious child!

7   May you obey me!

Christ:

28N:1   Oh how greatly you sadden me,

2   you noblewoman,

3   you who are my precious mother.

4   With words of affliction you have declared

5   how I will retreat,

6   how I will turn things around for myself,

7   so that I will not die.

8   Although you have declared many sad words to me,

9   not so will it be ruined,

10   that which my precious father has decreed,

11   that I will die.

29N:1   May you know,

2   oh noblewoman, oh my mother,

3   that God, the divinity, the sovereign, who lives forever,

4   he is a divinity of utterly surpassing goodness.

5   And he made Adam and Eve, and he placed them

6   there in terrestrial paradise.

7   He gave them orders

8   so that they would stay there,

9   in the very good place, in the very fine place.

10   And he gave them orders

11   so that they would not approach, they would not eat

12   the fruit of the tree of life.

13   But later on, the Devil, the demon deceived them,

14   so that they stretched out their hands to it, they ate it,

15   the fruit, the produce, of the tree of life,

16   which he had prohibited to them.

17   Thus they fell into the anger of God.

18   Thus here in the place of weeping, hither he exiled them.

19   He placed eternal death upon them.

20   But my precious father, God, has decided

21   that I will rescue them.

22   For this reason I will die.

Mary:

30S:1 You can well redeem,
 2 my sovereign son,
 3 the people, without dying.
 4 I know well that it's in your hands,
 5 if you want to make use of it.

31S:1 And as you can do anything
 2 with such strong power,
 3 why, son, don't you do it,
 4 as you can free the world
 5 with a decree if you like.

32S:1 If your immense divinity
 2 does not wish by this route
 3 to repair the human offense
 4 this that I am about to tell you,
 5 offer, Lord, as just compensation.
33S:1 Offer, God, your sacred works,
 2 and very profound mysteries,
 3 that to free a thousand worlds
 4 would well suffice, as there are so many
 5 and happy mysteries.

23 As it was with a tree that Adam and Eve erred,
24 likewise it must be with a tree that I die.
25 There will come forth eternal rescue,
26 and there my precious father will thereby be appeased.
27 And this:
28 oh my precious mother,
29 it is essential that I die,
30 for none soever will be able to enter heaven.
31 I alone must make things peaceful for them.

Mary:

30N:1 My precious child,
   2   may you know
   3   that I know this well, I consider it to be true.
   4   Even if you did not actually die,
   5   you would be able to rescue the people of the world
   6   with your very great, total power.
   7   You who are my precious child,
   8   since you are God, you are sovereign,
   9   therefore everything is in your hands.
31N:1 And may you want it to be this way,
   2   may you do it this way,
   3   such that it be entirely with your words: you will say,
   4   "May it be done."
   5   It is true
   6   that immediately the people of the world would be rescued.
32N:1 And if you do not desire that it be this way,
   2   that you do it this way,
   3   so that the people of the world will be rescued,
   4   then with these things may you make compensation
   5   before your precious father.
33N:1 The way that they cut your precious flesh a little bit,
   2   such that a great deal of your precious blood issued forth there,
   3   it along with all your wondrous deeds
   4   and your fasting, your good deeds,
   5   with these things may you make things peaceful for the people of the world
   6   before your precious father,
   7   so that he will be appeased.

34S:1 And since you have the power,
   2   my son, of this sort,
   3   cure humanity,
   4   and of mentioning to me your death
   5   think not, your divinity.

Christ:

35S:1 Sacred Virgin woman,
   2   oh mother, it is all right.
   3   Truly it seems to me
   4   that that which is prophesied
   5   cannot fail to come to pass.

36S:1 By my father it is ordained,
   2   be patient, Lady,
   3   by my hand it is signed,
   4   the sentence is pronounced,
   5   and the sad time has arrived.

34N:1 And this:

2   may you speak no more of your death!

Christ:

35N:1 You who are a blessed and perfect maiden,

2   you who are a noblewoman and sovereign,

3   you who are my precious mother,

4   what you have said is very true and correct.

5   It is true that I have total power.

6   Everything can be done,

7   whatever I may wish,

8   since I am the divinity, I am the sovereign.

9   But first may you know

10   that in no way will I turn things around.

11   It is true that I will cause to come true

12   that which the prophets left foretold.

13   Regarding me they left it said

14   that I would rescue people here on earth.

15   It will certainly come true,

16   that I will endure everything

17   that they left declared, which lies written in the sacred book.

18   Nothing whatsoever will be lost,

19   even if it is a little spatter of ink.

20   It will all come true.

36N:1 And it was he, my precious father, God,

2   he decreed it,

3   that is how the words were set down in this way.

4   And they will not be the least bit broken.

5   I will cause everything to come true.

6   Oh my precious mother,

7   may you not be very sad,

8   may you not be very distressed on my behalf.

9   The rescue of the people has already been left in my hands,

10   the sentence has already been set down.

11   I will endure everything that is hurtful to people.

12   And this:

13   already it has come to arrive,

37S:1   I might remove the mourning
     2   from this tested world,
     3   and the waiting and the payments,
     4   without dying on Calvary,
     5   with my most absolute power.

38S:1   But certainly you know,
     2   my Lady and mother of mine,
     3   that if it is not done in this way,
     4   what I promised to my God
     5   I would not be fulfilling in this.

39S:1   And God cannot lie,
     2   because he is truth itself.
     3   Thus I have to die.
     4   It truly is necessary,
     5   in order to redeem the world.

Mary:
40S:1   As you want, son and Lord,
     2   to open the celestial door
     3   with your blood and sweat,
     4   until I myself am dead
     5   let it not be, my Redeemer?

14 the day of sadness,

15 the day of sadness and weeping.

37N:1 It is necessary that I destroy

2 the garment of sad fasting for the dead, the winding-sheet of the dead,

3 that the people on earth go about wearing.

4 It is the old error, original sin.

5 Their souls are dressed in it,

6 the demon, Lucifer, enslaved them with it.

7 And this:

8 oh my precious mother,

9 if I am not stretched by my hands upon the cross

10 there on Mount Calvary,

11 then how will people be rescued?

38N:1 I speak truthfully to you,

2 oh my precious mother,

3 and indeed you know this well.

4 If I do not cause to come true,

5 if I do not carry out,

6 the command of my precious father, God,

7 then there can be no rescue.

39N:1 Therefore may you know

2 that absolutely never will God lie,

3 he will never break his word,

4 because he is a truthful divinity.

5 This:

6 oh my precious mother,

7 it is essential that I die,

8 it is essential for the people of the world.

Mary:

40N:1 My precious child,

2 may it be that you desire

3 that which I say.

4 May it be that I die first,

5 so that I will not see

6 how your precious blood will be spilled

7 and how your precious flesh will be broken

8 as you open, as you raise up the road to the refuge of heaven.

9 May I not see all that will befall you!

Christ:

41S:1 Mother, this will not come to pass,

  2 this argument is a great harm,

  3 because the day that it occurs

  4 in you alone will remain

  5 whole all the Faith.

42S:1 Everyone will abandon me,

  2 no friend will remain,

  3 my disciples will flee,

  4 only you together with me

  5 will feel the suffering and the laborious task.

Mary:

43S:1 Oh sad, afflicted Mother,

  2 with maddening and strong pain,

  3 as there is a definitive sentence

  4 that you must suffer death

  5 how might I continue living?

Christ:

41N:1 Oh my precious mother,
   2 Oh, how very piercing, how profound is the affliction
   3 that will befall me
   4 in that time, at that moment!
   5 Nothing is equal to it.
   6 That which you say,
   7 oh my precious mother,
   8 you say it as if you wish
   9 that you might die first.
   10 It must not be.
   11 It will occur in your presence,
   12 how I will be made to suffer.
   13 On the day of sadness,
   14 oh my precious mother,
   15 just with you alone will be in its entirety, will be kept in its entirety,
   16 the sacred belief, the holy Catholic faith.

42N:1 And also know,
   2 oh my mother,
   3 that at that time it will be most extremely piteous,
   4 for no one will be my friend any longer,
   5 for no one will follow me about any longer,
   6 for all of my students will hide, they will all flee.
   7 And just you alone will be left beside me.
   8 There you will know, there you will see me being hurt.
   9 You will be very faint of heart,
   10 oh my mother.

Mary:

43N:1 My precious child,
   2 how very piercing, how profound is the affliction
   3 that will befall you!
   4 Nothing whatsoever matches it, is equal to it,
   5 the aching, the hurting
   6 that your heart will know.
   7 How very strong is the sovereign command that was set down,
   8 the sentence of divinity!
   9 How will I be even a little bit happy?
   10 For I will see you then,

44S:1   Oh my broken heart
    2   Oh my anguished soul,
    3   Oh my much beloved son
    4   do not die an ignominious death,
    5   this alone I ask you.

An angel enters here with five letters sealed with five wounds.

Angel:

45S:1   Mother of sovereign God,
    2   listen, as I will inform you,
    3   that the time is very near
    4   in which God must suffer
    5   for the human lineage.

46S:1   By God the father it is ordained,
    2   ever since Adam sinned,
    3   also many prophets have prophesied
    4   what I am informing you of,
    5   and spoken of it.

47S:1   From Limbo I bring a message
    2   and a present, which you shall see,
    3   from the imprisoned people,
    4   and some letters. Don't be alarmed.
    5   Take them, sacred virgin.

11   when they tie you to the stone column by your hands.

12   Not just four hundred times will they flog you.

44N:1   Oh, my heart,

2   it is as if it is about to issue forth,

3   it is so distressed, I am suffering so much,

4   with sadness, with aching.

5   My precious child,

6   may you not become very short of breath,

7   as you are made to suffer fatigue,

8   but truly with all your heart, according to your wishes,

9   in this way the torments will befall you.

Here will come forth an angel. He will come bearing five letters. They will come emblazoned with Christ's holes in five places.

Angel:

45N:1   You who are utterly exalted,

2   you who are the mother of God,

3   may you exert all your effort,

4   may you be strong!

5   I have been sent hither to you.

6   Here is what I have come to say to you.

7   The time has come, it is now the moment

8   when your precious child will ache, will hurt,

9   for the sake of the rescue of the people of the world.

46N:1   And this:

2   God the father already decreed it.

3   He decreed it as soon as Adam erred,

4   that on behalf of every human being he will die,

5   and he will also die on behalf of the prophets,

6   who are in Limbo.

47N:1   And may you know,

2   you who are a precious noblewoman,

3   that I have been sent hither from there in Limbo.

4   I bear hither the words of those who are in Limbo.

5   Here are letters that you will read,

6   with which they entreat you.

7   May you accept them,

8   you who are utterly good and a maiden!

Mary:

48S:1   I want to see what's in them
    2   as they seem to be about suffering,
    3   and really just in seeing them,
    4   they have broken my heart.
    5   I cannot see to read them.

49S:1   Oh! I cannot understand,
    2   as the lettering is so fine.
    3   Five, and sent to me,
    4   I don't know what it could be,
    5   with five seals sealed.
50S:1   How large are these two.
    2   Did you see them written,
    3   tell me, angel of my God?

Angel:

50S:4   No, but I can tell you
    5   that they are all for you.

51S:1   This one is from father Adam
    2   first man made
    3   and these that here go together
    4   are from others who are
    5   enclosed there because of his sin.

Our Lady reads the letter from Adam, and it says as follows.

Adam's letter:

52S:1   Sacred Virgin Mary,
    2   daughter and mother of the living God,

Mary:

48N:1 May it be that I might see what they say,

2 our fathers who first came to live on earth.

3 It is as if I see words of torment,

4 with which they come to speak,

5 the way they appear on the outside.

6 I feel quite faint of heart

7 as I look at these letters.

8 Ay! May I not see

9 how very afflicted my spirit, my soul will be!

49N:1 It is truly very precious,

2 how the five letters are adorned.

3 This is not just purposeless.

4 It indicates some frightful torment,

5 the way each one comes emblazoned.

50N:1 Do tell me,

2 you who are the angel of my divinity, my sovereign,

3 did you perhaps see it

4 when these letters were written?

Angel:

50N:5 No, oh noblewoman,

6 but they all come to belong to you.

7 You will read them all.

51N:1 This one is the paper that the first person, Adam, sends you.

2 And the other four,

3 they are the papers with which four others write to you.

4 All of them are confined there in Limbo.

So that the letters can be read, it is necessary that a little child be dressed up. He will read them to our lady. And for the five passions of the rescuer, it is also necessary that five little children be dressed up. When one of his precious passions is mentioned, then an angel will come forth.

Our lady looks at and reads the letter from Adam and it says

Angel: [reads Adam's letter]

52N:1 You who are the blessed maiden,

2 you, Saint Mary,

    3   I, your father Adam, write you
    4   with more sorrow than joy,
    5   captive in this prison.

53S:1   I alone am the one who sinned
    2   by having too much gluttony
    3   I know that I erred,
    4   and he who made me from nothing,
    5   his command I trespassed.

54S:1   Where we all pay for
    2   my sin and betrayal,
    3   in this prison, where we are all
    4   awaiting Redemption,
    5   which we are all looking forward to.

55S:1   As you are a font of compassion,
    2   forgive me, if I have erred.
    3   And see, your goodness,
    4   that great need
    5   has emboldened me.

3   you who are the precious daughter of eternally living God the father,

4   I greet you,

5   and I write to you,

6   I, your father Adam,

7   here within the house of torments,

8   the place where people are tied, Limbo.

53N:1   May you know

2   that it was wretched me,

3   wretched me alone,

4   it was with me that the old error began.

5   It was because of my gluttony that I ate

6   the fruit, the produce of the tree of life,

7   which our lord God, the sovereign, prohibited to me,

8   there in terrestrial Paradise,

9   so that I would not eat it.

10   And this:

11   I erred,

12   thus I trespassed, I held in low esteem

13   the command of my divinity, my sovereign.

54N:1   In this other place, in the place where people are tied

2   we lie confined, we lie enduring afflictions,

3   because of my wickedness, my wretched misdeed.

4   Ever since, we lie about fretting,

5   as we lie about sighing,

6   while we lie about awaiting

7   the rescuer, your precious child.

55N:1   This is the reason why it is from you

2   that the river of life, the compassion has emerged:

3   may you know

4   that it is because you are very good and proper.

5   May you pardon me

6   because of my confusion.

7   And now I am going to be so daring

8   as to entreat you,

9   may you yield to your precious child,

10   for it is essential that he rescue people!

56S:1   This † I offer as a present,

    2   take it, daughter, and consent.

    3   The rest, more clearly

    4   King David will tell you,

    5   the prophet, and your relative.

Mary:

57S:1   Oh, what a sorrowful pain.

Angel:

57S:2   Rather not, divine light,

    3   as although today your son dies,

    4   the Cross has such virtue

    5   that it will provide total glory.

58S:1   And have patience, virgin,

    2   for what I have told you here.

    3   And please give me permission

    4   to return whence I was sent

    5   now without further detainment.

The end.

The cross will come forth here.

56N:1 And so that your heart will be filled,
   2 I present to you this †.
   3 May you accept it with all your heart.
   4 And may you know
   5 that it is very great,
   6 what your precious child will endure there.
   7 And this:
   8 this is all that I write to you.
   9 But much more straightforward
  10 is that which King David writes to you,
  11 who comes from your lineage.

Mary:

57N:1 Oh, how very lamentable are these words.
   2 And this cross!

Angel:

57N:3 Oh noblewoman,
   4 may you know
   5 that this cross is exceptional.
   6 Nothing matches it,
   7 in the way it will surpass all things,
   8 in goodness, in excellence.
   9 For it is by means of this that one will go to, that one will enter heaven,
  10 so that people will be rescued there.

58N:1 And this:
   2 oh precious noblewoman,
   3 may you endure the affliction, the sadness!
   4 For this is not all that will be,
   5 for there are things that are even more exceptional,
   6 which you will see and you will know.
   7 Now I am going.
   8 May you give me permission, your send-off,
   9 so that I may return there whence I was sent hither,
  10 in the presence of the divinity, the sovereign, God!

Mary:

58N:11 May all-powerful God go leading you!

David's letter:

59S:1   Oh mother of the Redeemer,
   2   have compassion for us,
   3   remedy our suffering.
   4   Let die your son and God;
   5   may the Savior come, come.

60S:1   May our medicine come
   2   may the cure not be delayed,
   3   let us escape from such sadness,
   4   take us, kind Virgin,
   5   from this dark prison.

61S:1   And, well, to you we entrust
   2   that you will thus do it.
   3   We all beseech it of you,
   4   that you will want to help us,
   5   all of us who are here.

62S:1   Do not consider our errors,
   2   font of all goodness,
   3   forgive the sinners,
   4   and from so much darkness,
   5   let your servants depart.

63S:1   This crown of thorns
   2   I present to you, mother of God,
   3   as with it they will make him king,
   4   perverse wicked people,
   5   because he established a new Law.
The end.

Moses' letter:

64S:1   Enclosed, sealed-off garden,
   2   well of fresh water,
   3   humbled before you,
   4   my powerful Queen,
   5   you will see Moses prostrate.

David's letter   Angel:

59N:1   Oh, you who are the precious mother of the rescuer,

    2   all the way from here I greet you,

    3   for the sake of your pain.

    4   May you be so compassionate

    5   as to yield to your precious child,

    6   so that he may die.

60N:1   May he come quickly to rescue us,

    2   we who are there in the place of gloom, the place of darkness, Limbo.

61N:1   Therefore we entrust ourselves to you,

    2   so that you will help us,

    3   all of us who are here in Limbo.

62N:1   May you pardon us!

    2   May you not look now at our wickedness,

    3   by which we offended God.

    4   And this:

    5   oh mother of God,

    6   may you help us,

    7   so that we will get out!

The crown of sour thorns will come forth here.

63N:1   Oh mother of God,

    2   here is that which I present to you,

    3   this crown of sour thorns,

    4   with which the wicked ones, the Jews, will mock him.

    5   And afterwards our riches, our prosperity will return.

    6   That is all with which I strengthen your heart,

    7   I, King David.

Moses' letter   Angel:

64N:1   Oh, you who are forever a maiden of complete goodness,

    2   you who are God's sweetness and delight,

    3   before you I bow, I humble myself, I kneel,

    4   I, Moses.

65S:1 Your Regal feet and hands,
   2 I kiss and bless a thousand times,
   3 as you healed our wrongs,
   4 with your face and great cloak
   5 you cured the mortals.

66S:1 Take these three ˌcoral beads
   2 as your gift.
   3 They are three mortal nails,
   4 with which he will be nailed
   5 on Calvary for my wrongs.

67S:1 You well know, Virgin entire,
   2 that God came here out of love
   3 and to grab the flag,
   4 which Lucifer took
   5 in a wily manner.

68S:1 To you, Lady, we ask,
   2 make an end to our pains,
   3 so that in Limbo where we are
   4 "Lift up your heads, O ye gates!"
   5 we may hear in the voice of God.
The end.

65N:1 And I kiss your feet,
   2 you who are a precious noblewoman.
   3 May you know
   4 that it is truly you from whom has bloomed, has blossomed
   5 the remedy for our misdeeds.
   6 You, you very humble one,
   7 he who has emerged from you
   8 will be the healing of the people of the world!

The nails will come forth here.

66N:1 Oh noblewoman and sovereign,
   2 here is that with which I greet you,
   3 three metal thorns,
   4 with which your precious child's hands and feet will be shot with metal arrows,
   5 there on Mount Calvary,
   6 because of my wretched misdeeds,
   7 with which I offended God.
67N:1 And well do you know,
   2 you noblewoman,
   3 that your precious child heartily desired so for it to be:
   4 that he would rescue people,
   5 that he would destroy the deceptions of the demon, Lucifer,
   6 with which he mocked the people on the earth.
68N:1 And this:
   2 oh noblewoman,
   3 all the way from here I beseech you,
   4 may your heart concede
   5 that our torment may finish, may come to its end,
   6 here in Limbo.
   7 And may you send him,
   8 may your precious child go,
   9 so that he will die!
   10 For that is when he will come to Limbo.
   11 Then we will hear him, he will say,
   12 "Lift up your heads, O ye gates!"
   13 Then it will abate, the way we suffer fatigue.
   14 That is all with which I console you,

Jeremiah's letter:

69S:1   Sacred temple dedicated
    2   to the holy Trinity,
    3   protected from sin
    4   which placed in need
    5   all the human lineage.

70S:1   Queen chosen from the beginning,
    2   you who so well guides us,
    3   as in you there is no vice,
    4   from your servant Jeremiah
    5   receive this service.

71S:1   This column I gladly
    2   present to you, and the cord
    3   with which he will be tied,
    4   your kind Emmanuel,
    5   and on the column flogged.

72S:1   Forgive, my Lady,
    2   if into this sorrow I bind
    3   part of your happiness,
    4   because our great travail
    5   gives me boldness, Lady.

15 I, Moses.

16 May you exert all your effort,

17 may you be strong in your painful sadness,

18 oh mother of God!

Jeremiah's letter   Angel:

69N:1 Oh, you who are the temple of the Most Holy Trinity,

2 you who are the sovereign noblewoman,

3 no misdeeds whatsoever will appear, will be seen, with you!

4 You are very great, you are a saint!

5 Right when you were placed inside your mother,

6 you were a saint.

7 And now,

8 may you know,

9 that there in Limbo we are weeping, we are sad.

10 Because of our misdeeds we are confined.

70N:1 And you, you were God's chosen one,

2 right when the world began,

3 such that you would be a precious noblewoman,

4 such that from you would emerge the rescuer.

5 And from you has emerged our help.

6 As to you,

7 no little misdeed whatsoever ever reached you.

8 And this:

9 here is that with which I greet you,

10 I, your father Jeremiah.

Then the stone column will come forth.

71N:1 May you accept

2 the very lamentable, saddening stone column,

3 so that your precious child may be tied thereto by his hands,

4 so that he may be flogged there,

5 so that he may feel very faint there.

6 And not just a few times four hundred times will they flog him,

7 the very humane one, the humble one.

72N:1 And this:

2 oh noblewoman,

3 all the way from here I bow before you.

4 May you pardon me!

5 I am a wretched wrongdoer.

73S:1 For this reason, he took flesh
   2   from you, excellent virgin,
   3   as for this reason, he came down here
   4   into the world, and to the people
   5   he promised the remedy.

74S:1 As he was born in order to suffer
   2   death for our errors,
   3   may he come to take us from here,
   4   the Lord of lords.
   5   Please do not impede it.

Abraham's letter:

75S:1 Mother of the sinners,
   2   hear us, sacred Virgin,
   3   the cruel cry and the sorrows
   4   of this imprisoned people;
   5   give us now your favor.

76S:1 And with your saying yes,
   2   the Redemption will take place.
   3   Thus allow it,
   4   may he take us to where he is going,
   5   may he come and take us from here.

77S:1 We all beseech this of you,
   2   that you will want to grant it,
   3   to you, Lady, we beg,
   4   that you will not wish to deny it,
   5   consider that we are entrusting ourselves to you.

78S:1 Mother of Emmanuel
   2   do not have such fear,
   3   and consider that from Heaven
   4   he descended, when to Gabriel
   5   you gave the "yes" of agreement.

79S:1 Man and God in one principle

6   For truly it will be done to your precious child,
7   oh mother of God.
73N:1   For it was not just in vain
2   that he emerged from your womb of complete goodness and took our vassal's flesh.
3   It was for the sake of the rescue of the people in the world,
4   and also of us,
5   we who are confined here,
6   we whom the great demon, Lucifer, enslaved.
74N:1   This is what your precious child wanted
2   as the third thing that he will endure on earth.
3   May you not delay our rescue,
4   by which he will come to rescue us,
5   we who lie suffering fatigue here in Limbo!

Abraham's letter   Angel:

75N:1   You who are the mother of God,
2   you who are the wrongdoers' advocate,
3   you who are utterly good and a maiden,
4   may you hear from us
5   our words of weeping, our words of sadness,
6   with which we humble ourselves before you,
7   we who lie tied up here in Limbo!
8   May you help us!
76–77N:1   We all firmly demand of you
2   that your precious child go
3   where he wants to go.

78N:1   May you remember
2   when Saint Gabriel the angel went to greet you.
3   When you answered him you said,
4   "May it so be done to me,
5   that which my divinity, my sovereign desires."
79N:1   Right then our precious rescuer assumed flesh in your womb.

    2   joined, and the two extremes
    3   by a "yes," as man and God
    4   were joined so that by this
    5   there would be a good effect on us.

80S:1   Oh, from Heaven to the world
    2   he descended by a "yes," our Lady,
    3   give us this "yes" now
    4   that he might descend to the depths,
    5   where your lineage weeps.

81S:1   If that "yes" rose to heaven,
    2   may this one bring down to us the light,
    3   and if that agreement came down,
    4   may this put him up on the Cross,
    5   and break the human vigil.

82S:1   This lance of glory
    2   I give to you, chosen Virgin,
    3   take it, and hold it in your memory,
    4   as it will give the final
    5   wound of victory.

Christ:

83S:1   As the time has now arrived,
    2   mother of mine, and you shall soon see
    3   everything that has happened here,
    4   I beseech you not to impede me
    5   from that which I have so much desired.

2 And it was in order that later, after he was born, he would endure many torments.
3 Furthermore, you know that it is so,
4 and we ourselves believe that it is so,
5 that he is God and man.
6 As he is your precious child,
7 thus he will suffer fatigue,
8 thus he will make things peaceful for us
9 before his precious father, God.

80N:1 And this:
2 oh mother of God,
3 here we are weeping,
4 and on earth it is greatly longed for.
5 In order that your precious child would rescue people
6 is truly why he went there to earth.

81N:1 May it be that he labors,
2 may it be that he serves,
3 may it be that he ascends upon the cross
4 so that there will be fulfilled, will be completed
5 the wishes of your precious child.

The lance will come forth here.

82N:1 Therefore, here is the joyful lance of glory!
2 With it I strengthen your heart for you,
3 so that you will be strong of heart.
4 That for which the lance, the metal staff will be needed
5 is that with it your precious child will be pierced in his side.
6 May you take it,
7 may you accept it,
8 may you take it to heart.
9 That which will be done to your child
10 is how he will overcome the great demon, Lucifer.

Christ:

83N:1 Oh! My precious mother,
2 may you be consoled
3 by all the words that you have heard
4 from the first fathers of people, the prophets,
5 of how essential it is that I rescue people

84S:1   Allow me now to rescue
    2   these my beloved children.
    3   Consider how lost they are.
    4   And in the spilling of my blood
    5   they will be redeemed.

85S:1   And as my Resurrection
    2   will be on the third day,
    3   may you suffer, your discretion,
    4   the travail and agony,
    5   for it is pure consolation.

86S:1   Thus, Mother and blessing of mine,
    2   I beseech you that you give me permission
    3   to go to Jerusalem.
Mary:
86S:4   What will I do in your absence,
    5   ay, my Jesus the Nazarene?

87S:1   And as you are going away, my God,
    2   this I wish to ask of you,
    3   please do not wish to deny me it,
    4   that you let me go with you.
Christ:
87S:5   That I cannot allow you.

6   from the hands of the demon.

7   And may you not hinder me,

8   because the time has now arrived

9   when I will be afflicted.

10   I have been longing for it for a long time.

84N:1   May this be all that you say,

2   may you yield to me,

3   may it be that I go!

4   It is for this reason:

5   my precious ones and a great many others

6   who were confounded, were confused by error,

7   I will rescue with my precious blood.

85N:1   And may you know,

2   oh my precious mother,

3   that although you will weep,

4   although you will be distressed for my sake,

5   because of my torments,

6   afterwards your joyfulness will return.

7   This is how it is:

8   when I myself have revived,

9   then you will be very happy, you will be consoled.

86N:1   And may you yield to me

2   so that I may go to Jerusalem.

Mary:

86N:3   What will I do,

4   and what will I say

5   in your presence,

6   you who are Jesus the Nazarene?

87N:1   But I do say,

2   and I do beseech you,

3   may it not be that you will leave me!

4   I will accompany you!

Christ:

87N:5   That which you say,

6   oh my precious mother,

7   I myself will not concede it to you.

88S:1 Because that would not be pleasing
    2   to God, my celestial father.
    3   Rather, you should stay here.
    4   Don't worry, holy mother,
    5   tomorrow you will learn of me.

Mary:

89S:1 As you don't want to take me
    2   with you, sovereign glory,
    3   please give me permission
    4   that I go to see you tommorrow.
    5   Please do not refuse it.

90S:1 And as you have such desire
    2   to leave here, my blessing,
    3   where will I find you tommorrow,
    4   if I go to Jerusalem,
    5   tell me, sovereign glory?
91S:1 Shall I go to the house of Zachaeus,
    2   or will I run across you in the streets?

Christ:

91S:3 John, son of Zebedee,
    4   will take you to where you can find me.

Mary:

91S:5 Ay! I will die if I don't see you.

Christ:

92S:1 You can go, Mother, if you like,
    2   Be consoled, for you give me pain.
    3   Certainly you will find me.
    4   Have Magdalene go with you.

88N:1 If this is how God wishes it to be,
  2 then may it be done so.
  3 But as for what I say,
  4 may it be that you just remain here
  5 so that you will not suffer such intense sadness.
  6 May it be that tomorrow you learn
  7 what will have befallen me
  8 there in Jerusalem.

Mary:

89N:1 Oh, you who surpass all things,
  2 you who are my joy and precious child,
  3 how can it be that you do not want me to accompany you?
  4 I ask for your authorization,
  5 so that I might see you there tomorrow.
  6 May it not be that you will return my words to me!
  7 May it be that you want me to go there!

90N:1 And this:
  2 where will I see you tomorrow?
  3 Will it perhaps be right there in the temple in Jerusalem?
  4 May you reassure me!

91N:1 But shall I perhaps go directly to the house of Zachaeus,
  2 or will it perhaps just be in the street that I will go to meet you?
    She will faint here.

Mary:

91N:3 Ay! Then I will faint, I will lose my breath,
  4 if I will not see you!

Christ:

92N:1 Oh my precious mother,
  2 may that be all,
  3 may you be consoled,
  4 for you will go.
  5 I feel very compassionate toward you.
  6 Because of you I am going to be very afflicted, I am going to be very sad.
  7 You both will see me there in Jerusalem.
  8 Magdalene, you will accompany my precious mother, you will go along and console her.

Mary:

92S:5   Ay! Will you become sad without me?

93S:1   Let God want, my heart,
   2   that when we see one another there,
   3   that it not be for more suffering.

Christ:

93S:4   Mother, it's time that we leave.
   5   Give us your benediction.

Mary:

94S:1   That doesn't make any sense.
   2   Give me yours, Redeemer.

Christ:

94S:3   Give me yours, as you are the mother.

Mary:

94S:4   Give me yours, as you are God
   5   as well as my son and father.
95S:1   Give me yours, my joy,
   2   light of divine loves.
Christ:
95S:3   Light that guides heaven,
   4   may it give you strength for your sorrows.

Mary:

95S:5   And may it be present in your guidance.

Mary:

92N:9	Ay! Oh woe is me,
10	if I am not to see you there!
93N:1	May God so wish it,
2	my precious child,
3	that when you look toward me,
4	at how I will faint with weeping,
5	may your agony not be greatly increased,
6	my precious child.

Christ:

93N:7	Oh, now that is enough,
8	now it is time,
9	may it be that I go.
10	Oh my precious mother,
11	may you give me your benediction.

Mary:

94N:1	May you not wish such a thing,
2	that I give you my benediction
3	so that you will go!
4	May it be that you are going to bless me,
5	my precious rescuer.

Christ:

| 94N:6 | May it be you, |
| 7 | because you are my mother in the fleshly sense. |

Mary:

94N:8	May it just be you,
9	because you are God the father's precious child, in the sense that you are a divinity.
10	And you are my child, in the sense that you are a man.

Christ:

95N:1	Oh, you who are the utterly good shimmering radiance
2	with which God guides those who lie in heaven!
3	May he strengthen your heart in your sad weeping,
4	you who are my precious mother!

Mary:

| 95N:5 | May he also go guiding you, |
| 6 | my precious child! |

Christ:

96S:1 As you are my beloved mother,

2 according to time and reason,

3 before my departure

4 I ask you for your benediction.

Mary:

96S:5 Benediction, light of my life?

97S:1 Lord, I will not contradict you.

2 May the benediction of God the father

3 always go with you,

4 and although I am daughter and mother,

5 I also bless you, son.

98S:1 And as I see that you are leaving,

2 my God and sacred son,

3 and my much beloved husband,

4 before you take leave of me,

5 give me a final embrace.

Christ:

99S:1 Oh, mother, with your suffering

2 you break me into a thousand pieces,

3 to see you filled with anguish.

4 Do not throw yourself into my arms.

5 Hold onto her, Magdalene.

Praise be to God.

[*Spanish text ends here.*]

Christ:

96N:1   Oh my precious mother,

     2   at last, that is enough,

     3   may it be that I go!

     4   May you also give me your blessing.

Mary:

97N:1   He who forever shines upon people, our lord God,

     2   may he bless you,

     3   my lord, my sovereign!

     4   May he go standing beside you, near you,

     5   your precious father, God,

     6   may he go leading you, in the sense that you are a man.

     7   And because I am the precious daughter of God the father,

     8   and you are my precious child, in the sense that you are a man,

     9   I give you my benediction.

98N:1   So now you are going,

     2   you who are my lord God,

     3   you blessed boy,

     4   you who are my repose.

     5   This do I desire:

     6   that before you set down one of your feet,

     7   first in a proper and religious way may you embrace me.

Christ:

99N:1   Oh, for my sake you are about to suffer such intense sadness,

     2   oh my precious mother,

     3   oh noblewoman!

     4   May it not be that you will fall,

     5   oh my mother!

     6   Oh Magdalene,

     7   take hold of her, embrace her!

     8   May it not be that she will fall!

Mary:

100N:1   My precious child,

     2   my son,

     3   may you wish it,

     4   may it be that I die with you,

     5   may it be that I accompany you in death!

     6   Fortunate was Jacob!

7   He did not know in advance of the torment of his son Joseph,
8   before they brought to him, showed to him
9   his mantle, all full of blood.
10   And fortunate was David!
11   He did not see his son Absalom
12   attached to an oak tree, hanging by his hair.
13   With three metal staffs they had pierced him.
14   They only heard how it happened.
15   And if Hagar, the slave of the noblewoman Sarah,
16   abandoned her child when he was about to die,
17   she said,
18   "I will not look at my child, he is about to die,"
19   then how my spirit will ache, will hurt!
20   Ah, my child, my son,
21   my life, my existence,
22   my jewel, my quetzal plume!

Christ:

101N:1   Oh my precious mother,
2   I make known to you now
3   that it is necessary that you not die.
4   You will remain here for now
5   so that you may console my sheep who are here.

Mary:

102N:1   My son, my child,
2   it is truly his desire, it is by his order,
3   your father, who lives forever.
4   May we praise him forever!
5   And as for you,
6   before you take leave of your mother,
7   may you bless me.

Christ:

103N:1   May you be blessed always and forever,
2   my precious mother!
3   May your head be forever blessed,
4   which always remembered what is proper and good!
5   May your maidenly womb be praised,
6   which for nine months carried me about!
7   May your breasts be praised,
8   which nursed me when I was still small, when I was a little child!

9   May your mouth be praised,
10 which is filled with true things!
11 May your hands also be praised,
12 which labored at what is good and proper!
13 May your soul be praised,
14 which is filled with grace and truth!

And they encouraged each other, then they took leave of each other, they said goodbye to each other, they embraced each other.

Commentary on the Plays

THROUGHOUT THE FOLLOWING ANNOTATIONS I make frequent reference to other Nahuatl texts, including those that are excerpted in the Appendix. I will briefly describe these materials before proceeding with the stanza-by-stanza commentary.

The Nahua playwright was surely familiar with some of the Nahuatl literature circulating at the time; even texts not directly known to the playwright may serve as comparative material, since they provide information on how certain subjects were discussed and ideas expressed in Nahuatl. Published Franciscan works such as fray Pedro de Gante's 1553 *Doctrina*, fray Juan de Gaona's *Coloquios de la paz y tranquilidad christiana* of 1582, and the 1583 *Psalmodia christiana* would have been readily available. The playwright could consult fray Alonso de Molina's 1571 dictionary regarding the meanings of Spanish words.

Published works from other religious orders may have been available as well. These include Dominican texts, such as the anonymous *Doctrina* of 1548 and fray Domingo de la Anunciación's 1565 catechism. The Augustinian Juan de la Anunciación had published a catechism in 1575 and a lengthy volume of sermons in 1577.

The playwright may also have had access to unpublished Nahuatl materials at Tlatelolco, such as the *Colloquios*, the *Exercicio*, and the sermons of the Franciscan preachers Alonso de Escalona and Bernardino de Sahagún. Excerpts from Escalona's sermons are included in the Appendix. The *Exercicio* is a collection of meditations and prayers for each day of the week. Sahagún claimed to have discovered this text among the Indians and rewritten it (or, more likely, had his Nahua students rewrite it) in order to correct its many errors (Sahagún 1574). Such works as the *Exercicio* and the *Psalmodia christiana* are particularly valuable because they were intended for native people to use on their own, in contrast to the sermons, biblical excerpts, and confession manuals that the friars employed for their own use. Included in the Appendix are the Easter songs from the *Psalmodia*.

I also consider in this analysis some less securely provenanced Nahuatl manuscripts dating to the sixteenth century. One of these is a fragmentary Passion text now in the Latin American Library at Tulane University (*Pasión* n.d.). It contains a recounting of the *despedimiento* (22r–27v) that is the closest parallel text I have located for the Holy Wednesday play. It is written in a native hand similar to that of the play. Though the work may well be Franciscan in origin, Moreno's tentative attribution to fray Juan de Gaona lacks a concrete basis (Moreno 1966:76). I have included a translation of this *despedimiento* text in the Appendix.

The most elaborate Nahuatl narrative of the harrowing of hell that I have found fills nine pages of an Easter sermon in an anonymous late-sixteenth-century text in Mexico's Biblioteca Nacional (*Sermones en mexicano* n.d.:213–21). Excerpts from the harrowing of hell narrative are reproduced in the Appendix. This Easter sermon is preceded by a lengthy sermon on the Passion, which features a brief farewell scene between Christ and Mary. This Passion sermon is very closely related to a Passion text in another Biblioteca Nacional manuscript (*Miscelánea sagrada* n.d.:201r–21r), an anonymous volume that Moreno (1966:76) very tentatively ascribes to fray Juan de Gaona. I have made use of both versions.

The John Carter Brown Library at Brown University houses a sixteenth-century Nahuatl manuscript containing a variety of religious texts, most of which relate to the cult of Mary (*Doctrina* n.d.). One of these is a hand-written copy of an otherwise unknown Nahuatl imprint of 1572, listing the papal indulgences granted to members of the confraternity of the Rosary. I have hypothesized that the manuscript belonged not to priests but to Nahua member(s) of a Rosary confraternity, who used it in their devotional practices (see also Burkhart 1995b).

A Nahuatl account of the Passion based very closely on the Gospels is found in the Biblioteca Nacional manuscript *Epístolas en mexicano* (1561), otherwise comprised of Nahuatl translations of Gospel readings. The manuscript, which bears the date 1561, is cognate with a set of Gospel translations known to have been produced under Sahagún's direction (Moreno 1966:67).

I have also made use of a few published works that slightly postdate the play: the Dominican Martín de León's 1611 *Camino del cielo* and 1614 *Sermonario*, as well as the Augustinian Juan de Mijangos's *Espejo divino* of

1607. León's volume of sermons includes a text on the Christ-Mary *despedimiento*, to which León assigns the Latin title *De ultimo vale Iesv, ad matrem virginem* 'Of Jesus's last farewell to the virgin mother' (1614:313v–317r).

In addition, the existence of significant comparative material in three early seventeenth-century Jesuit manuscripts now in Mexico's Biblioteca Nacional has prompted me to include them among the pool of sources. One of these manuscripts contains the famous collection of Nahuatl songs known as the *Cantares mexicanos* as well as a copy of at least one text written by fray Bernardino de Sahagún (*Cantares de los mejicanos* n.d.). The last text in the volume is a Nahuatl "History of the Passion of Our Lord Jesus Christ" (227r–293v), a text that includes a *despedimiento* scene so similar to León's that both are probably based on the same Spanish or Latin source.

The other two Jesuit texts share at least one redactor with the *Cantares* manuscript. The text known as *Sermones y ejemplos* (n.d.) contains a 60-page Passion narrative (353v–358v), the first page of which bears the date 1617 and the name Lorenço. It also contains an account of the harrowing of hell (306v–309v). The third Jesuit manuscript (*Santoral en mexicano* n.d.) contains a lengthy cycle of prayers to the Virgin Mary (1r–41v). One of these, "Oration to the Virgin when her precious son took leave of her," commemorates the Bethany farewell scene but does not provide any narrative details of that event.

In the following comments, Nahuatl words taken directly from the play or other texts appear as they are spelled in the original; for other Nahuatl terms I use a standardized orthography.

1   From the beginning, the Nahua author provides more extensive and more explicit information about the ongoing events than does Izquierdo. As well as providing the native audience with needed information, the inclusion of additional material was one strategy for making the text more elaborate, allowing the playwright to exercise his oratorical skill.

The terms by which Christ and Mary address one another are many and varied, especially in the Nahuatl text. Grammatically these vocative constructions take two forms in Nahuatl: second-person equative noun constructions of the "you (who) are" type, as in lines 1N:1–3 and 6, and exclamatory third-person constructions of the "oh my mother" type, as in line 1N:5. In the latter, men's and women's speech differed in Classical Nahuatl in that men added the stressed syllable *-e* to the end of the addressee's name or epithet while women stressed the final syllable without adding any suffix (see Andrews 1975:203–4). I suggest this gender difference in the translation by using the particle "oh" only for male speakers; hence Christ's "oh my mother" as opposed to Mary's "my precious child" (e.g. 4N:1). Male actors who played the role of Mary would have had to imitate women's speech in this respect.

The indigenous title *cihuapilli* 'noblewoman' was very frequently applied to Mary, serving in place of "Our Lady." This title located Mary within the native social hierarchy. Izquierdo's "great dignity" is rendered as "supreme noblewoman," the Nahua playwright associating the idea of dignity with Mary's social status and choosing a title familiar to his audience. Similarly, he changes "divine Father" to "God the father" (more literally, "God father-of-someone"), a form widely used in Nahuatl. Mary's humility is one of her attributes celebrated in the prayer cycle known as her crown (*corona*); fray Pedro de Gante's 1553 Nahuatl version refers to Mary as "you who are a completely and surpassingly humble one" (Gante 1981:128v).

The Nahuatl Christ explains that it is time for people to be rescued. The concept of salvation, in its spiritual sense not an indigenous concept, was translated into Nahuatl with forms of the verb *maquixtia* 'to remove (someone) from the hands (of others).' It is a more concrete notion than the Christian theological concept with its accrued connotations of spiritual blessedness and eternal reward. Christ appears in Nahuatl texts as a rescuer of captives, freeing people from the hands of demons.

The phrase *auh inin* 'and this' is a formula marking a break in discourse. Karttunen and Lockhart (1987:33; also Lockhart 1991:76) observe the use of this phrase to indicate that "a speaker is about to wind up, giving his summation or decision." In the play, the phrase is often used not at the end of a character's speech but to introduce a closing statement to a shorter segment of discourse, this shorter segment usually corresponding to one of the Spanish stanzas.

2   The Nahuatl Christ elaborates on his identity for the benefit of native people who might have trouble understanding his dual nature as man and god as well as his membership in the Trinity. He acknowledges that his mother understands these matters: this is the first of several occasions when the Nahuatl Christ, in contrast to his Spanish counterpart, defers to his mother's knowledge or authority. The Spanish Christ, on the other hand, here points out rather condescendingly that he is showing obedience by coming to his mother even though he is God; the Nahuatl Christ does not link his self-identification as God with his request for her permission.

The Nahuatl Christ calls himself a *teotl*, the Nahuatl word for sacred powers, which was used as a translation for "god" even though native divinities were more diffuse and less personalized than the Old World concept denotes. He uses this term in a triplet, also calling himself God (Dios), the proper name of the Christian *teotl*, and sovereign, literally "speaker," the Nahuatl word for a dynastic ruler. This translated the Spanish text's *soberano* but was also a title very frequently applied to Christ, often in the form of the paired terms "divinity, sovereign." The use of Spanish loanwords for "Holy Spirit" was standard.

The reference to Mary's pure womb is compatible with other Nahuatl literature. Christ's identity as a product of Mary's womb was reiterated constantly in the ubiquitous Hail Mary prayer, and her purity or cleanliness was a theme of many other texts (see Burkhart 1989:126–28; 1992c).

The compound word "precious child" (*tlazohpilli*), which translates Izquierdo's "son," can also refer to a child of favored status, such as a chosen heir or, in preconquest polygynous times, the child of a high-ranking nobleman and his principal wife. *Pilli* also means "noble." *Tlazohpipiltin* was used even in colonial times to refer to noblemen of high standing (e.g., Lockhart et al. 1986:64). Christ is describing himself not only as Mary's biological offspring but as a favored scion of her noble lineage.

For the second time, the Nahuatl Christ alludes to his impending fate and its purpose, topics not yet broached by Izquierdo. This contributes to a stronger sense of foreshadowing in the Nahuatl text, as well as its greater emphasis on Christ's physical agony.

The transitive verb stem of the passive construction in 2N:10 is *ihiyohuia*. This is the usual Nahuatl verb used for describing Christ's ordeal. The Spanish noun *pasión* is sometimes intruded into Nahuatl texts, but when a Nahuatl parallel or substitute is used it is *tlaihiyohuiliztli*, a noun derived from this verb. Fray Alonso de Molina's dictionary defines *tlaihiyohuiliztli* as "torment, fatigue, or pain that one suffers" (1970:121v). Today, among Nahuas in the Sierra Norte of the state of Puebla, the same term is used to refer to the ritual devotions of Lent and Holy Week (Montoya Briones 1964:138).

The verb *ihiyohuia* means "to apply one's breath to (direct object)." Karttunen defines the verb as "to endure hardship, to labor hard in order to subsist, to acquire something by one's own hard effort" (1983:98). With the generic direct object prefix *tla-* 'things, something,' the verb has the sense of exhausting oneself by working hard, becoming worn out to the point of fatigue and suffering. According to Nahua concepts of the human body, as analyzed by López Austin (1980:I, 291–92), hard labor increases one's level of internal "heat." Working to the point of exhaustion places one in a dangerous state of disequilibrium. This in turn invites more serious problems, as one is especially susceptible to sickness. Rest and food are required to return the body to a healthy state. Throughout this work I translate the verb *ihiyohuia* as "endure," its form *tlaihiyohuia* as "suffer fatigue" and the noun form *tlaihiyohuiliztli* as "torment."

I am using "misdeed," "error," "err," and "wrongdoer" to translate the Nahuatl words employed for the Christian concepts of sin and sinners. The Nahuatl term *tlahtlacolli*, though used for moral misdeeds, also encompassed a broad range of accidents, crimes, and other breakdowns of established order. It failed to convey the sense of personal moral responsibility, with its accompanying burden of guilt, that sin bears in Christian theology (see Burkhart 1989).

The Nahuatl passage is stylistically sophisticated. The initial 'And' (*Auh*) marks a break with the preceding discourse, corresponding neatly with Izquierdo's stanza boundary. Line 2N:3 consists of a triple construction, which itself forms a triple construction with the other two members of the Trinity, who are named in the following line. Christ's three different identities are listed with no intervening particles, while he, his father, and the Holy Spirit are separated from one another by two uses of *ihuan* 'and' or 'along with.' Christ is three-in-one, and he is also one of three. The point most crucial to the friars—that father, son, and spirit comprise a single being, a sole god—is, however, omitted; a friar would not have missed this opportunity to reiterate that point. The playwright is toying, subtly, with the notion of the Trinity.

Lines 2N:8–9 also comprise a parallel construction, in which the words *inic noquichtli* 'in the sense that I am a man' are repeated exactly but separated by a period and by the particle *auh* 'and.' This construction creates a bridge between two segments of discourse, the first of which (lines 2N:5–8) invokes Christ's past as Mary's child while the second (2N:9–11) alludes to his future fate. The repetition of "because" in lines 2N:11–12 works in a similar manner. It links Christ's upcoming task to the present moment, as he asks his mother's leave to depart.

The vocative "oh my precious mother" occurs three times within this opening speech of Christ's. Its reiteration breaks the speech into three segments of increasing length, and also marks the ending of Christ's turn in the conversation. It functions both semantically, as a periodic reminder of Christ's filial affection and respect, and discursively, as a formulaic "time-out" from the matters under discussion.

3   The vocative "You who are my consolation and precious child" is a single word in the Nahuatl, with twelve syllables. Nahuatl is an agglutinative language, and verbal artists exploited this fact by coining new and elaborate compound words.

Mary Magdalene, a silent presence onstage throughout both plays, is here acknowledged for the first time. For the Nahua audience, who might not recognize this character as easily as Spaniards would, her identification is made more explicit. The woodcut that accompanies Mary Magdalene's festival in the *Psalmodia christiana* shows her as a young woman with long, unbound hair (Figure 8).

The Nahuatl Christ's response to his mother is more elaborate and deferential than the Spanish Christ's.

4   The Spanish stanza's first two lines provided a model for the more elaborate quadruplet of third-person vocatives that the Nahuatl Mary directs to her son. His closing "oh my precious mother" she echoes with a "my precious child." Line 4N:2 is comprised of the single word *notzopelica-qualtilizneyollalilitzin*, at fourteen syllables the longest word in the play. It is echoed in line 4N:4 by an eleven-syllable construction. Having so effectively demanded her son's attention, the Nahuatl Mary proceeds to ask a couplet of questions, elaborating on the Spanish Mary's single query. In 4N:9 she concocts another eleven-syllable word to describe her son's face.

5   The Nahuatl word used for Christ's disciples was the usual term for students, including those who studied at the friars' schools. The apostles James and John were sons of a man named Zebedee (Matthew 4:21). Zebedee surely had a low level of name recognition among Nahuas in general, but his identity would have been familiar to the Nahua scholars from Gospel readings. A Nahuatl account of the Passion based on the Gospels, included in a collection of Gospel readings probably prepared under Sahagún's direction, refers twice to "the children of Zebedee" in its texts on the Passion (*Epístolas en mexicano* 1561:254, 276).

Mary's interpretation of the students' behavior, given in the last line of the Spanish stanza, is marked off in the Nahuatl by the "and this" formula. The Spanish Mary speculates, while the Nahuatl Mary declares the truth: she knows that something dreadful is going to happen. And she knows what it is.

6   The festival alluded to in the Spanish text is Passover, which Christ intends to spend in Jerusalem rather than in Bethany with Mary and the other

8. The penitent Mary Magdalene, secluded in a forest, prays before a crucifix. Woodcut from the *Psalmodia christiana*, 1583, f. 117v. Courtesy of the John Carter Brown Library at Brown University.

women. The Nahua author names this festival with the Spanish loanword *pascua*, or Pasch, modified by the Nahuatl *huey* 'great.' *Pascua*, in Spanish usage, can refer to Passover, Easter, Christmas, Epiphany, or Pentecost. Particular festivals are specified by descriptive modifiers: e.g., *pascua* of the Hebrews, *pascua* of the Nativity. Easter is *pascua de Resurrección*, *pascua de flores*, or *pascua florida*.

Nahuas adopted these names, partially translating some of them into Nahuatl, as in *xochipascua* 'flowery *pascua*' for Easter (Sahagún 1583:11r, 59v; León 1982). *Pascua* by itself is used for Easter several times in the *Codex Sierra* (León 1982). Nahuas also called Easter "great *pascua*" (Sahagún 1583:59v; Bierhorst 1985:272, 274), as here in the play. The Franciscan Alonso de Escalona criticized this usage in his Christmas sermon. He tells his Nahua listeners that they should not call Easter "great *pascua*" and Christmas "little *pascua*" because Christmas is every bit as great as Easter (Escalona n.d.:126). Pairs of festivals with the same name, distinguished as "great" and "little," were also a feature of the pre-Christian ritual cycle.

A Spanish audience would understand that Christ was referring to the Jewish festival of Passover. A Nahua audience very likely would have been unaware that such a festival existed or, if they knew of it, would not have understood the difference between it and their own *pascua*. Thus, they would very likely interpret the references to a *pascua* as referring to the approaching Easter, not distinguishing between the rite that Christ says he must celebrate in Jerusalem and the new rite that he is about to initiate.

A text on the Last Supper in the 1588 manuscript of Sahagún's sermons makes a rather feeble attempt to explain these matters. Discussing the escape of the children of Israel from Egypt, it mentions the eating of the paschal lamb, called *pascua*, and the marking of the doorways with the lamb's blood. God ordered Moses to commemorate this wondrous rescue every year. But then the text equates the celebration as conducted in Christ's time with that of the present: "And the people of Jerusalem rejoiced very much each year when they celebrated the festival of *pascua*, as we today celebrate the *pascua*" (Sahagún 1588:104r).

Line 6S:5 becomes 6N:6–7, the Spanish Mary's declarative statement of her own love being reworked, perhaps because the Nahua playwright misunderstood the Spanish *por mi amor*, into an admonitive construction in which she refers to Christ's love for her and reiterates again their relationship as mother and son.

Line 6N:5 parallels 6N:3. The addition of an intensifier adds a progressive emphasis and keeps the two phrases from being exactly the same. The entire passage is symmetrical. The two "I beseech" statements frame Mary's declaration of her desire in 6N:4. The admonitives in 6N:2 and 6N:6 form another layer outside of this petition, while at the beginning and end Mary invokes her maternal relationship to Christ.

7 The Nahuatl Mary here utters the phrase "my precious child" for the fourth and last time within this speech. Like Christ's "oh my precious

mother," it functions as a formulaic refrain to be reiterated at irregular intervals within her discourse. In 7N:2 she utters a direct command with no mollifying "may it be" or "would you." This is the only such command she makes in the play. Digression from her usual cautious politeness lends her words an additional forcefulness.

What I translate as "spirit" is the Nahuatl word *-yolia*. The *-yolia* is a life force located in the heart. It survives death and goes on to an after-life (López Austin 1980:I, 252–57). Of the several Nahua soul concepts, this was the only one similar enough to the Christian concept to be widely accepted as a parallel for the Spanish *ánima*. It was not entirely trusted, however, and the loanword *anima* was frequently used, both alone and paired with *-yolia*. In the play, the two terms appear both individually and as a pair.

The Spanish Mary speaks of what she truly believes; the Nahuatl Mary speaks the truth. She asserts her truthfulness twice, making 7N:6–7 into the third couplet in a row. Like the Spanish Mary, she foresees Christ's death, but her prescience extends also to his arrest, allowing her to make another couplet of his impending troubles.

Jerusalem has now been named four times in the Nahuatl text but has yet to appear in the Spanish. For the Mexica, the quintessential "great city" was Mexico. An implicit identification between the location of the play's action and the setting of its performance may be assumed, especially in the context of Holy Week, when processions with their crosses and images were about to take to the streets in commemoration of the Passion. If the play was staged in Tlatelolco, the "great city" within walking distance was Tenochtitlan, making Tlatelolco analogous to Bethany.

8   The Nahua author begins by echoing the content of the first Spanish line, though reversing "lady/noblewoman" and "mother" to keep the "oh my precious mother" formula in initial position. He then appears to mis-understand the meaning of the second line. In the Spanish this is another epithet applied to Mary. Ordinarily, the Nahua author is quite willing to list multiple epithets for Mary, but he reads this line instead as an allusion to the redemption of humanity.

His Christ goes on to discuss at further length the redemption and his predestined role in it. He makes explicit for his audience what Izquierdo vaguely refers to as a "mystery," contributing again to the Nahuatl play's stronger tone of foreboding. That his fate was something set down in the past by God is a subject to which he will return several times.

9 Like his mother, the Nahuatl Christ repeatedly asserts the truthfulness of his words. These statements act as a meta-commentary on the text itself, as if it is declaring its own authoritativeness.

The Nahuatl Christ speaks of going up or ascending (*nontlecotiyaz*) to Jerusalem. Jerusalem is indeed situated in a range of mountains and at a higher elevation than the nearby town of Bethany. While it is not inconceivable that the Nahua author had access to a description of Holy Land geography, it is more likely that he was extrapolating from other sources. In Luke 18:31, a verse sometimes used as the Gospel text for the Sunday before Lent, Jesus says to the Apostles, *Ecce ascendimus Ierosolymam* 'Behold, we go up to Jerusalem.' Nahuatl renditions of this verse use forms of the verb found in the play (e.g., Anunciación 1577:36r; play manuscript 51r). Jerusalem was typically depicted as a walled city upon a hill. The heavenly Jerusalem, Christ's celestial kingdom, was also imagined in this manner. A Nahuatl song in the *Psalmodia christiana*, based on the Book of Revelation, describes the location of the heavenly Jerusalem as "the top of some mountain, which was very high" (Sahagún 1583:72v). For sacred places to be conceived as mountains accorded well with indigenous mythology.

The "and this" formula in 9N:5 coincides with the phrase "and thus" (*y assi*) in 9S:3 and was probably suggested by it. Christ then ends his speech with a tightly ordered summary statement featuring the parallel constructions in 9N:6–7, 9N:8, and 9N:11. Where the Spanish Christ in 9S:4 gives his mother an order, the Nahuatl Christ instead issues a statement of fact. This makes his rejection of her plea seem less direct.

10 The Spanish Mary rejects the order Christ has just given her; the Nahuatl Mary responds appropriately to her own son's preceding words. The loanword *anima* 'soul' appears here for the first time. The line "God, true Messiah" in the Spanish is the basis for the Nahuatl Mary's reiteration of her son's dual nature as God and man, both of which states she describes in two ways. The term "Messiah" seldom appears in Nahuatl literature, "rescuer" being the standard manner for referring to Christ's prophesied role.

The Nahuatl Mary again shows her fondness for fancy vocatives by turning her counterpart's "my life" into a more elaborate paired construction and transforming "my joy" into the thirteen-syllable word that comprises line 10N:8. The word *contenta* in 10S:4 may have suggested the choice of "consolation" for the Nahuatl vocatives. The Spanish Mary's concern with her own personal happiness tends to be ignored by the Nahua author.

11 The initial "And" (*auh*) in the Nahuatl marks a discourse break, coinciding with the Spanish stanza structure. Through 11N:9 the Nahuatl Mary closely follows the sense of the Spanish text, though speaking with more formality and indirection and specifying Christ's Jerusalem destination. Izquierdo's *licencia* 'license, permission' is rendered by the Nahuatl term *teihualiztli* 'sending someone away,' as in bidding someone farewell or sending off a messenger.

12 The Spanish *desterrados* 'exiled ones, banished ones' might seem to suggest a more serious reason for absence than *cholotinemi* 'they go about fleeing' or 'they go about running and leaping.' The verb may imply that the subjects are fleeing from something, or simply that they are engaged in ongoing rapid movement; my translation is meant to convey this ambiguity. More precise glosses were available for *desterrado* (Molina 1970:45r). But the Nahua author's choice is culturally appropriate. In Nahuatl oratory, wandering about like a vagabond—whether by choice or necessity— is represented as a disapproved behavior that indicates a lack of proper upbringing. Uncontrolled movement was also frowned upon: the proper way to travel was with steady, measured steps (Burkhart 1986a; 1989:59–65, 137). Children who would leave home and go running around were poorly socialized. By saying that even such derelicts come home for the holidays, Mary effectively makes the point that Christ would be remiss to leave her at such a time.

13 The Nahuatl text's opening "this," though less emphatic than the "and this" construction, serves similarly to mark a break and call attention to Mary's subsequent words.

The epithet Jesus the Nazarene refers to the town where Christ grew up but also bears a particular association with the Passion. In Spanish iconography of the Passion, the name Jesús Nazareno is given to images of Christ dressed in a purple tunic and carrying the cross on his shoulder. Those who wear penitential costume and carry candles in the Holy Week processions of southern Spain are identified as Nazarenos (Mitchell 1990:40, 115). The name is also linked to the theme of prophecy. Matthew 2:23 states: "And he came and dwelt in a city called Nazareth: that it might be fulfilled which was spoken by the prophets, He shall be called a Nazarene."

According to John (19:19), the signboard placed above Christ's head during the crucifixion applied this name to him, calling him Jesus the Nazarene, King of the Jews. The Nahuatl Passion tracts in *Sermones y ejemplos* (n.d.:351v) and in the closely related *Miscelánea sagrada* (n.d.:217r) and *Sermones en mexicano* (n.d.:197) texts follow John's Gospel in this matter.

The *Psalmodia christiana*'s songs for the festival of the Circumcision invoke Christ under this name, in a passage modeled on the Latin hymn *O dulcis Iesus Nazarenus* (Sahagún 1583:18v; Morel 1866:67). One of the songs in the *Cantares mexicanos* also applies the name to Christ, rendering it Xesus Nazaleno (Bierhorst 1985:338). An image of Christ's head used in several sixteenth-century Mexican books, including the *Psalmodia* and Molina's confession manual, bears the inscription *IESV CRISTO NAZA-RENO* (Rodríguez-Buckingham 1993:297–300).

The Nahuatl Mary again refers to the upcoming festival as the "great *pascua*," or Easter, adding the intensifier *cenca* in response to the Spanish text's "solemn." In the last two lines, which have no counterpart in the Spanish, she tells Christ that he will safely escape the imminent events if he does not go to Jerusalem.

14 The prophets and their foretellings, an important theme of the play, are here mentioned for the first time. The loanwords *propheta* and *propheçias* are used in the Nahuatl, but native words are used for the act of prophesying. Similar passages appear in the *despedimiento* texts of fray Martín de León and the *Cantares* manuscript: Christ enumerates the sufferings that will befall him—points not discussed until later in the Holy Wednesday drama—and then cites the authority of the ancient prophecies. In León's version he speaks to his mother as follows:

The time has now come to arrive that my precious father God ordained, in which I will be made to suffer fatigue, I will be taken prisoner, I will be tied up, I will be buffeted, my face will be spit upon, I will be flogged, I will be stuck with thorns, I will be flayed, I will be stretched by my hands on the cross, I will be killed in regard to the rescue of the people in the world. All of the ancient speaking of the prophets will come true upon me, in the way that they left spoken about me, which as you are well aware lies written in the sacred book. (1614:315v)

The grounding of Christ's story in the prophecies of the Old Testament was vital to the development of Christian theology. For Nahuas, accustomed to looking to elders and ancestors—rather than deities—for moral guidance, the prophets and patriarchs of Christianity's ancient past lent the new religion an aura of ancestral authority. By emphasizing the authority of written texts, the playwright also supports his own position as an educated man with privileged access to Christian discourses.

In the hierarchical ordering of heaven's residents, the prophets and patriarchs rank higher than any other mortals except Mary (e.g., *Missale romanum* 1561:120r). The *Psalmodia christiana* recounts this heavenly hierarchy in its songs for All Saint's Day, placing "the very praiseworthy prophets, patriarchs, God's very precious ones, who lived on earth" after the angels and ahead of all the apostles and other saints (Sahagún 1583:202v).

One way to argue against Christian conversion was to appeal to the authority of tradition and respect for the ancestors. This argument is well articulated in the *Colloquios*, the fictionalized Franciscan-Mexica dialogues written by students of Sahagún. The spokesman for the Nahua nobles names a number of deceased native rulers, stating that they would have known how to respond to the friars' words. He professes an inability to challenge the elders' authority by destroying the old customs (Sahagún 1986:138). Further on, the spokesman for the native priests also invokes the authority of the ancestors:

Our progenitors, when they came to be, came to live on earth, they did not go speaking in this way. They bequeathed to us their customs. They believed in, they served, they honored the divinities. They left us trained in all the ways to serve and honor them. (Sahagún 1986:148–50)

To speak of the ancestors "believing" in the gods is an anachronism: "belief" as a test of religiosity was not an issue in native culture until the friars introduced their faith.

The Franciscans, meanwhile, have invoked their own ancient bearers of wisdom: the prophets and patriarchs to whom the "true divinity" long ago revealed himself (Sahagún 1986:114–16). Thus, the prophets are juxtaposed to the native ancestors as competing authority figures who received divine inspiration in the distant past. The two sets of characters are functionally equivalent and, thus, potentially interchangeable.

The *Psalmodia christiana* relates: "All that our lord Jesus Christ did here on earth, everything lies signified in the words of the prophets, the patriarchs" (Sahagún 1583:125v). Sahagún's Good Friday sermon clarifies the prophets' role in the Passion:

The prophets pronounced it, a very long time before it happened. Our lord showed them, taught them, and commanded them to write it down. They wrote it down.

And we keep their words, their writings. Especially Isaiah the prophet, he explained it. We keep his words. (1563:48r)

Isaiah was the prophet whose writings were most frequently cited by medieval Passion enthusiasts as predictions of Christ's afflictions (Marrow 1979).

In the Nahuatl Epiphany play "Comedia de los Reyes," written in Tlatelolco around 1607, Gaspar, one of the three kings, tells the infant Christ that the words of the prophets, Christ's ancestors, have been fulfilled. He adds that "the sovereigns, the patriarchs, the prophets, David, Abraham, Moses, Isaac" are rejoicing because of Christ's birth (Horcasitas 1974:312–13). Three of the four figures named are authors of letters in the Holy Wednesday drama.

The Old Testament prophecies did not, of course, speak of Christ directly but were thought to refer to him metaphorically; through his life on earth he fulfilled these signs. Izquierdo refers to *aquellas viejas figuras* 'those old designs' or 'those old figures' (14S:5). The Nahuatl term used here (14N:7) is *tlanezcayotiliztli*. This word is derived from the verb *neci* 'to appear' via the abstract form *nezcayotl*, which was used for figures of speech. The sense is of something hidden being made manifest, the sign being a revelation of its referent's hidden meaning.

15　It is possible, in Nahuatl, to make a comparative construction in terms of relative easiness or relative strength. But as written the Nahuatl passage is more emphatic: the earth and sky have *no* strength. It is also more fatalistic: earth, stars, and sky *will* come to an end. The apocalyptic destruction of the world, as described in Luke 21, was preached to the Nahuas on the first Sunday in Advent (Sahagún 1563; Anunciación 1577; Bautista 1606). These Christian beliefs resonated with native myths of world destruction.

Along with invoking the predictive powers of ancient prophets, an effective way to claim legitimacy for Christianity was to emphasize its foundations in ancient sacred writings, while claiming that these bore greater authority than the native manuscripts. In the *Colloquios* the Nahua lord speaks of how the native priests read the books and are in charge of the sacred words (Sahagún 1986:140). Later, the Franciscan spokesman explains the source of the friars' knowledge:

It is because we keep the sacred book, the sacred words, where lie visible, lie written, lie arranged in sections all the words of He of the Near, He of the Nigh. They were made a very long time ago. And these holy words, they are very true, very direct, very credible. (158)

The native people, he continues, keep no sacred book or sacred words.

The Nahuatl versions of stanzas 14 and 15 are structurally similar. Christ addresses himself to his mother, indicates that he is going to inform her of something, and then, after an "and this," explains that the preceding information applies to him because he is going to make it come true. In cases like these, it is clear that the Nahua author was taking the Spanish text one stanza at a time and building his own text in corresponding segments.

16 The Nahuatl Mary utters here an emphatic and graphic expression of her anguish. Nahuatl discourse employed imagery of the heart, seat of the *-yolia* life force, to describe a broad range of mental and emotional processes including understanding, memory, will, and affection (López Austin 1980:I, 207). Moral lapses also affected that organ; the preconquest purification rite of ritual confession, as well as the Catholic sacrament of penance, was called in Nahuatl "straightening one's heart." To feel as if one's heart were ripped apart by a knife suggests a severe disturbance in one's mental and emotional equilibrium.

Nahua hearts could be similarly wounded by a frightening experience. The verb used here for the breaking of Mary's heart, *tzayani*, appears in its transitive form in the compound *neyoltzayanalizpahtli* 'medicine for the breaking of the heart.' The medicine contained sticky latex intended to glue the damaged organ back together (Ortiz de Montellano 1990:178). Mary may, thus, be describing what she perceives as the actual condition of her heart: it *is* broken, due to the frightful shock her son is giving her, and feels *as if* he stabbed her with a knife.

The term *cochilo* 'knife' is a loan from the Spanish *cuchillo*, here adapted to Nahuatl pronunciation. Of the loanwords the Nahua author introduced spontaneously into the play, rather than taking them directly from Izquierdo's text, this is the only one that comes from everyday life rather than from Christian religious contexts. In the corpus of Nahuatl civil documentation analyzed by Karttunen and Lockhart, *cuchillo* makes its earliest appearance in 1570; it also appears in Molina's dictionary as a loan into Nahuatl (Karttunen and Lockhart 1976:62; Molina 1970:25v).

The Nahua author may be alluding here to the prophecy of the Hebrew elder, Simeon, uttered at Mary's post-partum purification ritual in the temple. According to Luke 2:35, Simeon told Mary that her soul would be pierced by a sword (*gladius* in the Vulgate). Interpreted as a prediction of her suffering at Christ's Passion, this prophecy became one of the so-called "seven sorrows" of the Virgin (Warner 1976:213, 218). In Miguel Pérez's Mary-centered account of the Passion, after Christ's death the Virgin cries out to Simeon that his prophecy regarding the "knife of extreme sorrow" has been fulfilled (Pérez 1549:30r).

References to Simeon's prophecy occur in a number of Nahuatl Passion tracts, with various Nahuatl constructions used to describe the cutting instrument. Some examples are "torment knife" (play manuscript, 145v); "metal blade, double-edged" (*Santoral en mexicano* n.d.:23v); "metal weaver's-reed cutting implement" (León 1614:315r); "metal cutting implement" (León 1614:316v); "metal *macquahuitl*," referring to the obsidian-edged wooden weapon used by native warriors (*Cantares de los mejicanos* n.d.:290v); or simply "torment" (*Sermones en mexicano* (n.d.:203). León also uses the Spanish word *lança* 'lance' (1614:316r). In the Tulane *despedimiento* text, Christ reminds Mary of Simeon's prophecy, though without mentioning a sword or knife (Appendix, Text I).

Iconographically, all seven of Mary's sorrows were represented as swords piercing Mary's chest. A late sixteenth-century relief carving by a native artist at San Andrés Calpan, near Puebla, is based on such a representation (Figure 9).

Line 16N:8 pairs -*yolia* with the loanword *anima* for the first time in this text. Such pairing of a Christian religious term and the native term selected as its closest equivalent served to support the fiction that native and European ideas were in fact cognate. The parallel construction suited native stylistic preferences. The friars could take comfort in the fact that the "right" word was there, while native people could focus on the familiar term.

The Nahua author did not translate line 16S:4. It is possible that he considered this petulant expression of jealousy inappropriate to Mary's character.

17 The Spanish Christ begins this speech by repeating his very first line in the play. This time, the Nahua author interpreted Mary's "dignity" by echoing the Hail Mary prayer's phrase "full of grace," itself taken from the angel Gabriel's greeting in Luke 1:28. He uses the same verb construction used in Nahuatl versions of the Hail Mary. The Spanish or Latin terms for "grace" were borrowed into Nahuatl renditions of the prayer, but in other contexts attempts were made to express the concept of grace in Nahuatl

9. Relief sculpture of the Virgin of the Sorrows, posa chapel of the Immaculate Conception, San Andrés Calpan, Puebla. Photograph by the author.

through derivatives of the terms for "good" or "proper." These were often paired with one another or with the loanword "grace," as in "you are filled with utter goodness, grace" (Gante 1981:143v), or "you are filled with utter propriety, grace" (*Santoral en mexicano* n.d.:52v). The Hail Mary was so familiar to Nahuas that many in the play's audience would have grasped this intertextual allusion.

Line 17N:7 presents the play's first reference to the cross. The Spanish *cruz* was introduced into Nahuatl for this object; the term and its referent would have been well known to the Nahua audience. Crosses were erected in the native communities not only at churches but also at crossroads, houses, and, according to Grijalva, mountains and "all places where there is some peculiarity"—anomalous features of the landscape that were associated with sacred power. People decorated the crosses with branches and flowers and made offerings of flowers to them (Grijalva 1624:73v; Mendieta 1980:308).

Mexico's Jesuit church boasted a fragment of wood believed to derive from Christ's cross. This and other relics, including a thorn from the crown of thorns and fragments of the clothing of Mary, Joseph, and Mary's mother Ann, were sent to the Mexico Jesuits by Pope Clement XIII. Their arrival was celebrated in November of 1578 with a grand festival in which native people participated extensively (Alegre 1956–60:I, 205–6, 220–23).

Three of the late sixteenth-century wills from the town of Culhuacan mention crosses among the testators' personal possessions (Cline 1986:28).

The verb used throughout the Nahua-Christian literature for the act of crucifixion was a compound of *maitl* 'hand' or, by extension, 'arm,' and *zohua* 'to stretch, spread.' I use a rather literal translation in order to retain the graphic, descriptive quality of this verb.

The Nahuatl Christ continues his pattern of alternating informative passages with more pointed "and this" statements. Here he describes what is going to happen to him, then relates this directly to his mother by telling her to be strong. The Spanish *esforçad* 'make an effort' is rendered well by the Nahuatl figure of speech *ma ixquich motlapaltzin*, a formula Karttunen and Lockhart call a "phrase of encouragement" (1987:34). Literally, the phrase means "may it be all your red color." Redness here alludes to the ruddy appearance caused by increased blood flow during physical exertion. Through a metonymic substitution of effect for cause, the red color symbolizes valiant effort.

18 Nahuatl preaching materials contain many usages of the metaphor by which Christ was equated with a doctor who "cures" sin (Burkhart 1989:173–76). Similar references occur later in the Spanish text (34S:3, 59S:3, 60S:1–2, 65S:3–5, 73S:5).

Lucifer makes his first appearance here. The Nahuatl term appropriated to translate devils and demons was *tlacatecolotl* (plural *tlatlacatecoloh*), a compound of the words for 'human being' and 'horned owl' (Burkhart 1989:40–44). The term seems to have had as a non-Christian referent a type of malevolent sorcerer who turned into a horned owl by night in order to carry out his malicious designs. The horned owl was considered an omen of misfortune. The associations with sorcery, malevolence, disguise, misfortune, night, and horns all coincided with Christian beliefs about devils. The friars relied on descriptions, pictures, and narratives to convey other attributes of these new embodiments of evil.

The term *tlacatecolotl* was used so often in Christian contexts that it did lose its original meaning and took on something closer to the meaning that the friars ascribed to it. But one aspect of that meaning was very different for Nahuas than for Old World Christians. The divinities worshipped by non-Christian native people were, according to the friars, demons one and all. These demons had held the native people in thrall until Christian armies and Christian priests came to liberate them.

Christian Nahuas, while they applied to the Christian sacra many beliefs, attitudes, and practices that had formerly been directed to the native deities, also learned to refer to the old deities as *tlatlacatecoloh* and to depict them in art according to European iconography of the Devil. The friars repeatedly reminded them that they were new in the faith and warned them against backsliding into the demons' clutches. When Christ speaks of liberating people from demons, the words resonate with Mexico's recent history.

The story of Lucifer's rebellion and fall appears in a number of Nahuatl texts. Sahagún asserted that the native deity Tezcatlipoca, a cosmic trickster and master of disguises, was Lucifer himself (1563:82r; 1579:10v; 1950–82:I, 38). The Nahua historian Chimalpahin calls Tezcatlipoca the "great *tlacatecolotl*" (1889:23); this is the same epithet used for Lucifer here in the drama, as well as in other texts (e.g., Sahagún 1563:48v, 51v; Appendix, Texts III and V).

The first Nahuatl play on record, the Judgment Day play of the early 1530s, most likely had demons in the cast to drag the condemned souls off to hell. A surviving script on this topic includes Satan and another demon (Horcasitas 1974:561–93). The first firmly documented appearance of Lucifer and his minions upon the Nahuatl stage occurred on Corpus Christi, 1539, at the Franciscan church in Tlaxcala. A dramatization of the temptation of Christ was performed, in which the demons consulted among themselves to determine which one would tempt Christ. Lucifer was chosen. He disguised himself as a hermit, but failed to cover up his horns and the long claws on his hands and feet (Motolinia 1979:73). A trio of unnamed demons vie for human souls in the didactic play dubbed "Tlacahuapahualiztli (Bringing up Children)" by John Cornyn, which probably dates to the sixteenth or early seventeenth century (Cornyn and McAfee 1944).

In preparation for Corpus Christi festivities in 1555, the Tlaxcala *cabildo* ordered that "some images of demons" be made (Lockhart et al. 1986:95). Already by that time, the demon was a recognizable figure with a stock appearance.

19 The first two lines of the Nahuatl text continue the discourse segment represented by 18N, but the opening vocative appears to have been suggested by the Spanish Christ's "mother of mine" in 19S:1. The Nahua author then constructs an "and this" statement relating the reason for Christ's coming to the present moment, and takes this opportunity to refer again to the prophets and prophecies.

20 The Spanish Christ here tells his mother to stop crying so much, while the Nahuatl Christ shows a bit more deference. Both Christs warn their mothers that worse suffering is yet to come. Line 20N:4 can be read as a comparative statement denoting the future pain as greater.

The Nahuatl in 20N:2 pairs the loanword *anima* 'soul' with heart, rather than, as occurs elsewhere in the play and is most common in other texts, with the heart-based *-yolia* soul. This usage may have been suggested by the choice of the verb *patzmiqui* to describe Mary's distress. *Patzmiqui* literally means "to be squeezed to death" and has the sense of anguish, distress, or oppress—emotions that may be experienced as a constricting pressure. This verb was also used in a compound with the word for heart, with the same meaning but alluding to pressure specifically on that organ (Molina 1970:41r, 80v). The heart was, thus, a customary recipient of this verb's action.

The Nahuatl Mary has already predicted her son's arrest in 7N:8. Here he alludes to it by referring to the tying of his hands. Christ was commonly depicted with his hands tied in scenes of his arrest, trial, and torture. He also predicts that Mary will see him in this state. Having told her how terribly she will suffer when he is merely under arrest, he clobbers her with a concluding "and this" statement regarding the imminence of his death.

21 Both Marys open their longest speech in the play by describing the pain caused by Christ's previous speech. The Nahuatl Mary again localizes her feelings in her heart. Rather than following Izquierdo's digestive metaphor, the Nahua author employs a medical allusion, in keeping with the imagery of Mary's torn and constricted heart. Her son's words should soothe and heal her; instead they make her feel worse.

22   Both Marys appeal to their son's divine status. Line 22N:3, regarding her son's relationship to his father, echoes Christ's address to her in line 1N:3. Christ having by now spoken repeatedly of his death, allusions to his father's immortality take on added relevance. The Spanish text's "cruelty" is softened in the Nahuatl to terms of sadness and suffering consistent with the heart-based feelings Mary has already been expressing. What I translate as "anxious" or "anxiety" (also 3N:5, 4N:11) literally means an overburdening or overpressuring.

Christ's Jerusalem destination is reiterated for the eighth time in the Nahuatl text; it has been mentioned only once in the Spanish. These references to his imminent journey, like the predictions of what will befall him upon arrival, contribute to the Nahuatl play's more intensive foreshadowing.

23   Having in the preceding passage invoked her son's divine nature, Mary now begins to play up his relationship to her. In both versions, she addresses him directly as her child for the first time in this speech. Where the Spanish Mary orders her son to remember what she did, the Nahuatl Mary takes a less direct approach by asking questions regarding her bearing of Christ and his early childhood. *Florentine Codex* orations ascribe value and prestige to pregnancy and childbirth, with successful delivery treated as an act of valor (Sahagún 1950–82:VI; Sullivan 1966, 1980).

The Nahuatl Mary refers to Christ's birthplace in a manner used in other Nahuatl texts. The early friars had had to introduce the Christmas story among people who had only recently become acquainted with large domestic animals and the buildings that house them. The Nahuatl term for deer was extended to cover horses, donkeys, and cattle. It became a generic term for large ungulates, although its principal referent remained "deer" and other terms were soon borrowed or coined for specific animals.

The manger (Spanish *pesebre*) in which, according to Luke 2:7, Mary laid the infant Christ was often translated into Nahuatl as "the deer's eating place." The Spanish term was introduced into some Nahuatl texts, but the Nahuatl phrase appears in a number of texts and in Molina's dictionary (Molina 1970:95v). In Nahua culture, the deer had strong symbolic associations with peripheral, uncivilized places and with poorly socialized individuals (Burkhart 1986a). In contrast to Europeans, Nahuas may not have read Christ's birth in a stable as a symbol of humility.

Sahagún's sermon for Christmas has Mary lay the newborn Christ "in the eating-place of the donkey and the cattle, which is called a manger, because there was no good place in a house there" (Sahagún 1563:8v–

10. The birth of Jesus Christ. Woodcut from the *Psalmodia christiana*, 1583, f. 229v. Courtesy of the John Carter Brown Library at Brown University.

9r). In fray Alonso de Escalona's sermons, Christ's place of birth is described as "the home of the deer"; the manger is "the eating-place of the horse" (n.d.:256r, 127r). In the prayer cycle from the Biblioteca Nacional, Christ's birthplace is "the sleeping-place of the deer" (*Santoral en mexicano* n.d.:13v). The *Psalmodia christiana* has Mary lay her newborn son "in the manger, the eating-place of the deer" (Sahagún 1583:234v). Figure 10 reproduces the woodcut that accompanies the *Psalmodia*'s Christmas songs.

A prayer to Christ in the *Exercicio* reflects upon the consequences of Christ's sojourn into human flesh: "In the sense that you are a man, milk will be necessary for you. Every day your precious mother will nurse you, you who give the angels their food!" (Sahagún 1574:9r). The text goes on to describe Christ's birth (10r): "You came to dwell in an old hut, and you came to place yourself among, in the midst of the deer, the four-footed animals. And straw and debris became your bed."

According to Mendieta (1980:432), Nahuas observed the Christmas holiday by erecting manger scenes at their churches. These featured statues of Mary, Joseph, the infant Christ, and shepherds. In the *Codex Sierra*, a canopy supported by rough-hewn posts, the setting for such a manger scene, is used to symbolize the festival of Christmas (León 1982). Durán mentions a Christmas Eve vigil: the native people gather in the church patios, lighting fires to keep warm, and stay up all night. Similar customs were, he states, followed at the preconquest temple patios during a ceremony that occurred at nearly the same time of year (Durán 1967:I, 288). Augustinians sponsored enactments of Mary's and Joseph's journey to Bethlehem (Weckmann 1984:I, 256).

24 The Nahuatl Mary tells Christ that he is her *octacatl*, her measuring device or model, such as would be used in constructing a building. In Nahuatl rhetoric this word was used metaphorically in regard to models for living well, including admonitive addresses regarding good behavior. According to the *Florentine Codex*, a lord addressing the common people would refer to his own discourse as an *octacatl* from which his listeners should learn how to live or speak well (Sahagún 1950–82:VI, 246–47). Fray Andrés de Olmos's list of figures of speech includes *octacatl* as a metaphor for a parent or leader and for doctrine or teachings (Olmos 1875:211, 227). A sermon of Sahagún's equates the preacher's *exemplum* with the Nahuatl *octacatl* (1563:45v). The Nahuatl Mary regards her son not just as a child whom she has nurtured but also as a behavioral model for her own life.

Mary then returns to the topic of Christ's childhood, reminding him of the flight into Egypt to escape the massacre of the innocents. King Herod, and the story of the Holy Family's flight, appear in two Nahuatl Epiphany plays, the "Comedia de los Reyes" from Tlatelolco, dating probably to 1607, and an "Adoración de los Reyes" known from a 1760 copy of what may be a sixteenth-century text (Horcasitas 1974:253–327). In "Adoración de los Reyes," an angel tells Joseph to hide the child and take him to Egypt because Herod is searching for him and all the little children are to be killed (Horcasitas 1974:276–78). In the other play, the escape is treated through indirect reporting. Herod's soldiers come upon a worker in the fields—a rustic character of a type well known in Spanish *comedias*—and ask whether he has seen a woman carrying a child pass by on a donkey, with a man leading them. He says that he has indeed: "She passed by here. And she was carrying her precious child in her arms. He was a wondrous little one, for his precious body was like snow, and great sunbeams streamed from it" (Horcasitas 1974:324).

25 In the *Exercicio*, a prayer to Mary relives this journey with her, using some of the same terms as the Nahuatl play:

And greatly your heart, your body ached, hurt, when you were traveling to Egypt. Not just a few plains and ravines did you pass through. And you carried your precious child in your arms. (Sahagún 1574:21r–v)

In the Nahuatl drama "Tlacahuapahualiztli (Bringing up Children)," Christ tells his mother, who has appealed to him on behalf of souls in Purgatory, that he will do as she wishes because he remembers how heavily burdened her hands were as she carried him about in her arms (Cornyn and McAfee 1944:348).

Indigenous women ordinarily carried (and still carry) their babies tied to their backs, not held in their arms, but images of Mary carrying her son always showed her holding him in her arms. This more strenuous manner of child transport, elaborated via the couplet in 25N:2–3, is used here to emphasize Christ's indebtedness to her. The verb for carrying in the arms, *napaloa*, was used by members of the Huexotzingo town council in a letter they wrote to King Philip II in 1560. Petitioning him for relief from their heavy burden of tribute, they describe how well they and their people had treated the newly arrived Spaniards, even carrying in their arms those Spaniards who were sick (Anderson et al. 1976:180).

The Nahuatl Mary further details the perils of her journey by telling her son how she could have stumbled and dropped him. Stumbling played a role in Nahua mythology; Quetzalcoatl stumbled as he fled from the lord of the underworld, thereby damaging the precious bones he had stolen with which he would create humanity (Bierhorst 1992:145–46; Garibay 1979:106). Under the old calendar system, stumbling on certain days was considered an omen of ill fortune. Stumbling and falling were dangerous because, like severe fright or any sudden blow, they could cause the *tonalli* to leave the body. The *tonalli* was a sort of soul, located in the crown of the head, that regulated body temperature and growth and played a major role in determining a person's character and fate. *Tonalli* loss resulted in illness and, if healing ceremonies were not performed, death. Small children were especially susceptible; if Mary had dropped her son on the ground, he might not have lived to fulfill his mission (Sahagún 1950–82:II, 35, 158; IV, 49; X, 162; López Austin 1980; Ortiz de Montellano 1990). Moreover, stumbling and falling were used in Nahuatl rhetoric as metaphors for moral deviance (Burkhart 1989:61–62, 65).

26 This passage refers to the story of the twelve-year-old Christ conversing with the religious authorities in the temple in Jerusalem (Luke 2:41–50). Mary and Joseph brought the boy with them to spend Passover in Jerusalem and inadvertently left for home without him. Discovering him missing, they returned to the city and, after three days, found him in the temple.

The Spanish text places this episode in the temple; the Nahua author chose to specify the city instead. He added line 26N:7, linking this past episode with the present circumstances. This highlights the fact that that earlier event foreshadows Christ's death, when Mary will again "lose" him in Jerusalem for the three days that his body will lie in the sepulcher.

The story is told in a number of Nahuatl texts, as narrative in the *Psalmodia christiana* (Sahagún 1583:52v) but in other sources as a prayer through which the worshipper seeks a connection to Mary's emotional experience. Mary's distress as she searched for the lost child was, like the flight into Egypt, enumerated among the Virgin's "seven sorrows," while her delight upon discovering him is one of the "joyful mysteries" celebrated in the Rosary (Warner 1976:218). The episode is, therefore, included in Nahuatl Rosary cycles (Anunciación 1565:77r–77v; Anunciación 1575:257) and is similarly treated in the Jesuit oration cycle (*Santoral en mexicano* n.d.:18r–21v). Such texts employ imagery of losing and finding Christ to describe metaphorically the moral condition of the soul.

The *Exercicio*'s texts for Thursday take as their subject the Gospel passage describing Christ among the sages in the temple. A narrative account of the event is followed by a prayer to God the father on the theme of prophecy and fulfillment:

For three days he admonished those who were sages of the sacred words, the priests, there in the great temple of Jerusalem. He questioned them there about the sacred words, as to how his coming was spoken of, how it lay in black ink, how it lay in red ink, the way the prophets left it. And he admonished them that they listen to him well so that they would know that it had now come true, it had now happened. (Sahagún 1574:20r–v)

Black ink and red ink in Nahuatl discourse represent books and, by extension, wisdom and ancestral authority.

This prayer is followed by one to Mary, which focuses instead on her anxiety:

And I contemplate the aching, the hurting that you endured when you lost your precious child there in Jerusalem. You went about seeking him for three days and three nights, and all the time your heart, your body ached with great weeping and distress. You did no sleeping. You went about wetting your lips, you went about with parched lips, you went about with misery in your guts, your tears were running down your face. (22v)

As in the drama, Christ's concern with fulfilling his destined role is juxtaposed with Mary's emotional involvement in his actions.

27 Both Marys conclude their speech with a plea that their son, based on his memory of her tribulations, will forgo death. The Nahuatl Mary concludes with a demand for obedience unparalleled in the Spanish text.

28 The Spanish Christ's flippant reply to his mother is handled with delicacy by the Nahua author. His Christ does not complain about Mary's nagging nor condescendingly reassure her that her behavior is understandable and to be excused. Just as his words have saddened her, her words sadden him. Unlike the Spanish Christ, he applies to his own feelings a term that Mary has previously used for hers. He comments on her words, showing that he has attended to her admonishments. Uttering his denial, he defers to his father's authority, thus indicating that he is not willfully disobeying her.

29 Here the Nahua author makes his longest digression from the Spanish text. He elaborates upon the mention of Adam's sin by recounting the story of Adam and Eve and explaining its relationship to his own destiny. The creation of Adam and Eve, the Devil's deception, and their expulsion from paradise were familiar topics in Nahua-Christian preaching. These primordial humans were typically called "our first father" and "our first mother" in Nahuatl.

The Nahuatl text's application to the Garden of Eden of the borrowed Spanish phrase *paraiso terrenal* 'terrestrial paradise,' and the formulaic couplet, "a very good place, a very fine place," is typical (e.g., Sahagún 1583:32v; 1986:192–93). Nahuatl versions of the Adam and Eve story vary in their content and degree of detail (Burkhart 1988a:74–78). The couple's sin may be described as a result of pride or a particular form of pride—disobedience or a desire to be like God—or it may be an unspecified misdeed inspired by the demon. The sin may be ascribed principally to Adam, to Eve, to both, or to the demon.

The Nahua playwright alters the biblical story by designating the tree in question as the tree of life. The biblical account is itself ambiguous. Genesis 2:9 mentions a tree of life and a tree of the knowledge of good and evil, both standing in the middle of the garden. God commands Adam and Eve not to eat from the tree in the middle of the garden, without specifying which one (Genesis 3:3). The serpent says if they eat this fruit they will know good and evil, indicating that it is from the tree of knowledge that he incites them to eat (Genesis 3:5). God expels them lest they also eat from the tree of life and therefore live forever (Genesis 3:22).

Most Nahuatl accounts do not mention these trees; some mention the eating of a forbidden fruit but not the tree from which it came. In the *Colloquios* there is one fruit tree from which Adam and Eve are, for no specified reason, not to eat (Sahagún 1986:192–93). The widely used Dominican *doctrina* of 1548 gives a detailed telling of the story complete with a tree of knowledge in the middle of the garden, but no tree of life (*Doctrina cristiana* 1944:32r–37r).

A version in the *Psalmodia christiana* closely follows the biblical account, but conflates the two trees. The tree with the forbidden fruit is designated the tree of knowledge. But when the authors translated Genesis 3:22, they read the reference to the tree of life as if it referred to the same tree. They have God tell the angels to expel Adam so that he will never *again* eat from the tree of *life* (Sahagún 1583:33r, 33v, 35r).

The elaborate dramatization of the fall of Adam and Eve staged at Tlaxcala in 1539 featured one tree in the middle of the mock garden, which represented the tree of knowledge (Motolinia (1979:66). The preconquest Nahua world view placed a tree at the center of a cosmos that, like Eden with its four rivers flowing from a central source (which were recreated in the Tlaxcala play), was divided into four quadrants.

Given the contradictions within and among these various accounts, it is understandable that the Nahua playwright would envision Eden with a single tree at its center and interpret the biblical passages as referring to a single tree by two names. That this usage was allowed to stand indicates that no friar inspected the playwright's work very closely to make sure that it conformed precisely to Catholic teachings.

The Nahua author pairs the Spanish word *diablo* 'devil' with the Nahuatl *tlacatecolotl* in line 29N:13. This is the only place in the play where any term other than *tlacatecolotl* is used for Christianity's forces of evil. However, it was not uncommon for the words *diablo* and *demonio* to appear in Nahuatl texts (Burkhart 1988a:69–70; 1989:40–41). The playwright here follows the common practice of pairing loanwords for religious concepts with the Nahuatl term customarily used to translate them.

Exile into a "place of weeping" is a motif belonging not only to the Adam and Eve story but also to the more frequently uttered Salve Regina prayer. This prayer to the Virgin was, like the Our Father and the Hail Mary, one which friars expected Nahuas to memorize and to recite daily. In Latin, the prayer contains the lines: "To you we cry out, we exiled children of Eve. To you we sigh, moaning and weeping, in this valley of tears." Renderings of the standard prayers into Nahuatl varied slightly from text to text, but some widely used Nahuatl treatments speak of being "exiled hither" (*hualtotoca*) into a "place of weeping" (*chocohuayan*) (e.g., Gante 1981:22r; Anunciación 1565:72r–v; Wagner 1935:4r). This intertextual link to a familiar prayer relates Christ's words about the primordial humans to the practices of the play's audience.

The analogy between the tree of Eden and the cross was well established in Christian doctrine. Elsewhere in the manuscript housing the play, a brief treatise on the triumph of the cross states that Christ rescued people on a cross just as the Devil destroyed "our fathers" with a tree (204r). The *Psalmodia christiana*, in its text for the festival of the Holy Cross, offers this explanation:

> When our first father had erred, then our lord God said: "As things were damaged with a tree, likewise with a tree will things be healed."
> Our lord said: "Where death emerged, likewise there will emerge life. With a tree it overcame people, likewise with a tree will it be overcome."
> The demon deceived our first father, but our lord Jesus Christ rescued the people of the world on a tree. (Sahagún 1583:83r)

The Nahuatl drama expresses this analogy not only in lines 29N:23–24 but also in 29N:14, where the playwright makes a clever play on words. To describe Adam and Eve reaching for the fruit, he uses an active form of the

11. The fall of Adam and Eve. Mural painting in the open chapel, Actopan, Hidalgo. Photograph by the author.

verb phrase that, in passive voice, was employed in Nahuatl texts to refer to crucifixion (see above, stanza 17). Here Adam and Eve *itech omaçouhque* 'on (or adjacent to) it they hand-stretched'; when Christ is crucified in Nahuatl, *mazoalo itech cruz* 'he is hand-stretched on (or adjacent to) the cross.' This reinforces the relationship that Christ is asserting between Adam and Eve's action and his impending death. The same pun occurs in the Tulane *despedimiento* text (Appendix, Text I). The author of one or both texts may have seen depictions of Adam and Eve similar to the mural painting by a native artist that survives in the Augustinian open chapel at Actopan, Hidalgo (Figure 11). In this painting, both partners have one arm extended toward the tree and hold a piece of fruit in that hand.

"Heaven," in Nahuatl, is *ilhuicac* 'in the sky' or *ilhuicatl ihtic* 'within the sky.' Christian teaching established this locus as a place of residence for God, angels, saints, and the souls of the virtuous dead. That Christ's actions serve to appease — literally, to "cool the heart of" — God is also stated in the *Psalmodia*'s Easter songs (see Appendix, Text V) and in Gante's 1553 *Doctrina*:

And [Christ's] death, his precious blood, his torment — for our sake he laid them as an offering before his precious father. In this way he appeased him in regard to us, so that he pardoned our misdeeds. (Gante 1981:72v)

The consequences of Adam's action and Christ's role in reversing them are also discussed in the *Psalmodia*'s songs for the festival of the Circumcision, which tell how no one, in five thousand years, had the power to reverse the effects of Adam's misdeed until Christ was sent by his father to rescue people (Sahagún 1583:16v–17r). In the play, the Nahuatl Christ's concluding "and this" statement makes much the same point; none but he can reverse the damage wrought by Adam and open heaven to humankind.

30   Her protestations of motherly anguish having failed to achieve the desired effect, Mary now begins to argue for alternative methods of salvation. Since God is omnipotent, he can save humanity by some other means. Mary offered this argument in the original *despedimiento* text, the *Meditations on the Life of Christ* (Ragusa and Green 1961:309).

31   The Nahuatl Mary here states more explicitly the power of Christ's spoken word; he can accomplish his mission entirely through speaking. In the brief *despedimiento* episode within the *Sermones en mexicano* Passion

narrative, this is the only argument that Mary musters against Christ's announced departure. He informs her that the time has come for him to rescue his vassals. Sad and tearful, she answers him:

My precious child, how is it that you wish to abandon me? Perhaps you are not all-powerful? May it not be that you abandon me! May it not be that we part from one another. You made your vassals with your words. Also with your words you made heaven and earth. May it also be just with your words that you rescue the people of the world. May it be that you utter forth your breath. Thereupon all the errors of the world will be destroyed. Thus heaven will be opened. (*Sermones en mexicano* n.d.:144–45)

He responds that he must obey his father and fulfill everything that the prophets wrote about him.

32 A second alternative is for Christ to argue that he has already done enough. The Nahuatl verb chosen to express the idea of compensation was also used for paying for goods, as at market, and for the restitutions that Catholic priests ordered as part of people's atonement for sins. Mary addresses Christ as "Lord" in the last line of the Spanish and as "God" in the first line of the following stanza. The Nahua author may have misread this as "offer *to* the Lord/God," and therefore brought "your precious father" into lines 32N:5 and 33N:6.

33 The idea that Christ's previous work on earth ought to be enough to earn humanity's redemption appears also in Miguel Pérez's life of Mary, with Mary raising this argument during the *despedimiento* scene and again when she learns of Christ's death sentence (Pérez 1549). In the farewell scene in the Tulane Passion text, Mary presents arguments similar to those she makes here in the play; she invokes Christ's early bloodshed and his fasting as well as his other good deeds and difficult labors (Appendix, Text I).

The Nahuatl Mary's observation that Christ has already shed blood is an allusion to his circumcision. The *Psalmodia christiana* describes the blood shed on that occasion as the beginning of Christ's work as rescuer (Sahagún 1583:15v). Fray Juan de la Anunciación's *Sermonario* also defines this event as the beginning of Christ's rescue mission, explaining that a little bit of his blood issued forth at that time (1577:16v, 17r). In the play, the Nahuatl Mary argues that he lost a lot of blood then, enough that he should not need to shed any more.

Bloodletting was an important aspect of the Nahuas' preconquest religion, both as a penitential practice and as a mythological motif. According to one myth, as transcribed by a Christian Nahua in 1570, the deity Quetzalcoatl contributed blood from his penis to the dough of ground bones from which humans were formed (Bierhorst 1992:146). Christian Nahuas were taught not to pierce their flesh directly in order to offer blood, but they could do it indirectly by flogging themselves. Teachings about the mystical power of Christ's blood fit well with their traditional attitude.

To the vague mysteries invoked by the Spanish Mary, her Nahuatl counterpart also adds Christ's fasting, an allusion to his forty-day sojourn in the wilderness mentioned in Luke 4:1–13. The term used here is the one used most often in Christian contexts for the fasting from meat required by the Church. In respect to non-Christian native practice it implied not only regimented eating but sexual abstinence and other restrictions. These penitential practices were, like bloodletting, important indigenous religious practices that were, to some extent, carried over into Nahua Christianity (Burkhart 1989). The Nahuatl play characterizes Christ as someone who engaged in activities that Nahuas recognized as pious and purifying.

34 The Nahuatl Mary concludes her speech with a brief and pointed "and this" statement. She has offered reasonable alternatives, and now demands to hear no further mention of Christ's death.

35 As in stanza 28, the Spanish Christ tells his mother, in effect, that her complaint is understandable and excusable but not worthy of serious consideration. The Nahuatl Christ again treats Mary with more deference, acknowledging the truth of her words. The Spanish Christ first called his mother "sacred Virgin" in line 2S:5, at which point the Nahua author responded with a simple "oh my precious mother." Here he tries to convey more of the sense of the Spanish, translating the Spanish word *sagrada* 'sacred' with the Nahuatl *teochihual(li)* 'made sacred,' which was used to express the Christian concept of blessing or blessedness. The term *ichpochtli*, used throughout the Nahuatl literature to translate "virgin," in Nahuatl means an adolescent girl or young woman.

The Nahuatl Christ then proceeds to turn Izquierdo's brief mention of the prophecies into a long defense of the prophetic power of the written word. Repeated allusions to truth authorize the words of the prophets — and the words of the playwright. Even accidental splashes of ink will find their fulfillment in Christ's upcoming actions.

36   Both Christs invoke the incontrovertible authority of their divine father, against which Mary cannot hope to prevail. The Nahuatl Christ refers again to words that were set down in the past and cannot be altered. He expresses concern for his mother's feelings, again using words that she has already applied to herself, while Izquierdo's Christ only urges patience.

Izquierdo's Christ takes partial responsibility for the situation, stating that he himself has signed his father's orders. The Nahua playwright could have translated this, as the custom of making signatures was familiar to Nahuas from wills and other legal documentation. Instead, though, all the responsibility is left with God the father, and the word "hand" in 36S:3 turns up in 36N:9, where Christ explains that he is stuck with the task that his father has assigned to him. By representing himself to his mother as a pawn in his father's game, the Nahuatl Christ appears to defy her wishes less willfully. The Nahuatl Christ manages to be more submissive to both his parents than does his Spanish counterpart.

The Nahua author takes the word "sentence" directly from the Spanish text, although he could have expressed this idea in Nahuatl through a derivative of the verb *tzontequi* 'to judge, decree, sentence,' which he uses in 36N:2. The Spanish term *sentencia* had probably become familiar through native people's involvement with the Spanish colonial courts. Karttunen and Lockhart document its appearance in non-doctrinal Nahuatl texts as of 1551 (1976:58). It is used for Christ's death sentence in fray Juan de la Anunciación's 1575 *doctrina* (270) and in fray Martín de León's 1614 *sermonario* for God's punishment of Adam (133r). Fray Juan Bautista's *sermonario* applies it to the Final Judgment (1606:100).

As is his custom, the Nahuatl Christ concludes his explanatory digression with an "and this" statement relating his previous words to the current moment.

37   The Nahua playwright here contradicts Izquierdo's text. The Spanish Christ admits quite clearly that he could save the world without dying at Calvary, while the Nahuatl Christ asserts, through the rhetorical question in his concluding "and this" statement, that there is no other way. The Spanish Christ toys with the idea of rejecting his fate. His Nahuatl counterpart, who speaks so often and solemnly of the truthfulness of the ancient prophecies and the authority of his father, does not presume to consider any alternative.

The Nahuatl text develops an elaborate metaphor comparing original sin to a garment. The Spanish word *luto* 'mourning,' used also for mourning garments, must have suggested this imagery. Izquierdo is referring in a general sense to the state of mortality into which Adam's sin plunged humankind. The term might also call to listeners' minds the purple cloths in which religious images and ornaments were swathed throughout the period of Lent, which itself represented the pre-salvation history of the world. For Easter morning services, these cloths were removed, symbolizing the achievement of eternal life through Christ's resurrection.

Line 37N:2's eleven-syllable *tlaocolmiccaneçahualiztlatquitl* 'sad-dead person(s)-fasting-garment' resembles *neçaualizmiccatlatquitl* 'fasting-dead person(s)-garment,' Molina's gloss for "mourning clothes" (*luto de vestidura*) (Molina 1970:79r). The word *tlatquitl* can, though, refer to any sort of accoutrement, not necessarily a cloth garment.

Mourning for the dead in preconquest times did not entail the wearing of a special category of garments, although the condition was represented through the use of particular insignia and styles of personal adornment. Thus, terms for mourning garments may be colonial coinages applying to customs introduced by the Church. A letter that fray Pedro de Gante wrote to Charles V mentions that the native people had the custom of dressing in conformity with the types of songs and dances they performed, "so they dressed of gladness or of mourning or of victory" (García Icazbalceta 1971b:224). Durán's chronicle describes ritual expressions of mourning following military defeats. The priests wore their hair untied; the old men and lords refrained from wearing their feather ornaments and instead went out with "insignias of much sadness"; wives of the dead and wounded also left their hair untied (Durán 1967:II, 435, 449).

It is interesting that the playwright included the reference to fasting, given that he could have described mourning garments without employing this term. Colonial texts do mention and depict special garments associated with the penitential fasting practiced in pre-Christian rituals. According to Sahagún's ethnographic consultants, a cloak called a *neçaoalizquachtli* 'fasting mantle,' decorated with a bone design, was worn by a new ruler and his attendant lords during the four days of ritual penitence that preceded his installation (Sahagún 1950–82:VIII, 62–64). Figure 12, from the *Florentine Codex*, shows six of these lords standing in front of a temple holding lit incense burners and maguey-thorn bloodletters.

In pictorial documents a flanged paper collar represented the term "fasting," as in the name glyphs of the famed Texcocan rulers Nezahualcoyotl 'Fasting Coyote' and his son Nezahualpilli 'Fasting Noble' (e.g., Sahagún 1979:VIII, 7r, 7v; Quiñones Keber 1995:32r, 36r, 43v). It was also

12. Lords wearing "fasting mantles" participate in penitential rites for the accession of a new ruler. *Florentine Codex*, Book VIII, f. 46v. Reprinted with permission from fray Bernardino de Sahagún, *Historia general de las cosas de Nueva España, Códice florentino*, Facsimile of the *Codex Florentinus* of the Biblioteca Medicea Laurenciana, published by the Archivo General de la Nación, México, 1979.

used in the place glyph for the town of Amaquemecan 'Place of Those of the Paper Vestments' (Schroeder 1991:33).

The compound term in 37N:2 is ambiguous. I chose the translation closest to the idea of mourning garments. But one could read it as "fasting-garment of the sad dead." In this case it would suggest the penitential garments—cloaks or collars—worn by the non-Christian ancestors, who are now dead and sad, still enslaved by the false deities/demons to whom they had directed their penances.

The Nahuatl Christ pairs this ambiguous fasting garment with the wrapping used for bodies of the dead (*miccaneolololli*, from *micqui* 'dead person' and *ololoa* 'to roll'). Both preconquest and colonial Nahuas wrapped their dead in white cloths, although placement in a flexed position, often followed by cremation, was replaced with burial in an extended position. A shroud is not a mourning garment, but the preceding reference to garments worn in connection with the dead, whether by the dead or in memory of them, may have suggested this addition. It effectively evokes the association between death and the state of un-redeemed (or un-rescued) humanity.

The Nahua playwright explains the cause of this mournful and morbid state by referring to original sin. He uses the Spanish phrase *pecado original*. The Spanish phrase is paired with the Nahuatl *huehuey tlatlacolli* 'old error' or 'old damage.' Original sin was more often expressed in Nahuatl as the origin or beginning of *tlahtlacolli*, but the phrase used here does appear in other texts. In non-Christianized usage, "old error" referred to a kind of hereditary servitude in which the original servant's obligations to his or her master were bequeathed to the descendants of both parties (Motolinia 1971:369; Burkhart 1989:114–15). Here the master is Lucifer, invoked now for the second time in the Nahuatl play.

38 The two texts differ here in a manner consistent with the two preceding stanzas. The Spanish Christ speaks as if he could choose not to act according to God's wishes, but he prefers to do it this way in order to keep his promise to his father. The Nahuatl Christ asserts again that there is only this one way to achieve the rescue of the people. Showing no sign of willfulness, he defers the responsibility onto his father. He acts not on his own promise but in response to God's command.

39 Here the Spanish text also speaks of truth; the Nahua playwright adds emphasis and parallelisms. Line 39N:5 serves the same purpose as Christ's

usual "and this" formula: it highlights his following words as a concluding statement, within which the reiteration of "it is essential" adds urgency to the speech's final lines.

40   Accepting the fact that Christ does indeed have to die, Mary now asks that his death might be delayed until after her own. She makes the same argument in the Tulane manuscript (Appendix, Text I). Where the Spanish Mary mentions her son's blood and sweat, the Nahuatl Mary refers to his blood and to the breaking of his body, twice asking to be spared the sight. And no wonder: in the *Cantares* manuscript's Passion text, Christ warns his mother in explicit detail of what she will see:

And my body, which the divinity Holy Spirit fashioned and assembled in your womb, you will see it particularly cut up, particularly broken up, particularly torn up, covered with bruises. It will be besmirched, covered with lumps, livid, beaten, drenched, particularly dripping with blood. (*Cantares de los mejicanos* n.d.:236r)

The Nahuatl playwright refers to a road to heaven rather than a door, even though he could have expressed the idea of a door in Nahuatl. The *Psalmodia christiana*'s songs for the Assumption of Mary declare that she opened the door to heaven (Sahagún 1583:72v–73r; 155r). But the songs for Easter twice state that Christ "opened the road to heaven for us" (Appendix, Text V). Gante's 1553 *Doctrina* explains that Christ "raised up for us the road to heaven" (Gante 1981:72r).

41   Where the Spanish Christ rejects his mother's argument as "a great harm," the Nahuatl Christ agrees with her that he will indeed suffer greatly. The idea of "harm" is here applied to Christ's torments, not to Mary's arguments; the Nahua author may not have understood line 41S:2's *el porque* as referring to her reasoning. Without contradicting his mother or commanding her that she must outlive him, the Nahuatl Christ explains the importance of her survival.

Miguel Pérez's life of the Virgin describes her on Holy Saturday as she sat in her chamber awaiting her son's resurrection "like a firm pillar and support of the Catholic Church, supporting with sure firmness the holy Christian faith" (Pérez 1549:34r).

The Nahua playwright expanded Izquierdo's "faith" to the Spanish phrase "holy Catholic faith" and paired this phrase with a Nahuatl explanation, "sacred belief."

13. The crucifixion, with Mary and John. Title page of the *Psalmodia christiana*, 1583. Courtesy of the John Carter Brown Library at Brown University.

42   Both Christs appeal to their mother's sympathy, asking her to share in their ordeal since no one else will do so. They somewhat overstate their plight, since the Gospel according to John (19:25–26) places at the foot of the cross not only Mary but her sister Mary the wife of Cleophas, Mary Magdalene, and a disciple conventionally identified as John himself.

Woodcuts of the crucifixion printed in sixteenth-century Mexico typically show Mary and John on either side of the cross (Figure 13). This

14. The crucifixion, with Mary, John, and Mary Magdalene. Mural painting in the Franciscan friary, Tepeapulco, Hidalgo. Christ's head is partially obscured by a later layer of ornamentation. Photograph by the author.

arrangement was so familiar that the artist who drew a picture of a chapel for the *Florentine Codex* depicted within the building's entrance a crucifix flanked by two figures recognizable as Mary and John (Sahagún 1979:XI, 243r). The crucifixion scene in Figure 17 also has this format. Another common arrangement was to depict Mary Magdalene at the foot of the cross while Mary and John stand to either side. A native artist's painting based on a woodcut of this type survives in the Franciscan friary at Tepeapulco (Figure 14).

43 The Nahuatl Mary's four opening lines mirror the beginning of Christ's previous speech to her (41N:1–5). No such resemblance exists between the corresponding Spanish stanzas. And nowhere else in the play does one character repeat another's words so closely. By echoing her son's words, Mary expresses solidarity and agreement with him. What makes this parallelism even more striking is that the Spanish Mary here continues to complain of her own suffering.

The Nahua playwright had already used the loanword *sentencia* in line 36N:10, but he apparently did not understand 43S:3's *definida* 'definitive, definite,' a word that Westmoreland determined to have been as yet relatively new in Spanish. The phrase *sentencia definitiva* was, though, in use in the colonial legal system, where it referred to a ruling by the Real Audiencia following an appeal (Kellogg 1995:41). The playwright assimilated *definida* to a Spanish word more familiar to him, *divinidad* 'divinity.' Nahuatl does not use the phonemes /f/, /v/, or /d/, and a Nahuatl speaker would not have distinguished between /f/ and /v/. This gave him the phrase *sentencia divinidad*, which he incorporated into his text. He paired it with *tlatocatlanahuatili* 'sovereign command,' a compound he may well have concocted as a Nahuatl parallel for the Spanish phrase.

The Nahuatl Mary goes on to predict Christ's flagellation. Having already shown empathy with him by repeating his words, she now displays prescience of the Passion, describing an event that the play has not previously mentioned. Mary here predicts that he will be given more than four hundred lashes. In the Nahuatl numerical system, four hundred was a unit of counting that also bore the figurative meaning "a great many."

44 The Spanish Mary tries one last time to place conditions on Christ's death, asking that he not die a vile and lowly (*abiltada*) death. Mary in the Tulane *despedimiento* makes a similar request, asking that Christ not die a shameful death in public view (Appendix, Text I). But Mary in the Nahuatl play does not say anything along these lines. She has ceased to pose counter-arguments and is focusing instead on a show of solidarity. She utters encouragements, hoping that her son will bear up well under his sufferings and that they go according to his will.

With the end of this first dialogue at hand, the Nahua playwright may have considered it necessary that the interlocutors resolve their differences and reach an agreement. His characters have throughout their dialogue adopted a less argumentative and more deferential tone toward one another than that exhibited by their Spanish models. It is now high time that these noble and sacred personages stop bickering. He represents their agreement via Mary's repetition of Christ's words, her prophecy, and her encouraging comments at the end. In this way the dialectical process of their interaction is completed and equilibrium is established. Mother and son are now prepared for the sudden and unexpected arrival of the angel.

In the Spanish play, mother and son are still disagreeing at the end of this first dialogue. The angel and the letters will play a mediating role, bringing Mary and Christ closer together and convincing her to stop protesting quite so much. In this way the play follows the classic model of Western drama, which goes back to ancient Greek tragedy; the dramatic action is driven by a conflict, resolved at the end into winners and losers (Schechner 1985:133). Though Izquierdo's drama is hardly action-packed, he represents the interaction between Christ and Mary as more of a clash of wills—with Mary the loser—than does his Nahua interpreter.

45 Angels were such familiar figures in Nahua-Christian texts and art that this figure, dressed no doubt in flowing robes and feathery artificial wings, would be recognizable to the audience as an angel. The word *angel* appears as a loanword in Molina's dictionary and was used in civil documents by 1555 (Molina 1970:10v; Karttunen and Lockhart 1976:59). Angels were sometimes also called by such titles as the nobles of heaven or the nephews of Christ.

Some Nahuatl texts associate angels with birds, specifically tropical birds such as quetzals and troupials. Though bird symbolism was associated with angels in the Old World as well, in the Nahua context this related the celestial beings directly to an indigenous complex of beliefs regarding the souls of the heroic dead, those who died in battle or sacrifice. These inhabited the heaven of the sun and took on the forms of tropical birds, spending their time singing praises to their solar lord and descending to earth to suck nectar from flowers (Sahagún 1950–82:III, 47; López Austin 1980:I, 384). The associations between angels and tropical birds are particularly strong in song texts, as in the *Psalmodia* and in some of the *Cantares mexicanos* (Bierhorst 1985; Burkhart 1992c).

Angels frequently appeared on the Nahuatl stage. At least one angel is cast in each of the five scripts thought to be copies of sixteenth-century compositions, as well as the early seventeenth-century "Comedia de los Reyes" (Horcasitas 1974; Ravicz 1970; Cornyn and McAfee 1944). During an enactment of the Annunciation performed in Tlaxcala in 1538, the archangel Gabriel was lowered to the stage on a platform, accompanied by several other angels (Las Casas 1967:I, 332; Horcasitas 1974:240). The

Tlaxcala *cabildo* records for 1555 authorize the purchase of wings, yellow hair, and other adornments for angel costumes for use in the celebration of Corpus Christi (Lockhart et al. 1986:94–95).

The nineteenth-century bibliographer Beristáin de Souza describes a Nahuatl Annunciation drama that he claims was in the library of the Tlatelolco friary and was authored by fray Luis de Fuensalida (1947:II, 309). In this play, the archangel Gabriel presents to Mary several letters from the fathers in Limbo, in which they beg her to accept the incarnation of Christ. Fuensalida was one of the famous Franciscan Twelve who reached Mexico in 1524. He left for Spain in 1535 and never returned to the colony. The participation of the Holy Fathers in the Annunciation recalls Saint Bernard of Clairvaux's fourth *Homily* (Bernard of Clairvaux and Amadeus of Lausanne 1979:53). If Beristáin's observations are correct, this lost script is a very early Nahuatl dramatic piece and one that establishes a precedent on the Nahuatl stage for the Holy Wednesday drama's letters from Limbo.

Angels were often associated with Mary in texts and art, in both the Old World and the New. Representations of the Annunciation showed her with the archangel Gabriel. Depictions of the Assumption surrounded her with angels. The apocryphal Gospel of James, source of the medieval tradition that Mary was brought up in the Hebrew temple, reported that as a child she received her food from the hand of an angel (James 1955:42). According to the widely used thirteenth-century hagiographic compendium called the *Golden Legend*, Mary "was visited daily of angels" (Voragine 1900:V, 103).

The *Psalmodia christiana* comments on Mary's familiarity with angels, stating that she "was not at all disturbed when she saw that Saint Gabriel was calling to her, for she often used to see angels" (Sahagún 1583:50r). Similarly, the John Carter Brown Library manuscript has Mary at this moment show surprise not at the angel's presence but at his adulatory greeting. She says to herself, "What are these words? Angels come all the time, but I have never heard such words" (*Doctrina* n.d.:105v).

In the stage directions, the Nahua author refers to the letters with the Spanish word *cartas*, as does Izquierdo. *Carta* was in use among Nahuas by 1565 (Karttunen and Lockhart 1976:61). The practice of sending letters was well known, and Nahuatl words such as *amatl* 'paper' or *amatlahcuilolli* 'paper-written thing' were used for them.

The letters bear seals depicting the five wounds that Christ will receive when he is crucified: holes in each hand and foot from the nails that attach them to the cross and the opening in his side from the lance of a Roman soldier. In Christian symbolism, the number five stands for these five wounds (Ferguson 1954:277). For Nahuas, the number five already represented the four directions and the center, a directional quincunx that coincided nicely with the markings placed on Christ's body. Five symbolized completeness and centrality but also excess. These associations were appropriate to the Passion, through which Christ set the world to rights while undergoing debilitating ordeals that left him bruised, broken, and drained of blood.

The Franciscan emblem used in the sixteenth century consists of a shield adorned with the five bleeding wounds, an allusion to Saint Francis's bearing of these wounds, or stigmata (from the Latin *stigma*, meaning a mark or brand). This shield was frequently used as a decorative motif in the relief sculptures and murals that Nahua artisans placed on the buildings they constructed for the Franciscans. Indigenous artists often depicted the wounds as beads, using the symbol that represented jade, with liquid streaming from them (Figure 15). This motif establishes a metaphor between Christ's bleeding wounds and the ideas of preciousness and precious liquid—the blood of sacrifice (Reyes-Valerio 1978:272–77). Atrium crosses, the stone sculptures placed at the center of church patios, often depict these wounds along with other symbols of the Passion (Figure 16). For the play's audience, then, the signs on the letters would be recognizable symbols associated with Christ, Saint Francis, and sacrificial bloodletting.

The Spanish text calls the wounds *llagas*; the Nahua playwright translated this as "holes." The Nahuatl term *coyonqui* 'hole, cavity' was not normally associated with wounds to the human body. Molina's multiple glosses for the Spanish words *herir*, *lamer*, *lastimar*, *llagar*, and their derivatives demonstrate that the Nahuas had a rich vocabulary for describing injuries of various sorts (Molina 1970:70v, 76v, 77r, 79r). Conversely, *coyonqui* and related terms designate a wide assortment of openings, fissures, hollows, and cavities, none of which entail the piercing of human flesh (Campbell 1985:82).

"Hole" suggests a permanent fissure, a structural feature such as an opening bored in an image of wood or stone, as opposed to a fleshly injury that will either close up and heal or become infected and putrid. In the iconography to which Nahuas were exposed, these wounds were indeed permanently open and frequently bleeding—Christ's body did not behave like ordinary human flesh. To conceive of the wounds as holes was, thus, an appropriate and descriptive analysis. However, it diverts attention from the painful sensations and frightful appearance associated with wounds to mortal bodies. It was precisely these emotional responses that European

15. An angel bears the Franciscan shield with the five bleeding stigmata. The crown of thorns surmounts the central wound; the other four are represented by the glyphic sign for jade. Relief sculpture at San Andrés Calpan, Puebla. Photograph by the author.

devotional practice sought to evoke through verbal and pictorial representations of Christ's wounds.

The designation of Christ's wounds, and those borne by stigmatics, as holes was fairly standard in sixteenth-century Nahuatl. It appears two other times in the manuscript that contains the play (110v, 204r). Gante's *doctrina* tells how Mary kissed the "holes" (*cocoyonqui*) in Christ's body when it was taken down from the cross (1981:141v). In the *Psalmodia christiana*, the resurrected Christ shows his "holes" to the apostles (Appendix, Text V). Marginal quotations indicate that this passage is based on a Latin hymn that uses the word *vulnera* 'wounds' (Nebrija 1549:34v). In the *Sermones en mexicano* (n.d.:218), Christ arises from the sepulcher with all of his injuries healed; the five holes no longer look like wounds:

16. The atrium cross at the Franciscan church at Tepeapulco, Hidalgo. Now set into the outer wall of the church, the cross originally stood in the center of the church-yard. Photograph by the author.

All that was left was his holes in five places, in his hands, in his side, in his feet. They were not like wounds. They were just like amethysts. They shimmered greatly, they shone greatly, as did all the rest of his body.

The *Psalmodia*'s account of the stigmatization of Saint Francis refers to the wounds as *plagas*, the Latin term from which Spanish *llaga* derives, but they are referred to in Nahuatl as Christ's "insignia" and as his five "holes," and are described as being more precious and attractive than precious stones (Sahagún 1583:174v–75r). These two passages also provide textual correlates for the iconographic association of the wounds with precious stones.

The Nahuatl angel's greeting to Mary is more polite and formal than that of the Spanish angel. His speech, like the stage directions that refer to his arrival, makes frequent use of the verb prefix *hual-*, which indicates that the action is performed while coming hither, or in this direction. He speaks, appropriately, as someone who has just arrived from elsewhere.

46   Limbo, mentioned here for the first time, is a place that Nahuas heard about in two principal contexts. One is Holy Week and Easter. Several lengthy Nahuatl accounts of the Passion and Resurrection make no mention of Christ's descent into hell, but a number of texts do describe it (e.g., Appendix, Texts III–V). The other and more common context is the teaching of the basic Christian catechism. The Credo, or Apostles' Creed, which all were expected to know by heart, states that Christ descended to hell and on the third day revived from among the dead. The fourteen Articles of Faith, also included in this basic instruction, state that Christ descended to hell, or to Limbo, and removed the souls of the Holy Fathers, who were there awaiting his coming.

Nahuatl versions of the Articles of Faith provided varying degrees of detail. The personages in Limbo were called by the Spanish title *santos padres* 'holy fathers' or by Nahuatl approximations. Hell was usually called by the Nahuatl name for the underworld, *mictlan* 'place of the dead' or 'among the dead'; the Spanish *infierno* 'hell' appears in some texts. Limbo is specified by the Spanish term. It is one of the few Christian religious concepts that had no widely used Nahuatl equivalent.

The 1565 *doctrina* by fray Domingo de la Anunciación provides this exegesis on the Article of Faith:

When [Christ] died, he descended to the place of the dead, hell. He went to bring forth the spirits of the good fathers, who were waiting for him there. And it is neces-

17. The harrowing of hell. Painting by an indigenous artist in the Franciscan open chapel at Tizatlan, Tlaxcala. Drawing by Ellen Cesarski.

sary here that you consider that our lord Jesus Christ did not rescue only those who were born after he came here in the world, but also those who were born earlier, when he made our first father, our first mother and those whom they gave birth to, all the time until the world will end. He rescued all of them with his precious death.

Heaven lay always closed up, all the time before the rescuer came, which is when he opened it. Therefore, long ago, the good ones, God's chosen ones, when they died in his grace, in the loving of our lord God, if they had not yet completed their penances, they always went to Purgatory, and afterwards they remained there within the earth, in a place called Limbo.

There in the place of darkness, the place of gloom they were enclosed, there they were waiting all the time until the true rescuer would come, so that he would rescue them and open heaven for them, where he would take them. (Anunciación 1565:24v–25r)

I know of only two sixteenth-century depictions of the harrowing of hell from the Nahua area. One is a mural painting by a native artist in the Franciscan open chapel at Tizatlan, Tlaxcala (Figure 17). Of the hell-mouth tradition, it shows Adam and Eve, already rescued from the beast's maw, standing to the left of the scene while Christ reaches toward those who remain inside.

The second is one of a series of Passion events depicted in a scene representing a Franciscan friar preaching to an indigenous audience with the use of pictures (Figure 18). This image, of the "architectural" variety, shows Christ extracting his friends from the doorway of a brick or stone

Spūs Dūi fupme: Euangelizare paupib'mifitme Efa.61

18. A Franciscan friar preaches of the Passion to a Nahua audience. Native art-ist's drawing in the manuscript of fray Gerónimo de Mendieta's *Historia eclesiástica indiana*. JGI 1120, Joaquín García Icazbalceta Manuscript Collection. Courtesy of the Benson Latin American Collection, University of Texas at Austin General Libraries.

edifice. The drawing, probably done by an indigenous artist, illustrates the original manuscript of fray Gerónimo de Mendieta's *Historia eclesiástica indiana*. An engraving of the same scene was published in Italy in 1579 by the Mexican Franciscan Diego Valadés, in his book *Rhetorica christiana* (Valadés 1989:478); both were probably based on the same source. In Valadés's engraving the wooden posts supporting the canopy above the pulpit partially obscure the harrowing of hell scene, while in the Mendieta drawing the artist depicts the canopy such that all the Passion pictures are fully visible.

47 The present mentioned in 47S:2 refers to the implements of the Passion which the letter-writers send to Mary. The Nahua playwright does not mention this present here, perhaps because he has a different strategy for bringing these objects onstage—his angel does not actually deliver these gifts.

48 The Nahuatl Mary identifies the people in Limbo as ancestral figures. Mary's "our" may be read as including only herself and her son, as she was believed to be descended from the old rulers, prophets, and patriarchs (e.g., Bautista 1606:464–65), or it may be given a more inclusive interpretation. Nahuatl texts occasionally do claim a more general "we" in this context. The 1588 manuscript of Sahagún's sermons has Christ descend to gather the souls of *qualtin totavan* 'the good ones, our fathers' or 'our good fathers' (1588:113v); the first-person prefix here substitutes for the usual usage of the generic *te-* 'someone's, people's.' The same construction appears in the Resurrection text by the play manuscript's friar-compiler (203r). The *Psalmodia christiana* calls these figures "[Christ's] precious ones, our fathers" (Appendix, Text V). If the Limbo inmates can be called "our" fathers, rather than an ambiguous "some people's," it implies that "we" are descended not from the damned but from those whom Christ rescued.

Mary, like Christ, bore a special relationship to the prophets and patriarchs because her role in the redemption was also, according to Christian interpretations of the Old Testament, firmly inscribed in the ancient prophecies. An account of Mary's life in the John Carter Brown Library manuscript tells how, when at age fifteen she declared her intention to remain unwed, the astonished priests said, "Perhaps she is the one of whom the prophets said, 'a maiden will give birth to the child of God'" (*Doctrina* n.d.:104v). The prophets and patriarchs are the first saints to greet Mary upon her assumption into heaven (*Doctrina* n.d.:60v–61r).

49 While the Spanish Mary professes bewilderment at the significance of the letters, the Nahuatl Mary displays a prescient understanding of the meaning of the wound symbols: precious signs that signify torment—the Nahuatl word for the Passion.

50 The Nahua author did not translate the first line of the Spanish stanza. Izquierdo's script gives no stage directions indicating how the five implements of the Passion are to be delivered. I suspect from this line that he assumed small reproductions of these objects would be wrapped inside the letters or depicted on them. The two letters that are larger than the others may be those containing the miniature cross and column.

51 The Nahua playwright has been using the loanword *cartas* to refer to the letters; this word was in use among Nahuas by 1565 (Karttunen and Lockhart 1976:61). Here he switches to the native word *amatl* 'paper.'

The subsequent stage directions indicate that in Izquierdo's play, Mary was to read the letters aloud. In the Nahuatl play, the content of the letters is to be announced to the audience by a child. That this child is to be dressed as an angel is indicated by the directions for the individual letters, which give "angel" as the speaker. This innovation maintains the play's structure as a dialogue: instead of launching into a prolonged monologue, Mary is addressed by another speaker, who acts as a representative of the letters' senders.

The Nahua author deals with the presentation of the Passion implements through another creative staging technique. Instead of having these objects enclosed in the letters, they are to be carried onstage at the appropriate moments by five other children costumed as angels. In this way the objects can be suddenly and dramatically revealed to the audience, as each child steps forth from behind a door or curtain. Larger versions of the objects can be used, whether three-dimensional reproductions or pictures. All five implements may be kept in the audience's view, something that would be difficult with five small objects or pictures that Mary had to handle by herself.

The addition of these six little boys to the cast also allowed a higher level of participation. Nahuatl theater was a theater of schoolboys. The author, himself a former schoolboy and possibly a former or current teacher, may have wished to allow as many children as possible to have a part.

The Mexico-born Franciscan spokesman Diego Valadés mentions in his *Rhetorica christiana* that the friars would place children dressed as an-

19. The Mass of Saint Gregory. Mural in the Franciscan friary at Tepeapulco, Hidalgo. A later painting of the Franciscan rope belt partially obscures the upper portion of the painting. Photograph by the author.

gels around the altar when they administered communion to indigenous people (1989:432–33). The Jesuit chronicler Pérez de Ribas records that native children were dressed as angels to march in the Holy Week processions from the Jesuits' church of San Gregorio in Mexico. This was "a favor that their parents greatly appreciate" (1645:737).

In these stage directions, the Nahua author refers to the implements of the Passion as "passions," using the loanword *passion*. In the characters' speeches he never uses this word but always expresses the concept in Nahuatl. His own use of the word is unorthodox. The word "Passion" properly applies to Christ's entire ordeal, not to the individual episodes of his torment nor to the implements employed therein. Since Classical Nahuatl did not use plural forms for inanimate objects or abstract concepts, a Nahua could easily fail to distinguish between a list of individual torments, such as were recounted in tellings of the Passion, and the entire ordeal that they collectively comprised. The playwright goes a step beyond this part-for-whole synecdoche, making a metonymic substitution of the implements for the suffering they caused. And, as with the pictures of Christ's wounds, he designates them as precious objects.

Nahua artists carved representations of the Passion implements on stone atrium crosses, such as that shown in Figure 16, and painted them in murals. The Mass of Saint Gregory, in which Christ appears surrounded by these insignia, is depicted in at least one mural painting (Figure 19) and one of the rare surviving featherwork pictures (*Mexico: Splendors of Thirty Centuries* 1990:258–60). Some murals and relief carvings show angels bearing these objects, a motif that may have suggested the use of angel-impersonators to carry them in the play (Figures 20 and 21).

The last line of these stage directions appears in the Nahuatl play in Spanish, presumably copied from Izquierdo's script. The Houghton Library imprint lacks the words *vee y* 'looks at and.' In place of the Spanish text's *dize assi* 'it (or she) says as follows,' the Nahua scribe wrote what looks like the Spanish word *diez* 'ten.' The scribe may have conflated the sounds of the two Spanish words, or he may inadvertently have misspelled *dize*. The line is in any case superfluous: the Nahua playwright has altered the performance such that Mary does not read the letters aloud.

52 The Nahuatl Adam gives three names for his place of imprisonment. The first, "house of torments," incorporates the Nahuatl term used for Christ's Passion and its component tortures. In this way Adam draws a parallel between what he and the other inmates of Limbo are undergoing and what Christ will undergo in the process of freeing them. To characterize the Limbo of the Holy Fathers as a place of torment contradicts Christian teachings. Locked in the darkness and deprived of the sight of God, the Holy Fathers had to wait patiently for a long time, but they were not in pain.

"The place where people are tied" (*teilpiloyan*) is one term that Nahuas called jails or prisons, including those that were in use during colonial times (Las Casas 1967:II, 385; Sahagún 1583:71r, 142v, 217r; *Códice Osuna* 1947:256). Thus, this word corresponds to the Spanish Adam's character-

20. An angel carries the crown of thorns. Relief sculpture, posa chapel of the Annunciation, Huexotzingo, Puebla. Photograph by the author.

ization of his abode. Preconquest-style prisons were dark houses with small doors, within which people were kept inside wooden cages. Prisoners were lowered into the cages through a trap door at the top. According to Durán, they suffered for lack of food and water. These jails were also called *teilpilcalli* 'house where people are tied' or *cuauhcalli* 'wooden house.' Mexico's was located at the site of the royal granaries, or *petlacalco* 'place of the mat houses (or coffers)'; this name was extended to apply to the prison. According to the *Florentine Codex*, this was where "they used to tie up, they used to enclose the wrongdoers." Since in Nahuatl criminals were called by the same term used in Christian contexts for sinners, this description could as easily apply to the Holy Fathers shut up in Limbo because of sin (Durán 1967:I, 184; Las Casas 1967:II, 385; Sahagún 1950–82:VIII, 42, 44).

21. Angels bearing instruments of the Passion (the lance, the sponge, and the ladder) flank a representation of Christ's IHS monogram, itself surmounted by a cross. Mural in the Franciscan cloister at Huexotzingo, Puebla. Photograph by the author.

22. Four prisoners languish in the jailhouse of preconquest Mexico, as depicted in the *Florentine Codex* (Book VIII, f. 27r). The prisoners' decorated mantles suggest noble rank. Reprinted with permission from fray Bernardino de Sahugún, *Historia general de las cosas de Nueva España, Códice florentino*. Facsimile of the *Codex Florentinus* of the Biblioteca Medicea Laurenciana, published by the Archivo General de la Nación, México, 1979.

Illustrations of Mexico's old prison, such as that shown in Figure 22, depict men confined in cages so low that they cannot sit up straight. The interior of the cages is colored dark gray or dark green to indicate darkness (Sahagún 1979:VIII, 27r, 39v; Durán 1967:I, plate 29). At the time the play was written, a hospital stood where this jail had been (Durán 1967:I, 184).

53 Nahuatl catechisms and confession manuals provide models for oral confession in which the penitent begins by saying *nehhuapol*, literally 'big me'; the suffix *-pol* carries a sense of deprecation or contempt (e.g., Gante 1981:97v, 148v; Molina 1565:5r; Molina 1569:19r). The Nahuatl Adam, by twice uttering this word at the beginning of this passage, frames what follows as a confession of his wrongdoing, representing himself as a penitent seeking absolution.

The Nahua playwright repeats the doctrinally incorrect identification of the fruit as pertaining to the tree of life. From Izquierdo's text he takes the non-standard attribution of Adam's sin to gluttony. The Nahuatl word he uses for this sin was a standard choice for translating the Spanish *gula* 'gluttony,' but friars customarily described Adam's sin as one not of carnal overindulgence but of pride.

54 The Nahuatl Adam again characterizes his abode as a place of misery. Not only are the prisoners confined, but they are tormented with afflictions: the verb here is the same as is used for Christ's Passion, but with "afflictions" rather than generic "things" as the object. The reiteration of compound verbs indicating that they are lying down while performing the various actions suggests both a state of exhaustion and confinement in a small space—like that of the prison depicted in Figure 22.

55 Adam in the Spanish calls Mary a "font of piety" and "your goodness." The Nahua playwright turns these epithets into a brief discourse on Mary's role in the redemption. Because she is so good, it is from her that the compassion—that is, Christ and his redeeming work—have emerged, like a river flowing from its source, the river image no doubt suggested by Izquierdo's *fuente*. The Biblioteca Nacional prayer cycle refers to Christ as a spring or fountain of life, with Mary as its vessel (*Santoral en mexicano* n.d.:12r, 13r).

The Nahuatl Adam asks that Mary pardon him because of his "confusion." This term was used in Nahua-Christian literature for the errors of heretics and idolaters. Adam's statement could be read as an allusion to his own non- or pre-Christian status, under which, like Nahuas before the friars came, he did not understand that he was doing wrong.

The Nahuatl Mary has already yielded to her son and accepted his fate. But the characters in Limbo nevertheless entreat her to do so, as the Nahua playwright continues to incorporate the sense of the Spanish text into his own work. Their entreaties reiterate the necessity of Christ's actions and relate the redemption to their own situation. Given indigenous models of discourse as a scattering of precious jewels rather than a linearly organized argument, such redundancy would not have been seen as interfering with the progress of the play's action.

56 The Nahua author indicates with marginal notes when the boys bearing the Passion insignia are to come onstage. For Adam to be associated with the cross makes sense given the symbolic link between the tree of

Eden and Christ's place of death. Christ was the "new Adam" who reverses Adam's sin and initiates a new era of human history. One of the Spanish dramas resembling Izquierdo's had Adam himself appear on stage carrying a cross; another had Adam send a letter sealed with a cross (Rouanet 1979:II, 418, 394).

The letters from Limbo frequently employ a verb prefix that indicates that the action is performed while "going," or moving in an outward direction. This is the opposite of the "coming hither" prefix favored by the visiting angel. The use of this prefix makes the letters sound, in Nahuatl, as if the speakers are indeed far away, sending their words forth toward Mary.

Adam finishes with an "and this" statement deferring to the second letter-writer. In Nahuatl texts, David is sometimes given the Spanish title *rey* 'king,' as the Nahuatl Adam does here.

David's kinship to Mary was a key link between Christ and the Old Testament prophecies. One oft-cited prophecy of Isaiah (11:1-2), interpreted as alluding to the birth of the Messiah, states: "And there shall come forth a rod out of the stem of Jesse, and a Branch shall grow out of his roots, and the Spirit of the Lord shall rest upon him." Jesse was David's father. Mary's genealogy was often represented in the form of the Jesse Tree: a tree grows from the body of Jesse, with other ancestors distributed along its branches. According to Motolinia, a representation of this scene was painted on the open chapel in Tlaxcala in 1539 (1979:65).

Sahagún's sermon for the festival of Saint Joseph says of Mary that God "made her from a very great lineage, that of the great sovereign and great saint David" (1563:98r). The authors of the *Psalmodia christiana* explain the Isaiah prophecy in their text for the festival of Saint Ann, describing Mary as a stalk that sprouted from the trunk of Jesse's lineage (Sahagún 1583:122v–23r). The same text also renders into Nahuatl this liturgical chant regarding the birth of Mary: "Today was born the favored one, Saint Mary, who is always a maiden, who came from the lineage of David" (Sahagún 1583:171v). The Nahua lineage, or *tlacamecayotl* 'human rope,' was not a corporate descent group but a cognatic descent line along which people traced relationships to ancestors and other kin (Kellogg 1986:106–11). For Mary to come from David's *tlacamecayotl* meant that she could trace her ancestry to him through male and/or female links.

57 The angel reassures Mary that the cross will bring joy as well as sorrow, the Nahuatl text explaining just what these positive results will be. The paired terms referring to goodness in line 57N:8 appear as a gloss for *virtud* 'virtue' in Molina's dictionary (1970:117v).

58   The Spanish script has the word *fin* 'end' at the end of the angel's part and two of the letters. The word was not meant to be spoken.

The Nahuatl angel encourages Mary to endure the upcoming sorrows. By using the verb employed for Christ's Passion, he indicates that her sufferings will be of that sort. He goes on to utter a vague prediction, with no basis in the Spanish text, of wondrous future events. The author may have been thinking of Christ's resurrection, ascension, or Mary's own assumption.

In line 2N:13, the Nahua playwright translated the Spanish *licencia* 'permission' as *motenahuatiltzin* 'your command,' a form consistent with Molina's glosses for *licencia* (1970:78r). This time he copied the word *licencia* into his text, though once again pairing it with a Nahuatl word for sending off a messenger or bidding farewell to someone. Karttunen and Lockhart found *licencia* as a loanword in a Nahuatl text from 1551 (1976:58).

The Nahuatl Mary bids the angel a brief farewell. This is the only place in the parallel play texts where the Nahuatl playwright introduced a character's turn at speech with no counterpart in the Spanish original. For Mary to let such an honorable guest depart without uttering a word may have seemed too flagrant a breach of Nahua customs for polite behavior.

59   Like Adam, the Nahuatl David begins by politely greeting Mary, even though his Spanish counterpart launches directly into his plea. Izquierdo here characterizes the Holy Fathers' condition as one of sorrow or suffering (*dolor*). Izquierdo too, then, although to a lesser extent than his Nahua interpreter, shows a tendency to depart from the official story in order to represent Limbo as a place of suffering. His Valencian predecessor Miguel Pérez (1549:28v) has Christ speak of freeing the Holy Fathers from the "tearful prison" where they sigh, counting the days of their "miserable exile." The two *despedimiento*-related dramas in the *Códice de autos viejos* allow Adam to speak of his sorrow or pain (*pena*), as in Izquierdo's line 52S:4 (Rouanet 1979:II, 395, 419). Emphasis on the Holy Fathers' discomfort served the narrative purpose of lending urgency to Christ's rescue mission.

60   The Nahua author calls Limbo by a pair of terms used also in fray Domingo de la Anunciación's book, as quoted above (stanza 46). His description of Limbo as a dark place is directly supported by the Spanish text. The term *tlayohuayan* 'in the place and/or time of darkness' was used in Nahua-Christian literature in reference not only to dark underworlds but also to the time before the creation of the world, the time before the coming of Mary or Christ, the time before the coming of Christianity to the Nahuas, the state of idolatry or paganhood, and the state of sin. It is also applied to Limbo in the *Psalmodia* (Appendix, Text V).

61 The verb phrase in 61N:1 literally means "we go to leave ourselves with you." This form does not number among Molina's glosses for the Spanish *confiar* 'confide, entrust' (1970:29r), which Izquierdo uses, but it effectively expresses the desired idea.

62 The Nahuatl David asks for help in getting out. He does not, as the Spanish David does both here and in 60S:4, speak as though Mary herself could free the prisoners. In this sense the Nahua author (and/or his Franciscan advisor) is more circumspect than Izquierdo in regard to doctrinal correctness.

63 David, himself a former king of the Jews, presents Mary with the crown of thorns with which Christ's mockers will crown him king of the Jews. David was considered a historical type, or model, for Christ, David's temporal kingdom standing for Christ's spiritual and eternal one. David, like Christ, was born in humble circumstances. He won his kingdom due to his defeat of the Philistine champion Goliath, an event taken to symbolize Christ's defeat of Lucifer.

When the archangel Gabriel spoke to Mary regarding her son's incarnation, he told her: "the Lord God shall give unto him the throne of his father David" (Luke 1:32); similar passages appear in a sermon of Sahagún's (1563:94r) and in the *Psalmodia christiana* (Sahagún 1583:57r). Another of Sahagún's sermons urges native rulers to view David as a model for benevolent rulership (1563:77r).

Three of the four Evangelists mention that a crown of thorns was placed on Christ's head (Matthew 27:29, Mark 15:17, John 19:2). The crowning with the crown of thorns was one of the five "sorrowful mysteries" contemplated in the course of praying the Rosary (Anunciación 1565:78r; Anunciación 1575:258).

The Nahua playwright calls the crown of thorns *xocohuitzcorona*, a compound of an indigenous plant name, *xocohuitztli*, and the Spanish and Latin word *corona* 'crown.' *Huitztli*, the Nahuatl word for "thorn," is the common element in all Nahuatl names for the crown of thorns, which otherwise vary considerably. In pre-Christian Nahua ritual, thorns were employed in penitential bloodletting and served as a symbol of such penances. This symbolism is appropriate to the context of Christ's Passion.

In Old World Christian symbolism, the thorn stands for grief, tribulation, or sin; sins puncture and lacerate the soul. After Adam and Eve sinned, God cursed the earth so that it would bring forth thorns and thistles (Genesis 3:18). These thorns were associated with those in the crown of thorns, which Christ wore while expiating that original sin (Ferguson 1954:49; Marrow 1979:100).

This is not quite the same thing as Christ engaging in ritual penances for the sake of people's rescue. It is doubtful that many Nahuas were aware of this connection to Adam and Eve. The text for Sexagesima (the second Sunday before Lent) in the other native-hand section of the play's manuscript does state that the cursed earth brought forth thorns and thistles (48r). But both the *Psalmodia christiana* and one of Sahagún's sermons describe the postlapsarian flora as thistles and datura (*tlapatl*) rather than thorns and thistles (Sahagún 1583:34v; 1563:29v). The *Psalmodia* mentions thorns in the translation of a liturgical chant, based on the Song of Solomon (2:2), that calls Mary a "lily among thorns," an allusion to her immaculate conception (Ferguson 1954:41). The *Psalmodia* version says, "All the children of Adam are considered to be thorns, thistles," while only Mary is a flower (Sahagún 1583:224v). Fray Juan de Mijangos's *Espejo Divino* has a similar passage in a prayer to Mary (1607:312); the figure also appears in fray Juan Bautista's *sermonario* (1606:473). Nahuas would not necessarily interpret such metaphors in terms of relative moral purity.

Xocohuitztli compounds the term *huitztli* with *xocotl* 'hog plum,' a type of fruit and also a generic category for sour- or acidic-tasting fruits. *Xocohuitztli* is identified by Anderson and Dibble (in Sahagún 1950–82:IV, 45) as cardoon; they cite Santamaría (1959:641), who assigns the botanical name *Bromelia pingüin* L. (which is not cardoon) and describes it as "a plant of tropical regions, which grows to about a meter in height and produces leaves similar to those of the pineapple."

One variety of *xocohuitztli* was called *tlacatecoloxocohuitztli*. *Tlacatecolo(tl)* is the term used in Christian contexts for demons and in non-Christian contexts for a type of sorcerer. This plant had ritual uses. According to Sahagún's ethnographic informants, on the day 4 Wind in the 260-day calendar, a day associated with sorcery, people would stuff their smokeholes with this plant as a protection against sorcerers (Sahagún 1950–82:IV, 45). During the festival of Tititl, youths would try to pelt women with bags filled with vegetation or shredded paper; the women would defend themselves by brandishing *tlacatecoloxocohuitztli* plants (Sahagún 1950–82:II,

23. The crown of thorns is placed on Christ's head. Woodcut in fray Melchior Vargas's trilingual *doctrina* of 1576, f. 18v. Courtesy of the Benson Latin American Collection, University of Texas at Austin General Libraries.

158). A plant thought to protect people from malevolence might be considered an appropriate accoutrement for Christ, the conqueror of demons.

Beginning in the thirteenth century, a tradition developed that the crown was not simply placed on Christ's head but pressed into it, in some versions piercing his brain or his eyes. Depictions show Christ's tormentors pulling on two staves in order to drive the thorns into Christ's skull (Marrow 1979:92–93, 141). One such image appears in the Augustinian friar Melchior de Vargas's 1575 *doctrina*, a trilingual text in Spanish, Nahuatl, and Otomi (Figure 23). A similar scene is included in the Passion sequence shown in Figure 18.

Fray Juan de Gaona's *Colloquios de la paz y tranquilidad christiana* describes how Christ's tormentors applied the thorns:

They placed very large thorns on his head, which entered in various places right into his skull. They cracked the back of his head, and they also they cracked his face [or eyes]. (1582:110r)

The onomatopoetic verb *tlatzini* describes explosive sounds like the cracking of an egg or a burst of thunder. Other Nahuatl texts also speak of Christ's skull being pierced by the thorns (Anunciación 1575:270; 1577: 60v; *Cantares de los mejicanos* n.d.:236r, 276r; León 1614:315v; *Sermones en mexicano* n.d.:189; *Miscelánea sagrada* n.d.:213v).

The Nahuatl playwright identifies Christ's tormentors as Jews (*Jodiosme*). For them to be so labeled is typical of Nahuatl Passion tracts, although frequently in shorter texts the involved parties are unidentified. The designation as Jews is made repeatedly in Escalona's Passion text, which, like the play, pairs "wicked ones" and "Jews" (Appendix, Text II). In no text have I seen the Holy Fathers in Limbo identified as Jews.

The *Psalmodia*'s authors make a consistent distinction between the Hebrew people of old, the chosen people whose experiences were thought to foreshadow many aspects of Christ's life and the Christian faith, and those of the time of Christ and the apostles. The former are called "the children of Israel" (*ipilhoa Israel*); stories about them are called signs or emblems of other stories the authors tell regarding Christ and the saints. These ancient folk function as positive and rather generalized ancestral figures. The latter are called Jews (*Iudiosme*). They are cast as nasty folk responsible for killing or attempting to kill various saints. They stone Saints Stephen, Matthew, and James the Less; they convince pagans to burn Saint Barnabas; they cast Saints Martha, Mary Magdalene, Lazarus, and others adrift in a boat, expecting them to drown. These Jews function as villains. Nahuas in Mexico would know that Spanish Christians derided Jews and that the Mexican Inquisition sought out and punished people accused of alleged Jewish practices.

In Izquierdo's text, the wicked people mock Christ "because he established a new Law." This line makes it clear that he considered the mockers to be Jews, who represent the old law of the Old Testament. The testament that Christ made with his followers was to supersede the old law of Moses. At the Last Supper, Christ said, according to John 13:34, "A new commandment I give unto you, That you love one another; as I have loved you, that you also love one another." Nahuatl texts translate this "new commandment" using the Nahuatl word for "command" (*nahuatilli*) or borrowing the Spanish word *testamento* (Sahagún 1574:30r, 30v; 1563:44r); the word *nahuatilli* is Molina's first gloss for the Spanish word *ley* 'law,' used here by Izquierdo (Molina 1970:77r). Thus, the Nahua playwright could easily have translated Izquierdo's line into his own text. Instead, he put very different words into David's letter.

Izquierdo makes a causal link between the mocking of Christ and his foundation of the new law; the Jews object to the replacement of their testament. In the Nahuatl text the sequence is temporal, not causal. After Christ is mocked by Jews, David and his companions, who have nothing to do with Christ's tormentors, will regain their riches and prosperity. This formulaic phrase could refer not only to precious goods but, metaphorically, to any favorable and desirable state of being.

Under Christ's "new law" the sin of Adam is atoned and the Holy Fathers are freed from Limbo and brought to heaven. But the reward in store for the Holy Fathers is not coterminous with life before the fall; David will go to heaven but he will not have restored to him the riches and renown he enjoyed as king of Judea. The Nahuatl text, though, implies a return to the past. Ancestral figures, imprisoned and tormented, will regain something that they have lost.

In 63N:6–7 David formally closes his letter. The Spanish David makes no departing statement, but it is possible that the playwright responded to the word *fin* printed in the Spanish text.

64   The Spanish Moses salutes Mary by alluding to two of the epithets from the Song of Solomon that were incorporated into liturgical chants as metaphors for her immaculate conception: the "enclosed garden" (*hortus conclusus*) of verse 4:12 and the "well of living waters" (*puteus aquarum viventium*) of verse 4:15.

Moses, the ancient leader to whom God imparted his old law, foreshadowed Christ as initiator of the new. The *Psalmodia christiana* states that Moses, in erecting the ancient tabernacle, signifies Christ, who erected the

Holy Church (Sahagún 1583:45r). In leading the Israelites out of captivity in Egypt, Moses foreshadowed Christ's role as savior; "The children of Israel fell into the hands of the Egyptian people. They were enslaved. And Moses became their rescuer" (Sahagún 1583:16r). The exodus from Egypt also foreshadowed the Nahuas' own recent rescue from the hands of the demons, according to a song in the *Psalmodia* (Sahagún 1583:148v–49r).

65 The Nahua playwright introduces flower imagery, suggested perhaps by Izquierdo's previous mention of the "enclosed garden." Christ as a flower blooming from Mary is an image grounded in the interpretation of Isaiah's prophecy, described above (stanza 56), and one which fit well with the flowery language of Nahuatl sacred song. The playwright, writing oratory rather than song, employs little such imagery. The statement here would indicate that the "remedy" of line 65N:5 is, metaphorically, a medicinal plant.

Izquierdo's reference to Mary's "great cloak" may allude to an iconographic tradition that depicted Mary as a central figure sheltering her worshippers under her cape. The John Carter Brown Library manuscript includes a text on how Mary's worshippers should prepare and adorn her mantle so that she will cover them with it when they die (*Doctrina* n.d.:98r–v). The play's friar-compiler includes in his Spanish text on the birth of Mary an exemplary anecdote telling how Mary, clad in a great mantle, appeared to a female devotee (206v–207r). The woman watches as all manner of vile and poisonous vermin crawl beneath the hem of the Virgin's garment. These creatures represent, the Virgin explains, human sinners who seek her assistance.

66 Moses' most direct links to the Passion of Christ came via two episodes recounted in the Old Testament. In one, God sends a plague of serpents to afflict the Israelites. When they repent their offenses, God orders Moses to make a brass serpent and put it up as a sign. Those bitten by the serpents will be cured if they gaze upon this contraption (Numbers 21:5–9). The comparison between the brass serpent and Christ, who cured people of sin when he was hung up on the cross, was made even in the Gospel of John (3:14). The *Psalmodia christiana* recounts the story of Moses' metal serpent, treating it as a symbol for Christ on the cross (Sahagún 1583:84r).

The second episode is that of Moses bringing forth water by striking a rock with his staff (Exodus 17:6, Numbers 20:11); this was interpreted as a symbolic foreshadowing of the piercing of Christ's side with the lance (Marrow 1979:166; Labriola and Smeltz 1990:125).

Izquierdo, however, assigned to his Moses not the cross or lance but the three nails. Called by the Spanish word *clavos* in the Nahuatl text's stage directions, the nails are referred to in Moses' Nahuatl letter in two ways. The first, "metal thorns," is the fourth of five glosses that Molina's dictionary gives for "iron nail," or *clavo de hierro* (1970:26r); it also appears for Christ's nails in León's sermons (1614:329r). Moses also compounds the word for metal with a verb meaning "to shoot arrows." A form of this compound is Molina's second gloss for *clavo de hierro*. Some other Nahuatl texts use this or related forms (Gante 1981:102r–102v, 133r, 139v; *Miscelánea sagrada* n.d.:216v; *Cantares de los mejicanos* n.d.:286r–288v). Molina's other entries are "metal instrument for planting things" (*tlatepuztoconi*), "metal bar," and "metal dart." All three are used to refer to Christ's nails, as are other constructions that speak of Christ being beaten or stricken with "metal stakes" or simply "with metal" (Escalona 1588:220r; Gante 1981:125v; Anunciación 1565:78v; Anunciación 1575:40, 271; 1577:61r; Sahagún 1563:50r, 1583:191r, 1588:109r; *Sermones y ejemplos* n.d.:349v, 352v; León 1611:34v, 1614:329r; *Sermones en mexicano* n.d.:195–96; *Cantares de los mejicanos* n.d.:286r).

Of the available alternatives, the playwright chose the two that are most evocative of bloodletting and sacrifice. "Metal thorns" suggests the penitential symbolism already invoked by the crown of thorns. To be shot with arrows, particularly in the context of a ritualized execution on a cross, recalls the arrow or scaffold sacrifice practiced by a number of preconquest peoples. Durán's informants told him that ritual arrow sacrifice was practiced in Mexico as part of the ceremonies for the female maize divinity Chicomecoatl. Prisoners of war were tied to wooden poles with their hands outstretched. Durán's Spanish phrase, *manos extendidas*, surely translates a Nahua informant's use of the "hand-stretch" construction applied to Christ's crucifixion. In contrast to Christ's position on the cross, however, these prisoners had their feet separated. Archers dressed to impersonate several deities then shot arrows at these suspended people (Durán 1967:I, 140). Blood from their multiple wounds would have run down the poles into the ground, revitalizing the earth's life-giving force.

67   Moses knows that Christ intends to die because he was present at Christ's transfiguration. According to the Gospel of Matthew (17:1–9),

Christ took the disciples Peter, James, and John to a mountaintop, where he was transfigured before them, his face shining like the sun and his garments shimmering white. Moses and the prophet Elias (or Elijah) appeared there as well. The story is told in Sahagún's sermon for the second Sunday in Lent (1563:34v–35r), but the *Psalmodia christiana* gives a more elaborate version for the August 6 festival of the Transfiguration. Moses is designated "the very great prophet, who was in Limbo" (Sahagún 1583:130r). Christ speaks to the assembled men of his forthcoming ordeal:

And even though I am great, I am a divinity, I am a sovereign, I am all-powerful, for the people of earth to be rescued it is necessary that I be seized, that I be flogged, that I be stretched by the hands upon a cross there in Jerusalem.

I predict this to you, and I reveal to you in advance my honor, my sovereignty. When you see me, when I have been flogged, when I have been stretched by the hands upon a cross, you will not be confused.

You will know that I am willing for this to be done. It was set down by my father, and the Holy Spirit, and it was set down by me. It is the rescue of the people of the world. (130v–131r)

This passage resembles some of Christ's speeches in the play.

68 In his "and this" statement the Nahuatl Moses refers to the experiences of the figures in Limbo as "torment," using the term that alludes to the Passion of Christ. The corresponding Spanish text gives *pena* (68S:2), which can mean pain and sorrow but also penalty or punishment. In line 68N:13 Moses describes their suffering with the verbal form of the Passion term. The first verb in this line literally means "to cool off": the excess heat associated with fatigue will dissipate once the Holy Fathers are rescued and have a chance to rest. The Nahua playwright has again chosen to represent the Holy Fathers as suffering actual torment, analogous to Christ's Passion, rather than mere imprisonment and frustration.

Izquierdo's line 68S:4, *Attolite portas vestras*, is an incomplete Latin quotation from the Psalm 24 verses interpreted as a prophecy of the harrowing of hell (see Chapter One). The Nahua playwright repeats this but, in accordance with the biblical text, inserts the word *principes*, giving *Atollite portas pricipes* (sic) *vestras* (both texts misspell *attollite*). It is possible that an earlier edition of Izquierdo's play included this word, but it would have made the poetic line awkwardly long in relation to other lines. More likely, the playwright recognized the text, or consulted with a friar about it, and chose to include the proper wording as given in the Psalm and the liturgical texts based upon it.

The Nahuatl Moses, like Adam and David, formally marks the end of his message.

69 Of the five Holy Fathers that Izquierdo chose as his letter-writers, Jeremiah is the one least often mentioned in Nahuatl literature. His association with the Passion stems particularly from his woeful laments, inscribed in the Old Testament books of Jeremiah and the Lamentations of Jeremiah. Some passages from these books were interpreted as allusions to Christ's afflictions during the Passion and were used in Holy Week devotions (Marrow 1979:65–66; *Manuale chori* 1586:40–53, 68–78). Jeremiah was also thought to have predicted Mary's suffering. Fray Martín de León's *despedimiento* text cites Jeremiah 9:1, 17, and 20, verses that refer to women's tearful mourning for the dead (1614:314v–315r).

Jeremiah was linked to Mary in another manner, to which Izquierdo alludes here by stating that she was protected from sin. Medieval scholastic theologians believed that Jeremiah had been purified of original sin while still in the womb. This tenet was based on Jeremiah 1:5, where the prophet quotes God as saying to him, "Before I formed thee in the belly I knew thee; and before thou camest forth out of the womb I sanctified thee."

Mary was also assumed to have received some sort of special prenatal dispensation in regard to original sin, the precise nature of which was long disputed. Had she been conceived in original sin and purified at some later point? And what was this point? Or, like Christ, was she conceived without original sin? The latter view is the doctrine of the immaculate conception, according to which Mary was sanctified and purified of sin not just before birth but at the moment of her conception. The immaculate conception did not become official Catholic dogma until 1854, but as of the sixteenth century it was firmly embraced by the Franciscan and Jesuit orders and by many other Catholics, though it was opposed by Dominicans (Børresen 1971:23–69; Warner 1976:236–45).

Nahua scholars were familiar with the doctrine. The *Psalmodia* compares Mary's preservation from Adam's sin to God's preservation of the Garden of Eden from the damaging waters of the primordial flood (Sahagún 1583:223r–224v). Fray Juan de la Anunciación's sermon for the festival of the Conception explains that, when Mary was placed inside her mother, "the beginning of error did not reach her in any way" (1577:213r).

The Nahua playwright expresses the idea of the immaculate conception by stating that Mary was a saint from the moment of conception. A prayer to Mary in the John Carter Brown Library manuscript also uses her identity as a saint in its explication of the immaculate conception, stating "when you were born, you were already a saint" (*ye tisancta*) (*Doctrina* n.d.:10r). The *Exercicio* also describes Mary as having been a saint when she was born (Sahagún 1574:10v).

Mary's metaphorical identification as a temple appears in some Nahuatl texts. The *Psalmodia christiana*, translating a line from the Latin Christmas hymn *A solis ortus cardine* (Nebrija 1549:22r), states, "The completely pure womb of a maiden became the temple of God" (Sahagún 1583:233r). The Biblioteca Nacional oration cycle addresses Mary as "the very fine temple of our Lord God" (*Santoral en mexicano* n.d.:39r). A prayer in Mijangos's *Espejo Divino* tells her, "you are the jade temple of our lord Jesus Christ" (Mijangos 1607:311).

The Nahuatl Jeremiah reminds Mary that he and his fellow Holy Fathers are weeping, sad, and confined, the playwright again taking an opportunity to emphasize the suffering of the imprisoned ones.

70   Izquierdo states, in misspelled Latin, that Mary was chosen *abinicio*, that is, *ab initio* 'from the beginning.' The idea of Mary's primordial selection was related to that of her immaculate conception, God having sheltered her soul from sin down through the ages while prophets uttered paeans to her purity. The *Exercicio* prayer cited above lists Mary's primordial selection as the first favor she received from God. He chose her *yn oc yohuayan* 'when it was still the time of darkness'; that is, before the creation of the world or the sun (Sahagún 1574:10r). Fray Juan Bautista's sermon on Mary's conception also places her selection *oc yohuayan* (1606:482). The Nahua playwright notes that her freedom from vice extends even to venial sins, called "little misdeeds" in Nahuatl.

The Biblioteca Nacional prayer cycle begins with a prayer on the conception of Mary that links the ideas of primordial selection, immaculate conception, and prophecy:

Oh rejoice, oh Saint Mary, oh fresh pure one who in a sacred way is a flower, for our lord God chose you, he appointed you to become his mother, before the world began. Therefore he chose you to be completely proper, he made you to be completely proper. Right when it was your being placed within someone, your conception, he took from you, he removed from you, the beginning of error, the origin of error. (*Santoral en mexicano* n.d.:1r)

The prayer proceeds to allude to the ancient prophecies of Mary's conception, referring to the prophets as Mary's grandfathers. Similarly, the
playwright represents the prophet Jeremiah as a progenitor of Mary. He
changes Izquierdo's "your servant" to "I your father." This recalls the
Nahuatl Mary's previous designation of the letter-writers as "our fathers"
(48N:2). By so designating himself, Jeremiah claims, at least rhetorically,
an authoritative and ancestral relationship toward Mary rather than a sup-
plicating, self-deprecatory identity as her servant. The Nahua playwright
also chose not to represent the Limbo inmates as servants when he translated stanza 62.

71 Jeremiah presents Mary with the column to which Christ will be tied
during his flagellation. Christ's flagellation by Pontius Pilate is attested by
the Gospels of Matthew (27:26), Mark (15:15), and John (19:1). According to Marrow (1979:134), the flagellation received greater elaboration in
late medieval Passion literature than any other of Christ's ordeals. Passion
tracts claimed that the episode left Christ completely covered with wounds.
The flagellation was one of the "sorrowful mysteries" contemplated in the
Rosary prayer cycle (Anunciación 1565:77v–78r; Anunciación 1575:257).

Since colonial Nahuas participated by the thousands in Lenten and
Holy Week flagellation rites, of all Christ's sufferings mentioned in the play
this was the one which people in the audience could most readily connect
to their own experiences. The fact that civil and religious authorities punished Nahua transgressors with the lash added a further dimension of local
meaning, especially as this was not a preconquest method of judicial sanction. Nahuas, like Christ, were sometimes flogged by the representatives
of an intrusive colonial power.

Although the Evangelists mention no column, medieval and Renaissance depictions show Christ standing at a column with his hands tied to
it. This column was a standard inclusion in representations of the Passion
instruments or Arms of Christ. In many, the cord with which Christ was
tied is shown wrapped around the column (as in Figure 19). The Spanish
Jeremiah sends this cord along with the column; his Nahuatl counterpart
sends only the column, but follows the Spanish text in referring to Christ's
being tied there.

Depictions of the flagellation, like that in fray Melchior Vargas's *doctrina* (Figure 24), typically show two men scourging Christ, one with a
whip and the other with a broom-like bundle of vegetation. A mural painting similar to Vargas's woodcut survives, in very poor condition, in the

24. The flagellation of Christ. Woodcut in fray Melchior Vargas's trilingual *doctrina* of 1576, f. 14r. Courtesy of the Benson Latin American Collection, University of Texas at Austin General Libraries.

Augustinian cloister at Yecapixtla, Morelos. At Actopan, Hidalgo, a mural on the second floor of the convent shows Christ at the column with Saints Augustine and Nicholas of Tolentino praying to either side.

Sahagún tells his Nahua congregation that Christ's flogging was much worse than any that they might have received as punishment for some wrongdoing (1563:49r). Fray Juan de la Anunciación's sermon on the Passion describes the results of Christ's flagellation in this way:

Then his body no longer appeared human, it was torn up everywhere, it was livid everywhere. And on his back, where the lash fell many times (while they were flogging him), his ribs were visible. (1577:60v)

Even though Mary was not present in Pilate's house at the time her son was flogged, she could nevertheless be represented as bearing witness to the event. The *Sermones en mexicano* Passion text tells how she overheard the sound of the lashes:

Oh our precious mother, oh noblewoman, oh Saint Mary, even though you are very sad, as you stand there listening outside the door while the whip is cracking upon your precious child, how much fainter with sadness you would feel if you could enter, if you could see how he stands against the column already bathed with blood. (n.d.:188)

The *Sermones y ejemplos* text tells how Christ's blood flowed like a fountain, painting the column red (n.d.:334v–36r).

Some Passion texts describe the flagellation in a manner that recalls an ancient method of human sacrifice: flaying. This is especially true of the Jesuit *Cantares* and *Sermones y ejemplos* manuscripts. The lashes stripped off Christ's skin, such that his body was flayed in various places. Later, when his garments were again stripped from him in preparation for nailing him on the cross, his skin stuck to the fabric and he was again flayed all over. The verb used for flay, *xipehua*, is the same as is used for the sacrificial practice (*Cantares de los mejicanos* n.d.:271r, 275r, 277r, 284r, 285v; *Sermones y ejemplos* n.d.:333v, 346r).

In line 43N:12 Mary predicted that Christ would receive more than four hundred lashes. Now Jeremiah multiplies that number several times, suggesting a number in the thousands, comparable to the figure of 6,606 given in the Tulane *despedimiento* (Appendix, Text I) or fray Martín de León's 4,200 (1611:34r). The playwright thus adds emphasis to Christ's sufferings.

72   The Nahuatl Jeremiah's "and this" statement brings the focus from Christ's future affliction back to the present interchange between the prophet and Mary. Like Adam in lines 53N:2–3, he speaks as though he were participating in ritual confession. The juxtaposition of his request

for pardon with his formulaic self-deprecation makes him sound as if he were asking Mary to pardon his misdeeds, as David appears to do in lines 62N:1–3.

73 The Nahuatl playwright follows Izquierdo in having Jeremiah speak of the redemptive purpose of Christ's incarnation. But he appends a reminder of the Holy Fathers' condition, drawing attention away from the plight of all humanity and toward this group of imprisoned souls.

74 The Nahuatl Jeremiah refers to the flagellation as the "third thing" that Christ will endure. Jeremiah's is not the third letter, nor is the flagellation necessarily the third of the many hardships Christ endured on earth. But the flagellation was invoked in relation to the third canonical hour, or Terce. Since the students at the Colegio observed the canonical hours, it is not surprising that the playwright would spontaneously make this association.

The canonical hours review, at three-hour intervals, the events of Good Friday, from Christ's midnight arrest through his entombment Friday night. Fray Pedro de Gante's 1553 *doctrina* supplies a complete Nahuatl rendition of the canonical hours (Gante 1981:132r–144r). For each hour, the observer is to make the sign of the cross, recite the Our Father, Hail Mary, and Apostles' Creed, and utter additional Nahuatl prayers given in the text. The relationship between each hour and the events of the Passion is also explained in words and with the help of an appropriate woodcut illustration. The text for the Office of Terce states: "When it was Terce, when there was a little sun, our precious rescuer Jesus Christ, the true divinity and true man, for our sake he was made to suffer fatigue, his precious body was flogged" (Gante 1981:137r).

The Nahuatl Jeremiah uses the verb for Passion sufferings in reference to Christ's endurance of the flogging (74N:2) and also in respect to the discomfort of the people in Limbo (74N:5). Hence, he once again characterizes their condition as one of torment, and represents it as being on the same order as Christ's imminent afflictions.

75 Like his fellow letter-writers, the patriarch Abraham prefigured Christ; God's original covenant with the Hebrew people, which was superseded by Christ's new one, had been made with Abraham. Mary and Christ were, like all Jews, Abraham's descendants. A liturgical chant for Mary's conception, printed in a Mexican psaltery of 1584, invokes Mary as having

been conceived *ex semine Abrahe* 'from the seed of Abraham' (*Psalterium* 1584:153r).

Abraham was not particularly well known to sixteenth-century Nahuas. However, a dramatization of Abraham's near-sacrifice of his son Isaac was performed at Tlaxcala in 1539 (Motolinia 1979:74). A Nahuatl script on this subject, known from a 1760 copy, which itself purports to be based on a manuscript of 1678, may derive from an earlier manuscript (Horcasitas 1974:185–229). Native paintings on the same theme survive at the Augustinian friary in Metztitlan, Hidalgo, and the Franciscan church in Tecamachalco, Puebla.

A Jesuit harrowing of hell text dating to approximately 1617 follows a medieval tradition in treating the Abraham and Isaac story as a prefiguration "when it was still the time of darkness" (*oc yohuayan*) of Christ's own self-sacrifice. Isaac, who carried on his shoulders the wood that was to be used for his sacrifice, prefigures Christ's carrying of the cross, just as Abraham's willingness to kill him prefigures God the father's sacrifice of his own son (*Sermones y ejemplos* n.d.:309v, 342r; Labriola and Smeltz 1990:123–24). Miguel Pérez, however, saw Abraham as a prefiguration of Mary, who showed even greater obedience to the divine will in allowing the sacrifice of her son (1549:29v). Fray Martín de León's *despedimiento* text follows this view: Abraham's obedience was surpassed by that of Mary. She let her son die as an offering to God even though she loved him more than Abraham loved Isaac. If God had wanted her to, she would have killed him herself (León 1614:316r–16v). Mary does not exhibit so submissive a character in either version of the drama.

The Nahua playwright replaces Izquierdo's figurative "mother of the sinners" with the more precise "mother of God" and "wrongdoers' advocate." Mary's role as an advocate or intercessor before Christ on behalf of the morally misguided is frequently attested in the Nahua-Christian literature, in prayers—including the ubiquitous Hail Mary and Salve Regina, miracle narratives, songs, and other genres, including drama. Two surviving scripts, both of which may be copies of sixteenth-century compositions, present Mary speaking to her son on behalf of souls in Purgatory (Ravicz 1970:224; Cornyn and McAfee 1944:348).

Intercession, expressed by the formula, "to speak for someone" (*tepan tlahtoa*), was not a behavior associated with preconquest deities. Nor is there clear evidence that the preconquest legal system employed lawyers, although Offner (1983) believes it is possible that some sort of advocate existed. But colonial Nahuas could relate advocacy to their own lives, in respect to the Spanish colonial court system as well as less formal contexts. The "speak for someone" formula appears in colonial documents such as wills, where the testators sometimes designate some trusted person to carry out their wishes after they have died (Cline 1986; Cline and León-Portilla 1984).

The Nahua playwright changes Izquierdo's "cruel cry and sorrows" into sad and tearful words; his Holy Fathers are, like Nahua elders, skilled orators who express themselves through speech, not through inarticulate cries.

Izquierdo's reference to imprisonment is again translated in regard to being tied up, as in lines 52N:8 and 54N:1, alluding to the manner in which offenders were confined in preconquest prisons. Being tied up is also something the Holy Fathers share with Christ during the Passion, for his hands are tied when he is arrested and when he is tied to the column (see lines 20N:6, 71N:3).

76–77   Here the Nahua playwright gives Izquierdo's text an exceptionally summary treatment. The verb in 76–77N:1 is also unusual. This is the only place where a Holy Father issues Mary such a strong command, as opposed to entreaties and requests.

78   Izquierdo begins to develop a complex spatial image that he will pursue through the next three stanzas. The imagery counterposes Christ's movement from heaven down to earth, up onto the cross, and down into the underworld, against Mary's agreement to those movements, her assent itself rising to heaven as a message to God. At the time of the Annunciation, she agreed to Christ's descent from heaven to her womb. She must now agree that he may ascend onto the cross in order that he may then descend to the underworld and free the Holy Fathers.

The Nahua playwright does not attempt to translate this imagery, but comments on the events to which Izquierdo refers. In this passage he elaborates on Izquierdo's reference to the Annunciation by quoting the oft-cited words with which Mary responded to the angel's message. Mary answers Gabriel with these words: "Behold the handmaiden of the Lord; be it unto me according to thy word" (Luke 1:38). The Nahuatl version in 78N:4–5 resembles other translations, such as this one from the John Carter Brown Library manuscript: "May it be done to me, what my divinity, my sovereign desires, for I am his vassal" (*Doctrina* n.d.:10v).

Fray Juan de la Anunciación's sermon on the Annunciation connects

25. Relief sculpture of the Annunciation, posa chapel of the Immaculate Conception, San Andrés Calpan, Puebla. Photograph by the author.

that event to the imprisonment of the Holy Fathers, as did the lost Nahuatl Annunciation drama described by Beristáin de Souza. Like the *Psalmodia*'s Easter songs (Appendix, Text V), Anunciación consigns all ancient people to Limbo rather than reserving that place for "good" people. There the prophets and patriarchs, bowing and sighing, cried out to God to send his precious child. When it was time, God sent Gabriel to Mary (Anunciación 1577:145v–146r).

Figure 25 is a native sculptor's interpretation of Mary's meeting with Gabriel. Individual elements, no doubt copied from an unknown wood-cut, have been arranged so as to grant prominence of place and size to the vase of lilies (included in Annunciation scenes as a symbol of Mary's purity) and the resplendent dove of the Holy Spirit. This treatment reflects the role played by flowers, birds, and radiance in Nahua conceptions of encounters with the sacred.

79 Mary's assent joined two opposite extremes, god and man, into a single entity, as Christ immediately became incarnate within her womb. The Nahua playwright, who probably did not conceive of god and man as simple opposites in this way, describes the incarnation in more straightforward terms and proceeds to elaborate upon the "good effect" that was to result therefrom, referring twice to Christ's sufferings.

80 Izquierdo's Abraham asks that Christ may descend to where he and his fellows are weeping. In an "and this" statement that returns the focus to the current situation, the Nahuatl Abraham mentions this weeping, but he also includes the people on earth among those who await rescue.

81 The Nahua playwright ends his triplet of optative statements with a reference to Christ ascending onto the cross. This is the only instance in which he retains Izquierdo's imagery of upward and downward motion.

82 John is the only Evangelist to state that a Roman soldier pierced Christ's side with a spear (John 19:34). This was, as Izquierdo states, the final wound inflicted upon Christ's body. The fifth of Christ's five stigmata, it was conventionally shown on the right side on images of the dead and resurrected Christ. In Miguel Pérez's telling, since Christ was already dead and could not feel this blow, it was Mary who felt its pain as it pierced her soul (1549:30v).

The Nahua playwright borrowed the Spanish phrase *lança de gloria* directly into his text, prefixing the Nahuatl *pahpaquiliz(tli)* 'joy, happiness' as a translation of *gloria*. In line 82N:4 he again uses the Spanish word *lança*, but pairs it with *tepuztopilli* 'metal staff.' This compound appears in several other texts that mention this episode (Gante 1981:102v; Anunciación 1575:40; *Miscelánea sagrada* n.d.:219r; *Sermones en mexicano* n.d.:202; Sahagún 1588:109v, 112v; the Tulane *despedimiento*). A *topilli* is a staff that is carried as an insignia of civil or religious office.

Like the other Nahuatl correspondents, Abraham seeks to comfort and encourage Mary. Nahua conventions for polite speech account for some of this, but there is also a sense that the Passion instruments will, as in lines 82N:2–3, somehow strengthen or empower Mary (see also 56N:1, 63N:6, 68N:14–17). If these implements are viewed as power objects in their own right, ritual insignia that channel sacred force into the here and now, her jurisdiction over them would indeed serve as a source of power and authority. The playwright's earlier designation of these objects as "passions" supports this view; the instruments embody the divine force represented by Christ's Passion.

Passion narratives follow the piercing of Christ's side with the removal of his body from the cross, the lamentation of Mary and others over his body as it lay in Mary's arms, the anointing and enshrouding of his body, and its entombment in the sepulcher donated by Joseph of Arimathea. A native artist at Epazoyucan, Hidalgo, depicted Mary and the other women lamenting over Christ's body (Figure 26).

83 With the letters read and the Passion implements presented, Christ and Mary now resume their conversation. As the play nears its close, the pace of the dialogue increases; the speeches become shorter and the speaker often changes in mid-stanza.

Like the authors of the letters, the Nahuatl Christ speaks of Mary's being comforted by those messages. He also reiterates the identity of the Limbo correspondents as ancestors and prophets. Both Christs express a desire to fulfill their destiny, but only the Nahuatl one mentions his afflictions as a part of what he desires.

84 Izquierdo's "these my beloved children" is the model for the Nahuatl text's "my precious ones." But to these elect the Nahua playwright adds "a great many others." In line 84S:3 the intended meaning may be "how many are lost": the word *quanto*, singular in the Houghton Library imprint, is pluralized in the 1603 Cuenca edition. But even if the version used

26. The lamentation over the body of Christ. Mural painting in the Augustinian friary at Epazoyucan, Hidalgo. Photograph by the author.

by the playwright did say *quantos*, or he interpreted *quanto* as if it were plural, the many lost ones would be equivalent to Christ's "beloved children." The phrase would merely emphasize that there are many of them. Yet the Nahuatl unambiguously refers to additional people (*yhuā yn oc cenca miyequintin*), who are to be included in the redemption along with Christ's "precious ones."

Christ's "precious ones" is one way the Holy Fathers are designated in other Nahuatl treatments of the harrowing of hell. The playwright is altering the story such that Christ rescues many people in addition to the Holy Fathers — perhaps all people who were "confounded and confused" by the doing of deeds that the Church deemed immoral. The Nahuas' own ancestors, who according to the friars had been deceived and imprisoned by the demons and so confused that they worshipped those demons and practiced idolatry, might be covered by this blanket amnesty. Thus, not only does the play allow for the Old Testament figures to be seen as generic ancestors that Nahua audience members might take as their own, it also states outright that many other people will accompany them on their journey out of the underworld.

85   Both plays refer here to Mary's suffering, the Nahuatl Christ noting that it is because of her sympathy for him in his own torments that she will be so distraught. Both Christs reassure their mother that she will be relieved of her sorrow when he is risen. The words used in Nahuatl for Christ's resurrection derive from the reflexive form of the verb *izcalia*, which has the sense of quickening, reviving, or resuscitating. As a transitive verb, *izcalia* refers to nurturing or educating someone, as in bringing up a child. Since the verb does not necessarily refer to a return from death, it imparts less of a sense of the miraculous than does the idea of resurrection as used in Christian contexts.

86   The Spanish Mary, expressing her characteristic concern with her own comfort and happiness, asks what she will do after Christ has left her. Her Nahuatl counterpart remains focused on their ongoing dialogue.

87   Even the Spanish Mary now desists from entreating her son to escape his fate, the letters having persuaded her that protest is useless. Conflict now centers on whether Mary will be allowed to accompany her son on his fatal journey. The Spanish Christ denies his mother's request outright.

88 Both Christs delegate to their father the ultimate responsibility for regulating Mary's actions, but the Nahuatl Christ does not venture to speak in his place or to issue direct commands. His request that Mary remain behind is phrased not in terms of God the father's authority but his own concern for her feelings.

89 Frustrated in her request to accompany him, Mary now asks that she might travel separately and meet him in the city the following day. The Spanish *licencia* 'license, permission' was glossed as "your command" in line 2N:13 and borrowed into the Nahuatl in line 58N:8. On this third occasion, it is glossed as *mohuelitzin* 'your power' or 'your authorization.'

90 With her "and this" statement, the Nahuatl Mary focuses on specifics. Without giving Christ a chance to deny that she will meet him, she demands to know where the encounter will take place. She asks if it will be at the temple. This statement, added by the Nahua playwright, alludes to their previous visit to Jerusalem, mentioned in stanza 26.

91 According to Luke 19, Zachaeus was the leading publican, or Jewish tax collector, in the town of Jericho. When Jesus passed through Jericho, he dined in Zachaeus's home. Although he was a wealthy man, Zachaeus showed himself to be generous and just, explaining to his guest that he gave half of his goods to the poor and restored fourfold anything that he took from another unjustly. Jesus declared that salvation had come to his host's house. The story is told in Nahuatl in fray Martín de León's *sermonario* (1614:161r–v). Torquemada mentions it in his chronicle, in a chapter where he praises native people for carrying out the restitutions assigned them as penances for their sins (Torquemada 1975–83:V, 272).

Since Zachaeus lived in Jericho, which was farther from Jerusalem than Bethany was, Mary would hardly have gone to his house if she was to meet her son in Jerusalem. However, the Spanish form of Zachaeus's name, Zacheo, rhymed, conveniently, with both Zebedee (Spanish Zebedeo) and *veo* 'I see.' Izquierdo may have taken this reference from the *despedimiento* play in the *Códice de autos viejos*. In that play, Mary asks her son, "Am I to find you in the house of Zachaeus, or in the house of Nicodemus?" (Rouanet 1979:II, 414).

Mary's next option is more appropriate, for it was in the streets of Jerusalem that she would see her son. Some versions of the story place this encounter at the time when Christ was being taken to Pilate's house after his arrest; others place it when Christ was carrying the cross en route to Calvary. Some, such as Gante (1981:136v, 138v), report both meetings, although neither episode is attested in the Gospels. Where Christ, in line 20N:6, predicts that Mary will see him with his hands tied, he alludes to this first encounter.

Christ's brief speech in this stanza is omitted from the Nahuatl play. This may have been an accident on the part of scribe or playwright, for Mary's name is repeated at 91N:3 as if this was the beginning of a new speech. It is the only place in the play where a speech in the Spanish text has no counterpart in the Nahuatl. The Nahuatl Passion narratives in the *Miscelánea sagrada* (n.d.:209v–211r) and *Sermones en mexicano* (n.d.:179–81) tell how John returned to Bethany after Christ's arrest in order to tell Mary, Mary Magdalene, and Martha what had happened. Mary and Mary Magdalene then proceed to Jerusalem. Mary meets Christ in the street as he is being taken (for the first time) to Pilate's house. Other versions send John to Bethany when Christ is already bearing the cross to Calvary. The women accompany him back to Jerusalem, where they see the beaten and bloodied Christ struggling beneath his cross (*Cantares de los mejicanos* n.d.:281v–284v; *Sermones y ejemplos* n.d.:344v–345r; Escalona's Passion narrative, Appendix, Text II).

The Nahua playwright inserts stage directions indicating that Mary will faint at this point. Mary collapses twice during the Tulane *despedimiento*, first after Christ tells her that he must be crucified and again after he describes to her how he will be tortured (Appendix, Text I). In Escalona's Passion sermon, she feels faint as Saint John approaches to report on Christ's condition (Appendix, Text II). The Nahua playwright has her faint out of fear that she will not be able to see Christ in Jerusalem. This is somewhat ironic, since in some texts it is when she does see him there, carrying the cross or hanging on it, that she faints (Gante 1981:139r; Anunciación 1577:60v; *Sermones en mexicano* n.d.:195; *Santoral en mexicano* n.d.:24v–25v).

92 The farewell text in the *Meditations on the Life of Christ* ends with Christ agreeing that the women shall travel to Mary Magdalene's house in Jerusalem (Ragusa and Green 1961:309); this text set a precedent for Mary and Mary Magdalene making this journey together.

Both Christs imply that Mary's presence will add to their own woe, but the Nahuatl Christ makes this point more gently by prefacing it with an expression of sympathy.

In the Nahuatl text Christ addresses Mary Magdalene directly. This is the first time in either play that she has been spoken to, and the first time since stanza 3 that her presence has been acknowledged.

93 The Spanish Mary, as at line 16S:3, uses the word *passion* in its generic sense of "suffering," at the same time alluding to the fact that the upcoming event is "the" Passion. Her statement, though, is ambiguous as to whether the increased suffering will be hers, his, or shared by both. The Nahuatl Mary states more clearly that it is his suffering with which she is concerned.

The Spanish Christ uses plural pronouns in lines 93S:4–5. If these are royal plurals, this is the only time in the play that Christ makes use of such. He is probably including his disciples, who will accompany him to Jerusalem. The Nahua playwright translates these pronouns as singular.

The Nahua author borrows the term "benediction" from the Spanish text. Molina's dictionary gives *teteochiualiztli* 'blessing someone' as a gloss for *bendicion* and does not list this as a loanword (1970:19r). Gante's *doctrina* does, however, apply the word *bendicion* to the priest's blessing after Mass (1981:116v). The word appears once in the *Psalmodia christiana*: Saint Martin's soul, before rising to heaven, gives a farewell benediction (*iBendicion*) to one of the saint's followers (Sahagún 1583:210r).

94 Mother and son now disagree over which one should first bless the other. Given that the fate of humanity hung in the balance during their initial argument, this final quibble is so trivial that it provides some comic relief. It reflects, though, the ambivalent nature of their relationship: as his parent she has higher status than he, but as God he outranks her.

The Nahuatl text does not convey this ambivalence. The Nahua playwright seems to have read Mary's initial protest not in respect to this argument over proper social graces but as yet another effort to delay Christ's departure. Adding "in the fleshly sense" at 94N:7 dilutes the Spanish Christ's attempt to defer to Mary's status as his mother; 94S:5's "as well as," which contrasts Christ's identity as God with his identity in relation to Mary, is lost in the Nahuatl version. Also lost is Mary's potentially confusing figurative reference to her son as being also her father. The Nahua playwright seems more concerned with correctly describing Christ's dual nature and relationship to his mother and father than with following Izquierdo's teasing repartee.

95 The Nahua playwright either misunderstood or chose to reinterpret line 95S:1, reading it as an epithet for Mary. In the Spanish, the wording of the second line makes it clear that Mary herself is not the light; God, presumably, is. The Nahua playwright does involve God in the equation, since it is he who is asked to give Mary strength and whom she, in turn, invokes. Accustomed to opening his speeches with maternal epithets, the Nahuatl Christ here coins a thirteen-syllable word, reminiscent of the similarly lengthy outpourings that Mary concocted for him in their earlier dialogue. The Nahuatl Christ's characterization of his mother as a "guiding light" is consistent with Marian devotions of the period. Indeed, Izquierdo gave Mary the epithet "divine light" in line 57S:2.

96   Here the Nahua playwright introduces the noun form of the Nahuatl verb for "bless" (*teochihua* 'make sacred') instead of borrowing the Spanish noun.

97   Izquierdo has Mary introduce the rank issue again; she gives her son her blessing only because he insists. She defers to his father, who does have the authority to bestow blessings on him, before she adds her own blessing "although" she is (only) daughter and mother. Again, the Nahuatl text does not express this status difference in the same way. Indeed, the Nahuatl Mary, instead of making excuses for herself, asserts her status in lines 97N:7–8: she blesses Christ because of who she is, not in spite of it. Her opening invocation of God is not framed as a show of deference to his authority. Rather, and in contrast to the Spanish Mary's blessing, it echoes the imagery of light and guidance that Christ introduced in his blessing. In this way Mary's blessing reciprocates Christ's in a display of like-mindedness and solidarity.

   The Nahuatl Mary elaborates on what God's blessing of her son actually entails, using words reminiscent of a priest's benediction. She asks God to lead Christ "in the sense that he is man"; that is, through the torments that his human body will endure. She then repeats the phrase in reference to her own maternal relationship to Christ, as both she and Christ employed it in their previous dialogue (2N:8–9, 3N:3, 17N:8, 24N:3). The repetition places God the father and Mary in the same category in regard to their concern for their son's human aspect. She refers to all three of them as "precious." Again, her words convey solidarity and equivalency.

98   Izquierdo has Mary refer to Christ as her God, her son, and her husband, thus alluding to all three members of the Trinity. The Holy Spirit played the role of Mary's husband when he engendered Christ within

Mary's body. The Nahua playwright, however, avoids this designation as husband, which might have seemed aberrant to Nahuas in his audience. His substitution of "repose," though, suggests that he has connected Izquierdo's "husband" reference with the Isaiah text about the Spirit of God "reposing" upon the flower that sprouts from Jesse's root, which was interpreted as a prophecy of Christ's conception by the Holy Spirit (see comments to stanza 56). Both Marys have already addressed Christ as their "repose" during their earlier dialogue (4S:2, 4N:4), providing a precedent for the usage here.

99 The Spanish Christ shows sympathy with Mary's suffering. But he then rejects Mary as she attempts to cling to him, and orders Mary Magdalene to hold onto her—the Spanish Magdalene is here addressed for the first and only time. The Spanish play ends with the two women holding one another while Christ stands separate from them, an arrangement represented in some of the pictorial treatments of the *despedimiento*. It also prefigures their stance at the time of Christ's death, as imagined by commentators such as Miguel Pérez (1549:29v), who has Mary collapse, almost dead herself, into Magdalene's arms.

The final *Laus Deo* 'Praise be to God' is not part of Christ's speech but marks the end of the printed text.

The Nahuatl Christ does not complain that his mother's pain adds to his own, but rather utters a sympathetic prophecy of what she is to suffer. Whether or not mother and son embrace at this point would depend upon individual staging choices; stage directions indicate such an embrace at the very end of the Nahuatl play. Like his Spanish counterpart, the Nahuatl Christ orders Mary Magdalene to hold Mary, but here he does not, at least verbally, reject her embrace; rather, he is trying to prevent her from falling. His concern is expressed in his repetition of his wish that she not suffer such a collapse. Falling could, according to Nahua medical beliefs, result in serious injury (see comments to stanza 25). Christ's command to Mary Magdalene is direct, not preceded by a polite *ma* or *tla*. This reflects a sense of urgency—Magdalene must act immediately; it may also reflect the fact that she is of lower status than he and his mother.

100 The last four speeches of the Nahuatl play may be based on some unknown *despedimiento* text, available to the playwright in a Nahuatl, Spanish, or Latin version. This speech of Mary's is, in my opinion, her most eloquent and evocative utterance in the entire play; it is understandable why

the playwright chose to include it. Its opening argument is, however, out of context. Mary knows she is destined to outlive her son, for she asked in stanza 40 whether she might be allowed to die first, and was denied. Her request here, to die at the same time, is different, but Christ's reply in stanza 41 nevertheless applies; she must remain alive while he is dead because she alone will represent the faith. Again, the Nahua playwright shows a lack of concern with the linear development of the text. Avoiding redundancy is less important than providing his characters with eloquent speeches.

Line 100N:2 is the first time Mary addresses Christ as *notelpotzin* 'my son' or 'my boy'; she repeats this construction in 100N:20 and 102N:1. The introduction at this late stage of this new mode of address might indicate the incorporation or adaptation of a separate text that already existed in Nahuatl.

Mary proceeds to compare her sad lot with that of three Old Testament predecessors, none of whom, she asserts, suffered as grievously as she will suffer. The first bereaved parent is the patriarch Jacob. Jacob believed his favorite son, Joseph, to be dead when Joseph's jealous brothers brought their father his bloody coat and claimed the boy had been eaten by a beast (Genesis 37:23–36). Joseph was actually alive, having been sold into slavery by his brothers; he would eventually become the Egyptian Pharaoh's chief assistant and interpreter of dreams and would save the Hebrew people from starvation.

Medieval interpreters saw Jacob grieving over Joseph's bloody coat as a prefiguration of Mary's lamentations over Christ's body (Wilson and Wilson 1984:190). Miguel Pérez has his Mary, after Christ has taken leave of her, contemplate various prefigurations of Christ's death. Among these is the story of how Joseph was sold and stripped of his clothing (Pérez 1549:27r).

Fray Martín de León's 1614 *sermonario* provides a Nahuatl version of this figure. Joseph's brothers tell their father of Joseph's death and show him Joseph's torn and bloody mantle. Joseph laments: "No longer will I be consoled. So long as I shall live here on earth, always I will weep for my child." If Jacob was this upset at losing Joseph, the text continues, even though he had ten other children to comfort him, "then how much more will she weep, our precious mother Saint Mary, for her only child, Jesus Christ." No woman, the story concludes, ever loved her child as much as Mary loved hers (León 1614:87r).

The Jesuit *Sermones y ejemplos* Passion tract introduces the Jacob and

Joseph story at the point where Christ's bloody garments are stripped from his body in preparation for the crucifixion. The congregation should weep over Christ's garments in the way that Jacob lamented over Joseph's. This prefiguration of the Passion is described as Jacob having "revealed the torments" (*quimotlaìyyohuiliznextili*) of Christ "when it was still the time of darkness" (*in oc yohuayan*) — that is, in the pre-Christian epoch (*Sermones y ejemplos* n.d.:346v–347r).

The playwright uses the same word for Joseph's ordeal as for Christ's Passion. Here Mary says that her suffering will be greater than Jacob's not because he had other children but because he had no foreknowledge of, nor did he actually witness, his son's (reported) torments.

The death of King David's son Absalom is told in 2 Samuel 18:9–14. Absalom rebels against his father's rule and plots to overthrow him. David orders that his soldiers not harm the youth. Absalom is accidentally trapped when his hair becomes tangled in an oak tree. Joab, one of David's captains, then pierces Absalom's heart with three darts. When David finally learns of this, he laments, "Oh my son Absalom! My son, my son Absalom! Would God I had died for thee, O Absalom, my son, my son!" (2 Samuel 18:33). The parallels with Christ's death include not only a parent's grief but also the suspension of the young man in a tree (analogous to the cross) and the piercing of his body with three sharp objects. Here in the play, Mary draws a parallel not with the three nails but with the lance; she refers to three "metal staffs," a term Abraham used for the lance in line 82N:4.

The Absalom and David story is cited in various contexts in Nahuatl literature; for example, David's reluctance to punish Absalom for plotting against him is treated in Gaona's *Coloquios* as a model for patient endurance of worldly tribulations (1582:98r–98v). Some texts link the story to the Passion. In one *despedimiento* text, the bereaved David is mentioned as a model for how everyone should cry over Christ's fate (*Cantares de los mejicanos* n.d.:237v–238r). León's text on the descent from the cross digresses into a telling of Absalom's story; his disobedience is contrasted with Christ's obedience (León 1614:328v).

Mary's third example is the story of Hagar and Ishmael (Genesis 16–18, 21). Hagar was the Egyptian maid of Abraham's wife Sarah. Frustrated by Sarah's failure to have children, Abraham takes Hagar as a concubine. She bears a son, Ishmael. Later, when Abraham has made his covenant with God, Sarah miraculously conceives and gives birth to Isaac. Sarah catches Ishmael making fun of her Isaac and complains to Abraham. God promises Abraham that he will "make a nation" from Ishmael. Abraham gives

Hagar bread and a bottle of water and sends her away into the wilderness. When the water is gone, Hagar fears the child will die and places him under a bush. Sitting down a ways away, she laments, "Let me not see the death of the child." God causes a well of water to appear, and Ishmael is saved.

The banishment of Hagar is the subject of one of the Spanish *autos* in the *Códice de autos viejos* (Rouanet 1979:I, 22–34). Her story also constitutes part of the possibly sixteenth-century Nahuatl drama on the sacrifice of Isaac (Horcasitas 1974:185–229). In this play, Hagar and Ishmael serve as examples of how not to bring up children. They are banished from Abraham's home for fear that Ishmael, who devotes all his time to frivolous amusements, will have a bad influence on the dutiful Isaac.

In the Holy Wednesday script, Hagar's name is given as *aca*. Spelled "Agar" in Spanish, it has lost the final *r*, a sound that did not exist in Nahuatl, and the *g* has been assimilated to the nearest Nahuatl phoneme. *Acah*, with a final glottal stop—a phoneme rarely represented in sixteenth-century texts—means "someone." A Nahua unfamiliar with Hagar's story might have interpreted this usage as designating an unspecified "somebody" rather than a personal name. A scribe taking dictation may, somewhere along the line, be responsible for this change. Thus, the line could be read as "And if so-and-so, the slave of the noblewoman Sarah." The implications of social rank probably would have been salient for an urban Nahua audience; if a mere slave had these feelings, then a noblewoman like Mary, with her more sophisticated sensibility, would suffer more grievously.

The last line of Mary's speech introduces metaphors of preciousness frequently employed in *huehuehtlahtolli* discourses addressed to children (Sahagún 1950–82:VI; Bautista 1600). That a Nahuatl-speaking Mary should use such formulaic terms of affection in speaking to her son is not surprising; what is surprising is that this is the first and only place in the script that she does so. This supports my hypothesis that the playwright is, in this final section, working from an existing text in Nahuatl.

101   Christ now gives a new reason why Mary must not yet die. Christ's "sheep" are, of course, his followers, with whom Mary will continue to associate until her own death and assumption. Escalona's Easter sermon (Appendix, Text III) defines both the Holy Fathers in Limbo and Christians in general as sheep, with Christ as their shepherd. The Biblioteca Nacional oration cycle quotes Mary awaiting her son's resurrection with these words: "Do come out again on the earth, come show yourself, shep-

herd, come to gather together, come to bring together your sheep" (*San-toral en mexicano* n.d.:28r).

A text on the Assumption of Mary in the John Carter Brown Library manuscript enumerates four reasons why Christ left his mother on earth when he ascended to heaven: to console the Apostles, to teach the Gospel to the Evangelists, to encourage the martyrs, and so that people would know her and see that she was not a god (*Doctrina* n.d.:54r–54v).

102 Mary capitulates to God the father's wishes and then asks Christ for his blessing. Both points are redundant, given earlier statements in the play. Only the Nahuatl verbal form of "bless" is used in these final speeches.

103 Christ already gave his mother his blessing in stanza 95. But this second blessing is much longer and more laudatory than the two-line commendation to God's care that Izquierdo assigned to his Christ. It is an elaboration upon Luke 11:27, in which a woman amid the throng listening to Christ preach calls out to him, "Blessed is the womb that bare thee, and the paps which thou hast sucked." Christ in the Gospel rejects this praise of his mother, answering, "Yea, rather, blessed are they that hear the word of God, and keep it" (Luke 11:28). However, as Warner notes (1976:15), "The Catholic Church has consistently overlooked the apparent hard-heartedness in Jesus' words and stubbornly fastened on this passage as an example of the honour given Mary in the Gospels."

The Nahuatl Christ provides a model for the rendering of high praises to Mary, not only in respect to her bearing and nursing of him but also because of her own moral and mental excellence. He has the last turn at speech in the script, as he does in Izquierdo's script. However, Izquierdo's Christ ends by commenting on his mother's suffering and weakness, while the Nahuatl Christ devotes his closing words to her exaltation.

The Nahua playwright's addition to the text, though in some ways redundant, permits both mother and son to express praise and affection for the other in terms unparalleled elsewhere in the drama. They close their dialogue on a note of harmony that contrasts with Izquierdo's ending, in which Christ brushes off his mother's embrace. This harmony is also indicated by the Nahua playwright's closing stage directions, which represent the pair's actions as mutually shared, not carried out by one upon the other. That is, instead of Christ taking leave of his mother, as the event is characteristically designated in Old World contexts, they take leave of each other.

The embrace, delayed since Mary's request in stanza 98, brings them into a physical closeness that mirrors the closeness they have expressed through their words. The harmony they achieved at the end of their first dialogue is here expressed in an even more graphic manner.

Nahuas at the time may have had a custom of embracing one another at the close of formal meetings and exchanges of dialogue. This is suggested by a 1583 document from the town of San Miguel Tocuillan, reproduced and discussed by Lockhart (1991:66–74). It records the town *cabildo*'s granting of a house site to a woman who was the sister of one of the council members. To mark the close of the transaction, the woman, her husband, and the five council members all embrace one another. The same verb for "embrace" is used as in the play.

The characters end the performance by bidding one another farewell and dispersing. Closing the drama with these goodbyes symbolically marks the exit from the performance frame back into mundane reality. The actors will now change back into Nahua youths; the audience members will take leave of their neighbors and go their separate ways.

Appendix: Comparative Texts

THE FOLLOWING FIVE SELECTIONS treat in some detail subject matter connected with the Holy Wednesday drama: the Christ-Mary farewell
scene, the Passion, the harrowing of hell, and the Resurrection of Christ.
All come from sixteenth-century Nahuatl texts that are earlier than or approximately contemporary with the drama. Texts I through IV are from
unpublished manuscripts. Text V is my translation of the Easter songs from
Sahagún's 1583 *Psalmodia christiana*; these have also been published in English by Arthur J. O. Anderson (Sahagún 1993).

Text I, from an anonymous Passion tract, is the lengthiest Nahuatl
treatment of the farewell scene that I have located (other than the Holy
Wednesday drama itself). Texts II and III, from sermons by the Franciscan Alonso de Escalona (prepared, no doubt, with native assistance), show
how the Passion and Christ's descent to Limbo were treated in homiletic
discourses directed at Nahua congregations. Text IV is an unusually detailed anonymous telling of the harrowing of hell, from a manuscript that
appears to have been prepared by native writers. And Text V, from the
Psalmodia, is a rich collection of Easter lore, including native-style chants,
narrative accounts of the harrowing and resurrection, and translations from
the Latin liturgy.

I. The Tulane *Despedimiento. Pasión en Lengua Mexicana*, Latin American Library, Tulane University. Anonymous, sixteenth century.

How our lord addressed his mother there in Bethany

The Tulane manuscript begins its Passion narrative with three episodes that
precede the Passion proper: the plot by the Jews to kill Christ, Judas's betrayal, and
"how our lord addressed his mother there in Bethany." The opening lines set their

dialogue on Holy Thursday rather than Holy Wednesday, but the text contra-
dicts this at the end, where it states that the following day is Thursday.

[22r] Here is the third thing that I will cause you to hear. It is how our lord addressed his mother Saint Mary when it was Thursday. Do listen. Our lord, Judas sold him on [22v] Wednesday. Then he went there to Bethany. And when it was Thursday in the morning, in this way he addressed his mother. He said: "Oh my precious mother, now we have arrived at the time when I will die, so that because of my death the good, the righteous may be rescued. That is why I descended hither from heaven, I came to become a man within you. And that is why I came to be born from within you, so that I would die on behalf of those who are to be rescued. And now, this is how it is, it is now the time for me to die. Therefore, oh my precious mother, be consoled. May your heart, your body not be disturbed. Do not be sad. It is very necessary that I die. It has been greatly longed for, that it come true, that which my precious ones, the prophets, said about my death. And now, oh my precious mother, may you be joyful. My death, my torments, will become the joy of the good, the righteous." And [23r] Saint Mary, when she heard this, then she wept very much. Then she said: "Oh my precious child, you are all-powerful. May it be like this, that you will not die. You could rescue us. May this be the price for which the errors of the world will be destroyed: your fasting. May it be your blood, and your prayers. May it also be your blood that was spilled when you were still a child, when they cut your flesh. May this also be the price: that you went to fast there in the forest. May it also be the way your heart, your body ached, the way it hurt when you were going about teaching people in the city. May it also be all of the good and proper things you did on earth. May these also be the price for the errors of the world. Well do I know that they are many, the errors of the world. [23v] May these things become their price." And when she had said this, then she knelt before our lord. Then she fervently beseeched him: "My precious child, have compassion for me. My heart, my body aches very much, hurts very much." And then our lord said: "Oh my precious mother, this cannot be. It is essential that I die. If I do not die the sacred words will not come true, which say that I will die on account of the errors of the world." And then his mother, Saint Mary, said: "My precious child, may you remember that you commanded that children should obey their parents. And now, my precious child, I beseech you, may you obey me. May you not return there to Jerusalem." And then our lord said: [24r] "Oh my precious mother, it is true that it is necessary

for me to obey you. For you are my mother. But much more so he who is my precious father, it is necessary that I obey him. He wants me to go to Jerusalem." And then she said: "My precious child, in this way do I wish it, that you will obey your precious father very well. But now if your precious father wants you to die, may it not be right now that you will die. May it be when you have become strong, when you are old." And then our lord said: "Oh my precious mother, if my death is delayed for a long time, our first fathers and mothers, our relations, the prophets, our friends, who are there in Limbo, they will be very anxious. For a long time already they have been waiting for me. And my older brother Saint John the Baptist, he has gone to console them, he has gone to tell them that I will soon be going so that I will go and rescue them. And therefore it is essential that I die now." [24v] And his mother said: "My precious child, may you still wait until I am dead. May it not be that I see your death." And our lord said: "Oh my precious mother, we have arrived at the time when I will die. And it is also said in the sacred words that I will die now. Even if heaven and earth were destroyed, not thereby would I avoid my death. And now, oh my mother, may you remember that when you went to leave me in the temple when I was still a little child, you placed me in the hands of Simeon. May you re-member what he said to you, that because of my death, my torment, your heart, your body would ache very much." And then his mother said: "My precious child, even if it cannot be that you avoid your death, may it not be in front of people that you die. May it not be a shameful death, the way you die. If you die a shameful death in front of people, my heart, my body will ache extremely." And then our lord said: [25r] "Oh my precious mother, the way you speak, it cannot be. In this way was done the mis-deed by which the people of the world were destroyed. Likewise, it must be this way so that I may make recompense, so that they will be revived. Because when they erred, our first parents, it was very great, the way they erred. And they erred in front of people. Therefore my death, which will be its recompense, it is also necessary that it occur in front of people. And it is also necessary that it be very sickening, that it be very shameful. And because Adam stretched his hand to a hog plum tree, as he erred, as he cast his children into the hands of the demons, likewise it is necessary that on the cross I stretch my hands, as I rescue Adam's children from the hands of the demons." And when his mother heard this, then she was very sad, she cried out very much, she wept. And Saint Mary Magdalene, it was in her home that they were when they were addressing one another. And when she heard how much Saint Mary cried out, wept, [25v] then she ran there and she entered upon them, where she and our lord were. And then she saw Saint Mary lying fallen at our lord's feet. Then she too wept. She said: "My precious lord, what are you saying to your precious mother? For she has died, my lord. May you have compassion for her." And Magdalene, then she called to Saint Mary, she said: "My child, how are you doing? May you be consoled." And then she lifted her to her feet, she embraced her from behind. And then she called to, she cried out to her sister Saint Martha, that she bring water with which they might wash her tears. And then she said to our lord: "My lord, perhaps you do not see your mother, she is dying already. Why don't you help her?" And our lord was very sad. And then he said to his mother, "Oh my mother, may it be that you revive." And [26r] when our lord had said this, then his mother revived. And when she had revived, then she said: "My precious child, may you be saddened, may you have compassion for me. May it not be that you desire to die in a very sickening way." And then our lord said: "Oh my precious mother, may you be consoled, may you be strong, for it is just the truth that I tell you. No one dies the way that I will die, for it is very sickening, very shameful. Because it will take a very long time, my torment, my death. Every place will hurt very much. Greatly they will torture, greatly they will afflict my face. And on my head they will lay sour thorns. And they will stab my heart with a metal staff. And every place on my body, so will they flog me, 6,606 times, thus will come true what the prophet Isaiah said about me, [26v] he said my head, my face, my hands, my feet, every place on my body will suffer greatly. And now, oh my precious mother, may you be consoled, may you be strong. And so that you will not suffer greatly, imagine that you have no child." And his mother, when she had heard this, it was as if she fainted. And it was as if her words could no longer fall forth. She said: "My precious child, the way you speak, already my heart, my body suffers greatly. It can bear no more. Already I am about to die." And when our lord saw that his mother already suffered greatly, she was already about to die, then he wept sadly. And Saint Mary Magdalene, who was there, she also wept very much, she was very sad. Then she fervently beseeched our lord, she said: "My precious rescuer, may it be that you remain here with us until the pascua is celebrated. May it not be that [27r] you will go there to Jerusalem." And when she had spoken in this way, and the Apostles, who were together in the house, thus heard how Magdalene cried out and wept so very much, then they rushed in and they saw the three of them weeping, our lord and his mother and also Magdalene. Then they all wept. And then they asked: "Why are you weeping?" And then Magdalene said: "His mother is in pain. We beseech our lord that he remain with us until the pascua is celebrated, but he will not agree. And now you, may you also beseech him. Perhaps he will listen to your entreaty." And when the Apostles had heard this, then they all knelt before our lord. Then they all beseeched him not to go there [27v] to Jerusalem. They said: "Oh our lord, have compassion for us. May you not go there to Jerusalem. The people there want very much to kill you. May the pascua occur while you are still here." And our lord, when he had heard this, he was very sad. Then he said: "Oh my precious children, it cannot be. My father greatly desires that the pascua occur with me in Jerusalem." And when they had heard this, then they were very sad, then they stopped. Not one more time did they tell him not to go. And then our lord determined that he would go the next day, Thursday. Then they were very sad, all night long. No longer did they sleep.

Then, on Thursday morning, this brief farewell dialogue takes place between Christ and his mother:

[30r] And then our lord addressed his mother. He said: "Oh my mother, do not be distressed about my death. For [30v] it is what my precious father desires. And everyone who lies in the world, it is necessary for them that I die. And now, oh my mother, I say to you that I, even though I will die, on the third day I will revive again, I will appear to you, you yourself will see my body. Never again will I die. Not one more time will I die. Thus you will again be joyful." And then his mother said: "My precious child, it is what your precious father desires. And if it is what you desire, so be it." And then our lord went there to Jerusalem. And all the Apostles went with him.

II. Scenes from the Passion of Christ. *Sermones en Mexicano,* Biblioteca Nacional de México, MS 1482. Fray Alonso de Escalona, 1588.

Of the Passion of our lord

Fray Alonso de Escalona was a Franciscan who came to New Spain in 1531. According to Mendieta, Escalona quickly mastered Nahuatl and wrote sermons that many other friars used, since no others had yet been written. This suggests that they were written during the 1530s. The extant copy of his sermons is dated 1588, indicating that the sermons were still in use near the time of the play's com-

position. It is possible that the text had been emended over the years. Escalona
himself died in 1584 (Mendieta 1980:668–673).

The following are some excerpts from Escalona's sermon on the Passion of
Christ, which would have been used on Good Friday. I have selected passages that
relate most closely to the Holy Wednesday drama. The Latin text Miseremini
mei, miseremini mei *'Have pity on me, have pity on me' is from Job 19:21. I*
join the narrative just after Christ's arrest in the garden of Gethsemane.

[215r] Do listen, oh my children. Our lord Jesus Christ was tied up, he who
is truly a divinity and truly our rescuer. And his students all abandoned
him. They were very frightened when they saw that our lord was being
held. They abandoned him in the hands of the Jews. And now our lord is
in the hands of the Jews. No one has compassion for him. No one rescues
him. Oh my children, if our mother Saint Mary saw that her precious child
is tied up, that he is in the hands of the wicked ones, the Jews, perhaps she
would not weep very much? And we, let [215v] us also have compassion
for him. He calls to us, he says *miseremini mei miseremini mei.*

Christ ends up in the hands of Pontius Pilate, who would free him except that
the crowd of angry Jews demands he free Barabbas instead. The following excerpts
draw on the four Gospel accounts and popular tradition. The reporting of events
to Mary, and her lamentatious responses, recall the medieval literary tradition
of the Virgin's complaint. The scarlet robe of Matthew 27:28 is described as a
camixtli, *a word derived from the Spanish* camisa *and applied to the tunic-like*
shirts worn by colonial Nahua men.

[217v] Then [the Jews] cried out very much. They said, *tolle crucifixe cruci-*
fixe eum. "May you stretch him by the hands. May you stretch him by the
hands." And Pilate said, "Why? What has he done?" They cried out even
more. *tolle tolle crucifixe eum.* "May you seize him. May you stretch him by
the hands." And our mother, Saint Mary, she knew nothing of it. Let us
tell her. Your precious child will be stretched by the hands. And if Saint
Mary knew it, she would be very sad, she would faint because of it. Let us
have compassion for them, our lord and his precious mother, for they were
very sad. Do listen, oh my children. Pilate would have rescued our lord,
he would have consoled the Jews. He ordered that our lord be flogged.
He was thinking that perhaps thus they would be appeased, the great multitude who were gathering together, Pilate's friends. Then our lord was

flogged. They tied him by the hands to a stone column. They tormented him very much. His blood came out all over. And the floggers exerted themselves, they wore themselves out. But our lord received it happily, for our sake. And when he had been flogged, then they untied him. So very much of his blood came out that he could not sit down, he was in great pain. And now, no one has compassion for him. Everyone just afflicts him. But us, let us have compassion for him, for we belong to him, we are his children. And when they had tormented him very much, then they made what was like a flower garland. It was made with sour thorns, which were very painful, very afflicting. Then they placed it on his head. It entered in all places. It lay very tightly. Thus it was very afflicting. Then they put him in a red shirt so that they could mock him. Then they placed a staff in his hand. [218r] They kneeled before him. They said, "Perhaps now it is you, perhaps you are the sovereign? May you endure fatigue, you who are the sovereign of the Jews." And when he had been made fun of in this way, Pilate brought him out to show him to the Jews, so that they would be appeased, so that they would be satisfied. Our lord just came out calmly. He came wearing the red shirt and the crown that was like his flower garland. Then Pilate said, "Know that I see no reason for punishment." Then he said, *Ecce homo.* And when they saw our lord, then the Jews cried out very much. They said to Pilate, "May he be stretched by the hands! And if you release him you are not the friend of Caesar the Emperor." And now, oh my children, you will learn that although it is not written in the Holy Gospel, some say that Saint John the Evangelist was there. And when he saw our lord with his blood coming out profusely all over, he wept profusely, he was very sad. He was thinking that our lord was about to die. He was weeping very much, he was crying out as he went to tell his precious mother Saint Mary so that she would come to see him before he died. And when Saint John was still approaching her, Saint Mary heard his cries. Then she felt very faint, she shed tears, it was as though she fainted. Thereupon Saint John called to her, "Oh my precious mother, may you arise. If you want to see your precious child, I will take you. They have tormented him very much. They have flogged him all over. All over his body his blood is coming out. Let us hurry away so that we go after him before he dies." And our mother Saint Mary, who can say how profusely she wept, how very sad she felt, how very distraught was her heart? Then she arose and went out, then she accompanied Saint John, and also Magdalene, the three of them. [218v] They went crying profusely. And they entered Jerusalem.

Mary asks some residents of the city whether they have seen her son, whom she describes as being exceptionally pure and beautiful. They tell her that they did see someone, who is about to be crucified. But this person had been tortured; they could not see his face because blood was running down all over it. The narrative then returns to the scene at Pilate's house. The Jews continue to clamor for Christ's crucifixion, and Pilate concedes. The cross is placed on Christ's shoulders and he is tormented by the crowd. Mary and her companions struggle through the throng until she is able to see her son walking between the two thieves.

[219v] She did not recognize him. He came with his face covered in blood. Then she said to Saint John and Magdalene: "My children, which one is my child? I do not see him. Do you perhaps see him? May you tell me." And Saint John called to her sadly. "Oh! Oh my mother, my older brother comes very tormented." Then and there the three of them wept profusely. And when our lord reached our mother Saint Mary, she embraced [220r] her precious child. They both were very sad. Our lord was very sad on behalf of his mother. And his mother also was very sad on his behalf. Then and there he fell. And the Jews were so very wicked that they shoved our mother Saint Mary away. They said, "Here is your child. Soon you will see him there in front of you, stretched by his hands." And this: oh my children, perhaps someone could say how our mother Saint Mary wept? Then they lifted our lord to his feet. They left our mother Saint Mary, Magdalene, and Saint John there. The three of them were weeping there.

The Jews and the three prisoners reach the place where the crucifixion is to take place. When they remove Christ's mantle, some of his flesh sticks to it and he bleeds some more. They attach him to the cross by beating on his hands and feet with metal. Mary goes to stand at the foot of the cross, accompanied by John, and the other noblewomen. The Jews taunt Christ. The thief to Christ's right shows him reverence and Christ tells him that they will go together to his palace. The text then recounts Christ's commendation of Mary and John into one another's care (John 19:26–27), and goes on to tell of Christ's death.

[220v] Do listen, oh my children. Our lord has now reached the point at which he will become our offering and at which he will be sold for our sake. He will become our merit. His torments are about to come to an end. Then he called to his father, he said, *pater manus tuas commendo spiritum meum.* It means, "Oh my precious father, in your hands I leave my soul." Then he died, his soul emerged. Thereupon there was an earthquake and the rocks shattered. And the sun did not shine; darkness spread in the

world. All of our lord's creations revealed the torments; they were sad on behalf of their divinity, their creator. And the dead revived. He showed the people of Jerusalem. Before he died it was not apparent that he was a divinity. But when he died, then it became apparent that he was a divinity, since all of his creations were sad. And there was a person standing there, who was called a centurion. He was very frightened. Everyone said, "He is truly the child of God." And a person called Joseph of Arimathea placed him in a sepulcher in his garden. And who could say how very sad our mother Saint Mary and Saint John and the other women were? They left our lord right there. Let us feel compassion for them, let us weep for them, as it is said, *miseremini mei etc.*

III. The Harrowing of Hell. *Sermones en Mexicano*, Biblioteca Nacional de México, MS 1482. Fray Alonso de Escalona.

On the day of the holy pascua

Escalona devoted a large portion of his Easter sermon to the harrowing of hell. The Latin text on which the sermon comments is the line from the Apostle's Creed that mentions Christ's descent to hell and resurrection. The Latin passages in the dialogue between angels and demons are from Psalm 24.

[224v] *Descendit ad inferos tertia die resurrexit a mortuis.* It means, our lord descended to the place of the dead; on the third day he revived, he came to life again. You will hear three things. First, why our lord descended to the place of the dead. And second, where he descended, because there are many places in the place of the dead. And third, what our lord did there in the place of the dead, and how he revived. [225r] Oh my children, our lord Jesus Christ, when he died on our behalf, it was for three days. It says in the Gospel that they buried our lord's body then. And his soul descended to the place of the dead. He went to seize the good ones who were waiting there for our lord. He went to seize, he went to rescue those who lay there. They were so very sad, they were praying to our lord that he descend there, that he rescue them. Likewise is it done here on earth. You know well, oh our children, if someone is a great sovereign, and if some people offend the sovereign, their sovereign will cast them in the place where people are tied. Then he will tie them up, with metal doors it will be closed up. Perhaps

they will be able to rescue themselves? Perhaps someone will be able to rescue any one of those who are tied up there? All the rest of their friends are tied up there. You can see that it is not possible, because they all are tied up, they all are enclosed with metal doors. Who among them will be able to rescue the others? None soever. Therefore in order for them to be rescued it is necessary that someone come to rescue them. In this way it happened to those who were sitting there in the place called Limbo. Our first fathers, they offended God, and so he became angry with them, so they were cast into the place where people are tied, they and all their children. There they were enclosed with metal doors. Therefore it is necessary that our lord God rescue his sheep. Because as if they were sheep they were closed up. They will not be able to get out unless the shepherd comes to let them out. This is how it happened. We are called the sheep of our lord. As David says, *nos autem populos eius, et oves pascue eius*. It means, "We are the vassals, we are the sheep of our lord." [225v] And our lord is called a shepherd. He said, *ego sum pastor bonus & cognosco oves meas*. It means, "I am the good shepherd; I recognize my sheep." You know, oh my children, that a shepherd looks for his sheep. Wherever they go, he seizes them, then he brings his sheep back. This is what our lord does. His sheep lay in the place of the dead, they were in the place of the dead. David says, *sicut oues in inferno politi sunt etc*. It means, "Those good ones who were cast into the place of the dead, it is as if they are sheep." And they who could not be rescued, they went about very sad, they called sadly to our lord to rescue them. They were saying to He by Whom One Lives, *adiuuanos deus salutatis noster & propter gloriam nominis tui liberanos: et propitius esto peccatis nostris propter nomen tuum etc*. It means, "Oh our lord, oh God, may you help us, may it be by your name, rescue us. May you pardon our misdeeds." And our lord Jesus Christ had compassion for his sheep. He went to seize them in the place of the dead. Here it is apparent, oh my children, for what reason our lord died and descended to the place of the dead: he went to sieze his servants, his sheep, who lay there. And his precious children the angels accompanied him, went before him. And the place of the dead is enclosed with metal doors. Therefore when our lord and the angels descended there, then they beat on the doors. Then they said to the demons *attollite portas principes vestras: et eleuamini porte eternales et introibit rex glorie*. It means, "Oh demons, may you open your doors, you people of the place of the dead. The sovereign of heaven will enter there." And the demons then said *quis est iste rex glorie*. It means, "Who is the sovereign of heaven? Do we perhaps know him? Have we perhaps seen him here once before? We do not recognize him." They said *dominus fortis et potens: dominus potens in prelio*. It means, "He is the sovereign everywhere. He is the all-powerful contender." But they did not agree to open them. Therefore our lord pushed, [226r] he shattered the metal doors. Then he entered there in the place of the dead. Thus he went to rescue his vassals.

The second part of the text describes the four parts of the underworld: the hell of the damned, labeled by the Spanish term infierno; *the place where small children go who have not been baptized;* Purgatory; *and* limbo patrorum, *the Limbo of the Holy Fathers, which is the only one of the four that Christ visited. Escalona makes it clear that those incarcerated there did not undergo physical torment.*

[226v] And the fourth part is the place called Limbo of the Fathers. There were sitting the good ones, the servants of God, they who had lived serving our lord. They were just sitting there, they were not suffering, for they were good. And therefore [227r] before our lord died in order to open heaven, those who were placed there were waiting for our lord there. They were calling to him so that our lord would descend. And when our lord had died, when he had therefore spilled his blood, then he descended there, he went to rescue them. Therefore in the Creed it is said, *descendit ad inferos: tertia die resurrexit a mortuis etc*. It means, "Our lord Jesus Christ descended to the place of the dead; on the third day he revived, he came to life once more."

The third part of the text tells what Christ did in the underworld. After he shattered the doors:

[227v] He finally tied up Lucifer, the great demon, there in the place of the dead, so that he will never come out. And when our lord entered there, the demons were very sad, they wept profusely, they were very frightened. They feared our lord very much. But they, who can say how happy they were, how very joyful their hearts were. Then they all kneeled, they all took our lord as their divinity, then they said to him, "Oh our lord, oh our sovereign, you have come, you have had mercy on us, your heart has consented. For a very long time we have been waiting for you, we have been longing for you, we have been holding vigil for you. We were saying, 'When will he come, our lord, our rescuer?' And now you have come, your heart has consented." And then our lord blessed them. Then he cut,

he untied the chains. They came out very joyfully, they came happily, as David says. *Sedentes in tenebris & umbra mortis vinctos in mendacitate & ferro* [. . .]. It means, "The good ones, the just ones who were tied there in the place of torment, in the gloom, in the place of the dead, who were very afflicted with chains, because our first fathers erred, they did not keep well the command of our lord, therefore they were greatly afflicted, none soever had compassion for them." And when they had come out happily, then they beseeched our lord that he have compassion for them, that he rescue them. And our lord indeed had compassion for them, he indeed rescued them, he made them very joyful. All of them came out joyfully. When it was the third day after he died, then our lord accompanied the good ones, [228r] his servants. Then he came to his body, then he entered inside the sepulcher. He came to life again. He came out, he was very shimmery, very shiny, very pure. And the sepulcher, nothing happened to it. As it is said, *tertia die resurrexit a mortuis*, on the third day our lord revived, he arose, he came to life again. Thus we rejoice today, thus we are happy, as the great pascua is celebrated, because our lord had died, as the wicked ones, the Jews, the demons, their friends killed him. Today he really pushed away the demons, as he tied them up in the place of the dead. He rescued his servants. Finally today he has revived, he has come to life once more.

The Harrowing of Hell. *Sermones en Mexicano*,
Biblioteca Nacional de México, MS 1487.
Anonymous, late sixteenth century.

On the day of the holy pascua

This version of the harrowing of hell comes from an anonymous and un-dated manuscript written in a typical late sixteenth-century native hand. The last section of the manuscript is comprised of material copied from fray Juan de la Anunciación's 1577 Sermonario, *indicating that at least that part of the manu-script postdates the publication of that book.*

The story of Christ's descent is told as part of an Easter sermon, which takes as its text the passage Surrexit non est hic *'he is risen; he is not here.' These are the words with which, in Mark 16:6, the angel guarding Christ's tomb informs the three Marys of Christ's resurrection.*

The scribe incorporates lengthy passages in Latin, and has considerable dif-

ficulty with the spelling of Latin words. I have truncated the longer passages and standardized the spellings. Full, exact transcriptions are given on the diskette.

*The sermon is in three parts. The first section discusses Christ's death and entombment, the coming of the women to anoint his body, and their encounter with the angel who sends them to notify Christ's disciples. The second section consists of the following narrative about the harrowing of hell. Like Escalona's text, this one quotes, in Latin, from Psalm 24. It also quotes Zacharias's canticle from Luke 1:68 (*Benedictus dominus . . .*); this text was placed in the mouths of the liberated Fathers in two of the Spanish plays discussed in Chapter I. Lucifer is given an epithet belonging to the Nahua deity of the underworld, "lord of the place of the dead" (Mictlantecuhtli).*

[213] *Surrexit non est hic.* It means, our lord Jesus Christ has risen, he is no longer here. Oh my children, you have heard the Gospel that is said today in Mass, as it is in the book of the sacred words, how our lord revived. May it be that you hear all that happened when our lord died, all the time until he arose. Not all of it is written in the Gospel. In a book of very holy words we see other things that happened, and the saints remembered them, they agree. Do listen. The saints say that when our rescuer Jesus Christ had died upon the cross, his soul came forth. It went there to Limbo, within the earth, where the saints were waiting for him, Adam, Abel, Noah and the others. And as to how he descended there, it is to be believed, it is the truth, it is necessary for us to believe it, because it is the eighth thing to be believed. It is said, "I believe that our lord descended to the place of the dead. He went to seize his precious ones, the good fathers." And when he had not yet come and entered there, the demons, when they saw our lord, how he was shimmering brightly, he was shining brightly, then and there [214] they realized that he was truly God and man. Thereupon they were scared, they ran away, they went to slam shut the doors to the place of the dead. But our lord just came in a tranquil manner. Angels came along with him. And when he had not yet arrived, some of the angels spread out in front of him. When they reached the doors of the place of the dead, then they cried out to the demons, they said to them: *Attollite portas principes vestras: et elevamini porte eternales: et introibit rex glorie.* It means, "Oh demon sovereigns, oh chiefs of the demons, open, withdraw your doors! And you doors, open! For the sovereign of eternal joyfulness is going to enter!" And the demons, then they were scared. They answered them, they said to them: *Quis est iste rex glorie.* It means, "Who is the sovereign of joyfulness?"

And the angels once again spoke to them: *Dominus fortis et potens: dominus in prelio*. It means, "He is the personage who is the wholly strong sovereign." And when our lord came, then he breached the doors, he shattered them, even though they were very strong. Then great radiance entered. And when the demons saw it, they were very scared, they were very frightened. Then they ran into the abyss where Lucifer was, the lord of the place of the dead. With trembling words, with shaking words they said to him: "Oh! Oh! Oh how wretched we are! Who has come in? Whom have we let in? He is not like a captive of ours. He is just like a great sovereign. He broke, he shattered our metal doors. And he shines brightly, he shimmers brightly." And when the great demon heard this, he was very frightened by it, as were all the demons, when they saw the radiance, because they had never before seen radiance there. Even though [215] there is fire there, it does not shine, it is just black. Not just in vain were they frightened. And our lord Jesus Christ, when he had entered, then he went to Limbo. And when he had gone in, then radiance spread about where the good fathers were. And when they saw him they were very joyful, they were very happy, they were very grateful to him. Then they knelt before him, thereupon they prayed to him, thereupon they praised him, straightaway they said to him: *Benedictus dominus deus israel* [. . .]. It means, "May he be preciously praised, the sovereign everywhere, the divinity everywhere, because he has come to greet us, for he has come to rescue us, us vassals, as taught the prophets who have lived. He has rescued us from the hands of our enemies who hate us. Thus he has had compassion for us, he has remembered his promise, what he promised us. Thus tranquilly we will love him, thus no longer will our enemies the demons frighten us, thus always before him we will be completely good. He wished to have compassion for us, he sent his precious child, he came to rescue us. You shined on us in the place of darkness, in the gloom we were, so that you would rescue us, so that you would give us the place of tranquil living in heaven." And this, the men, it is their way of praising, their expression of gratitude. And [216] then the women gathered around, Eve, Sarah, and Rebecca, Saint Ann, etc. They too thanked him, they said to him: *Advenisti redemptor noster qui portas aereas conflixisti: et visitasti infernum et dedisti eis lumen qui erat in penis tenebrarum*. It means, "Our lord, our rescuer, you came hither, you breached the metal doors! You came to greet us and you came to rescue us, we who were in the place of darkness, in the gloom." And our lord Jesus Christ, oh my children, perhaps he answered them with nothing? Perhaps he said nothing to them? Yes indeed! We think that he addressed them with many things. We think that he said to them: "Oh my precious children, now may you rejoice! May you be consoled! It is over! It is ended, all of your sadness, your distress, all the time that you have been doing penance here. And as to how I took a long time, I came slowly, it is not just in vain, for thus was the decree of your [sic] precious father. And now I have come, I have come to rescue you. Oh my precious children, never again will you be sad. May you be happy! Forever you will be joyful. Now let us leave. Come! Let us go there to terrestrial paradise. There you will be until it is the time when we will ascend together to heaven." And when they heard him they rejoiced very much, they were very happy, and they thanked him very much. Straightaway they lined up, our lord led the others, he went accompanying Adam, our first father, and then all the other saints, the patriarchs, the prophets. And the angels went surrounding them. They went thanking him humbly, went expressing their gratitude to him. And our first father thereupon began the praises; he said to him: *Cantemus domino gloriose eum honorificatus est* [. . . 217]. It means, "Let us sing for our divinity, our sovereign, for he is quite worthy of precious praise! For he has rescued his vassals who were in the house of wood. He is our means of becoming strong, he is our means of becoming invigorated. And he is our honor. He has rescued us. It is true that he is our divinity, our sovereign. We will honor him, we will celebrate him, we will exalt him. He is our rescuer. He is like a great captain. There is no one like him. All-powerful is his name. In the abyss, in the gloom our lord closed up the great demon and his fellow demons. Very strong is your power, you are all-powerful. You beat, you afflicted our enemy the demon. And so just you alone, you will be honored. You deposed our enemy, oh our lord. Is there perhaps anyone who is equal to you in strength? Is there perhaps anyone who is equal to you in goodness, in propriety, in renown, in honor, in the doing of wondrous deeds?" Thus did the saints go praising him until they reached terrestrial paradise. And when they reached terrestrial paradise, our first father Adam was very grateful to our lord, he thanked him very much, because everything that [Adam] had damaged, [our lord] healed, thus [Adam] was greatly favored, and all his children. Thus beseechingly he said to him, "Oh my lord, oh my sovereign, I pray to you, I am grateful to you, for you are my creator, for you are my rescuer, for you are my favorer. Even though I erred greatly and I harmed my children, you [218] have healed me, you have made me right, and you have healed all that I damaged. Much more precious is that

which you have given me; what you had given me at first is not like it.
Thus I am very grateful to you, as you have favored me." And, oh my children, our lord was there with them on Saturday.

*The third and final section of the sermon tells of Christ's resurrection. He brings
all of the liberated saints along with him as he rejoins his body and then pays a
call upon his mother. A popular legend with no New Testament basis, this visit
is attested by Mary's sixteenth- to early seventeenth-century Spanish biographers
Miguel Pérez (1549:38v), Alonso Villegas Selvago (1760:100), and Pedro de Rivadeneira (1835:20). It was staged in Juan de Pedraza's Passion play of 1549 (Gillet
1933; see Chapter I). Sahagún's Easter sermon also describes this visit (1563:54r),
as does the* Psalmodia *(see Text V). Here in the* Sermones *text, after Mary and
Christ greet one another several of the saints greet Mary with biblical and liturgical passages in Latin and Nahuatl. These speaking parts are assigned to Adam,
Abel, Noah, David, John the Baptist, Eve, Sarah, and Elizabeth. The angels
then greet her. Finally, the narrator admonishes his listeners to join them in their
praise of Mary. The narrative then returns to the story of the three Marys and
the empty tomb.*

V. The Harrowing of Hell and the Resurrection of Christ.
Psalmodia christiana, 1583. Nahua scholars,
with fray Bernardino de Sahagún

On the day of the resurrection of our lord Jesus Christ

*These songs for Nahua Easter celebrations were composed by Nahua scholars under
the direction of fray Bernardino de Sahagún. First written around 1558–1560,
they were published in 1583. The individual stanzas or cantos are titled "psalms":
the* Psalmodia *as a whole was intended to serve the Nahua Church as a source of
religious lyrics, as the Book of Psalms served the Latin liturgy.*

*There are three songs or sets of songs, assigned to three successive days of
Easter festivities. The first day's song alludes to the Easter morning procession of
the Nahua worshippers. The singer envisions the church patio transformed into
a sacred garden in which the women are flowers, the men are trees, and angels
circle above in the form of tropical birds.*

*Occasional Latin passages in the margins of the text indicate sources used by
the authors; these are transcribed along with the Nahuatl text on the diskette. In
the songs for the first two days, a few liturgical chants are quoted. These quotations*

become much more frequent in the text for the third day, which is derived almost entirely from the Latin hymns "Aurora lucis rutilat," "Rex aeterne Domine," and "Ad coenam agni providi," plus a few antiphons and responsories from the Easter week liturgy (Nebrija 1549:33r–35r; Hours of the Divine Office 1963:II, 1185, 1187–1188). Allusions to the paschal lamb, the [Red] Sea, and Pharaoh are from the "Ad coenam agni" hymn.

[58v] First Psalm

[59r] You green-corn flower, you heart flower, you cacao flower, you red jar flower: put forth a shady ring of fronds, send forth boughs! You have come to arrive in your place of sprouting.

You ceiba, you bald cypress, you cypress, you fir, pine: why do you still stand sadly? It is time, it is the moment for you to renew your flowers, your leaves, for you to send forth boughs, [59v] for you to bloom!

You oriole, you blue grosbeak, you mockingbird, you hummingbird: where had you gone? Where had you entered? And all you various spoonbills, you various troupials, come! Let there be flying, let there be unfolding, let there be unfurling! May your speech resound! May there be chattering, may your songs resonate like bells!

Our flowery pascua, our great pascua has come to arrive, has come to pass, the reviving of our lord Jesus Christ!

All of you little birds, all of you spread out above those that stand sprouting, that stand swaying, the various precious trees! Surround our sacred patio!

Let us sing together, let us be joyful together, let us praise together the great sovereign Jesus, for he has revived!

The ice, the chill have left. The softness, the warmth have come to arrive. The little insects, [60r] the various butterflies are now flying, are now rejoicing!

Let there be singing, precious spoonbills, various birds, let the festival of the reviving be exalted! For a long time it was awaited, for a long time it was longed for!

Second Psalm

Divine anger lay closing up the compassion. No one yet knew about the reviving. The people of the world were weeping there in Limbo.

The angels were not befriending the people of the world, because the dispute had not yet healed, which was established when Adam erred. Alleluia, alleluia!

The demon was the sovereign of the world. All the patriarchs and prophets went on being his captives. The door to heaven was closed, heaven still lay closed up.

When our lord Jesus Christ died on the cross, the anger disappeared, the weeping disappeared, the dispute ended, the reviving began.

And when our lord Jesus Christ revived [60v] among the dead, great rejoicing began, the reviving began.

Not just our lord alone revived, but also many saints revived with him. Alleluia, alleluia!

The angels then befriended us. In many places they appeared to people, in many places they consoled people.

When our lord Jesus Christ had died on our behalf, the angels did not want us to kneel before them. They said: "You are our fellow vassals, you are our fellows." Let there be rejoicing, let there be happiness!

Third Psalm

Let us praise our divinity, our sovereign, for he has performed a very great marvel!

For our sake he appeased his father. With his death he acquired for us life in the world. He led us to heaven.

Those who were weeping, who were sad in Limbo, [61r] he brought them out. He placed upon them great rejoicing, great happiness!

He opened the road to heaven for us. Let there be rejoicing, let there be happiness!

He consoled, he encouraged his precious ones, his students, who were intently searching around for him.

He appeared to them, he ate among them, he fed them his leftovers, and he admonished them with sacred words.

He ordered them to teach people everywhere, and to baptize people, and to pardon people's misdeeds.

He gave them the Holy Spirit, with which to untie those who are tied up with error, and to tie up those who do not want to obey the Holy Church.

Fourth Psalm

You who in a sacred way are a heart flower, a crow flower, a green corn flower, a red jar flower, you child of Holy Church, you who are a woman: rejoice, be happy!

[61v] You who in a sacred way are a bald cypress, a cypress, a fir, a pine, you child of Holy Church, you who are a man: rejoice, be happy!

When you die, you will burst into bloom, you will blossom, you will sprout, you will bud, you will send out boughs, you will become a jade, you will become a turquoise, you will become a quetzal feather!

Your very body will revive, will arise! Then nothing will disturb it. It will be quite pure, quite strong. It will live forever. It will be transparent, it will shimmer. With many heavenly vestments will our lord Jesus Christ adorn it!

You who in a sacred way are an oriole, a blue grosbeak, a mockingbird, a hummingbird, all you other children of God, you who are angels: come! Surround our sacred patio!

For now you are our friends, now you are our fellow vassals. With his death, with his reviving our sovereign, Jesus, has joined us together!

Oh our friends, be joyful, rejoice! [62r] For our reviving, our eternal life has appeared! Our happiness, our contentment has appeared, which Adam destroyed for us!

God the child, Jesus Christ, acquired it for us by command of the father and the Holy Spirit, the sole God, the sole sovereign. Let us always praise him!

For the Second Day
First Psalm

May the golden drum, the jade log drum, the lordly flowers stand forth! May there be exaltation! May there be adornment!

May the golden garland be taken, may it be worn! May the jade rattle be shaken!

May the golden flute resound, may it ring out! [62v] May our song, our words resound everywhere!

Happily, joyfully let us raise in song the marvelous deed of our divinity, our sovereign, Jesus!

A great battle, a war took place upon the cross. Jesus battled against our enemies!

Death and the great demon were taken captive, were overcome. The sovereign, Jesus, overcame them, captured them! Alleluia!

When the war had taken place, our lord left death stretched by the hands upon the cross. He quickly tied up the great demon. Alleluia! May there be rejoicing! Alleluia!

Then he went there to the home of the great demon. There he closed up the abyss, the place of utter darkness. Let us still be joyful!

Second Psalm

[63r] When the great sovereign's splendor went to appear, when it was seen, there in the place of the dead, all the demons were very afraid, were very fearful!

Then he broke, he shattered the bonds of those who lay tied there, his precious ones, the patriarchs, the prophets.

Then with heavenly vestments he adorned those he had rescued, the saints.

They came shining brightly, they came shimmering brightly when he brought them out, his precious ones, our fathers, the Holy Fathers.

And the seraphim, the cherubim, and all the other residents of heaven came to meet them with great rejoicing. They praised them. Alleluia!

Early in the morning he again took his body, when it was Sunday. With very great happiness was our divinity honored. Let us sing to him! Alleluia!

Then he appeared to, he consoled [63v] his precious mother Saint Mary, when it was still dark. And when the sun came out, he appeared to Mary Magdalene, there in the garden.

May there be rejoicing, may there be joyfulness! For our rescuer, the great sovereign Jesus, has revived!

Third Psalm

And once again, on the road, he appeared to the two Marys. He advised them, he consoled them. They kissed his feet! Alleluia!

And he appeared as well to Saint Peter there in the garden. And to the [other] ten apostles he appeared indoors. Thus did he greet them: "*Pax vobis*: Be tranquil." Alleluia!

May it be marveled at, you children, how our great sovereign Jesus honored his mother! Alleluia, alleluia, alleluia!

When it was Sunday, near dawn, Jesus's precious soul was bearing divineness, [64r] was there in terrestrial Paradise, was gathering together the souls of all the prophets and patriarchs.

Then he came to where his body was buried, which was also bearing divineness. Then his precious soul entered within his body. Thus he came to life. Then he passed through the rock outcrop; he did not open the sepulcher.

And the souls of many prophets and patriarchs entered within their bodies, which had died long ago. They revived, they came to life, by Jesus's command!

This happened in the presence of many angels, who were accompanying Jesus about. And our lord Jesus ordered some of them to tell his mother: "Your precious child Jesus has come to life, has revived!"

And then many angels went directly, went to greet the noblewoman, who was keeping vigil, who was waiting for her precious child.

[64v] Fourth Psalm

Then they joyfully said to her: "Oh heavenly noblewoman, oh queen, rejoice! Alleluia! For your precious child—alleluia!—has revived, as he said. Alleluia!"

When the heavenly noblewoman had heard this, she was very joyful, she was very consoled. She said: "May the precious child come to his garden, his orchard! May his eat his hog plums, his fruits!"

And then our lord Jesus Christ suddenly arrived. He greeted his precious mother. He said to her: "Arise, oh my precious mother! For the mist has departed, for there is now good weather!"

And his precious mother, when she saw her precious child, who was shining brightly, who was shimmering brightly, said to him: "How very sweet and fragrant are your words!"

And when the prophets and patriarchs who had revived along with [65r] our lord Jesus Christ saw the noblewoman, they greeted her with great admiration.

With a wondrous song they greeted her. They said: "You are the sovereign's blessed one, you are our daughter, because indeed by means of you, through you, we have merited life!"

There they made greetings, Adam, and Eve, and Abel, and Noah, and Abraham and Isaac, and Jacob, and Sarah, and Rebecca.

And the great sovereign David played his harp before her. There he intoned: "Arise, oh sovereign, be happy, you, and your ark, who is completely good."

Fifth Psalm

And Saint John the Baptist greeted the noblewoman. He said to her: "You are the happiness of Jerusalem, [65v] you are the joy of Israel. You are the fame, the honor of our city!"

All the prophets and patriarchs, there each one greeted her. With very admiring greetings they greeted the mother of God, Saint Mary.

Let us marvel at, let us listen gladly to how the noblewoman, the mother of Jesus responded. For she is very wise, very compassionate!

She entreated them, she said: "You are precious people. You are your divinity's, your sovereign's chosen ones.

"You my precious fathers, you are indeed the saints, the acquisitions of your divinity, your sovereign. This is now your command.

"You will cause people to hear, you will tell people of the strength of him who removed you from the place of darkness, who put you into his place of wondrous light.

"Not long ago you were closed up, you were captives of the demon. [66r] But now you are vassals of God, you are rescued!

"For a long time you lived with affliction. But now the compassion of God is upon you.

"Be grateful! Tell people everywhere about the mercy of God who rescued you from the place of darkness, who put you in his place of wondrous light.

"With the will of the father, with the love of the Holy Spirit it was done. With his work, with his torments my precious child, God the child, brought together those who are here."

For the Third Day
First Psalm

Let us marvel now at the song of our mother Holy Church, with which she praised our lord Jesus Christ on account of his reviving. It says:

Oh! How brightly does the light of dawn come shimmering! And in heaven they spread about twittering with song! And in the world they are joyful! But in the place of the dead there is howling, there is the raising of cries!

[66v] It was when the utterly strong sovereign, Jesus, conquered in the place of the dead, and he untied those who lay tied up there.

He was enclosed with stones. The enemy guards were guarding him. He arose, he revived! And death he conquered with his death.

When our lord Jesus Christ revived, he consoled those who lay sadly in the place of the dead. And the angel came shimmering brightly to tell people that he had revived.

The apostles were sad because of the death of our lord Jesus Christ.

The angel with soft words notified the women that our lord Jesus Christ would be seen there in Galilee. And when the women had gone to notify the apostles, our lord Jesus Christ appeared to them on the road.

Second Psalm

[67r] When the apostles learned, when they saw that our lord had revived, then they went straight to Galilee to see our lord Jesus Christ.

And when our lord Jesus Christ appeared to them there in Galilee, he was shining brightly, he was shimmering brightly. He showed them his holes.

Oh eternal sovereign, oh our creator, well do we know that in the sense that you are a divinity you are forever beside your father, but today, in the sense that you are a man, you revived!

You began the world, you made our first father Adam, and you made him your image.

But our first father was deceived by the Devil, our common enemy. But you took Adam's flesh. Thereby you became a man.

For this reason did you become a man: thereby you rescued your creations, which had fallen into the hands of the demon.

[67v] All the people of the world greatly marvel at how you were born from she who is forever a maiden.

And we are all waiting to revive because of you, through you, when the world ends!

Third Psalm

You, our rescuer Jesus Christ, destroyed our misdeeds with baptism. Our souls were tied up with misdeeds!

You, our rescuer Jesus Christ, accepted the cross death. Your precious blood became the price of our rescue.

You, our rescuer, our creator, to you we pray: give your vassals that which is the reason they rejoice, your reviving!

Let us adorn ourselves with pure adornments! Let us praise our [68r] great sovereign Jesus Christ! For he rescued us from the sea!

The precious body of our lord Jesus Christ was tormented on the cross. But because of his precious blood we attain eternal life!

With the precious blood of our lord Jesus Christ we were protected against the deadly messenger, from the hands of Pharaoh, the great tormentor.

The death, the precious blood of our lord Jesus Christ goes on being our rescue. He is a sacred lamb who was killed on our behalf. And his body goes on being our offering.

Oh! Oh precious offering, you breached the place of the dead! You went to bring out those who were captives there! You gave them eternal life!

Fourth Psalm

Our lord Jesus Christ revived in the sepulcher. He went to conquer in the place of the dead. He went there to close up our enemies, and he opened for us the road to heaven.

[68v] Our lord God's angel descended from heaven, when our lord had revived, and he moved the door of the sepulcher.

And then he sat upon the stone, and he advised the women. He said to them: "Do not fear! Jesus, whom you seek, has revived!

"Come, come to see where they had lain him. There is no longer anyone there, for he has revived!"

When our lord Jesus Christ revived, there was a great earthquake, and an angel descended from heaven.

The angel's face shimmered brightly, shone brightly. Like lightning was his glance, quite blinding.

The enemy guards fainted with fright, they swooned, when they saw the angel.

You who are our divinity, you who are our sovereign, let us always praise you! For [69r] you revived among the dead, and through you we will all revive!

Notes

Scenario

1. Michael Mathes identified the two library brands, in consultation with Alfred L. Bush at the Princeton library.

2. *Bibliotheca Mejicana* 1968; *Diccionario Porrúa* 1964:552–53.

3. *Bibliotheca Mejicana* 1968:215; price list, p. 27. The data on subsequent sales of the manuscript are from David Szewczyk's documentation. According to Szewczyk, the Sotheby's sales were June 24, 1919 (lot 219) and May 25, 1948 (lot 4862). The manuscript itself bears the Phillipps collection catalog number and is listed in the published catalog of the Phillipps collection (*Catalogus* n.d.:394).

4. I use the word "Christianizing" rather than "Christianized" in order to denote an ongoing process in which the indigenous participants were actively engaged, as opposed to an accomplished event of which they were passive recipients.

Chapter 1

1. Pérez Gómez could find no sixteenth-century edition in existence in Spain. Nor could Willard King of Bryn Mawr College, who checked the Biblioteca Nacional in Madrid at the request of Alfred Bush at Princeton. She did find Pérez Gómez's article on the *auto*, for which I am grateful. Efforts by Alfred Bush and other librarians at Princeton, and by Wayne Ruwet of the University of California, Los Angeles, to locate other early editions proved unsuccessful.

2. All translations from foreign-language sources are my own unless otherwise stated.

3. Of the 99 stanzas, 74 follow this pattern. Of the others, 11 show an AAAAA pattern, another 11 an ABBAB scheme, 2 are ABAAB, and 1 is ABABC, with the penultimate syllable of the last line corresponding to the A rhyme.

4. Maurice Westmoreland noted these dialect features. "Easternisms" within the text include the placement of an article before a possessive pronoun, as in *la mi muerte* 'the my death' (line 29S:4) and *la mi partida* 'the my departure' (line 96S:3); the use of the form *aquesta* 'this' (lines 60S:5, 82S:1); and the full usage of the present perfect tense, a feature of eastern Spanish dialects which at the time was not yet very well established in Castilian.

5. I am grateful to Judith Wilson of the Houghton Library for providing me with information on the volume's content and accession. Pérez Gómez (1976–77:501) mentions an undated edition of the *auto*, listed as c. 1595, offered in a catalog from Christie's of London, from the collection of Thomas Croft. This edition was part of a two-volume set of Spanish imprints, one volume containing 14 pieces and the other 17. Since the Houghton Library imprint is part of a volume containing a total of 17 pieces, it is possible that this is the edition sold by Christie's.

6. Most of my information comes from McKendrick (1989) and Shergold (1967). Both of these are synthetic works incorporating a great deal of earlier research, much of it by Spanish scholars. I have provided page citations to these two books with regard to some specific points; other works are cited where used.

7. All biblical citations in English follow the King James translation of 1611. Numbering of the Psalms also follows that version. Note that these are one number higher than in the Latin Vulgate. Biblical citations in Latin are from the Vulgate.

8. It was Rouanet's notes on this *auto* that first alerted me to the existence of Izquierdo's play.

9. Wilson and Wilson (1984:plates III–11 and III–24) reproduce two miniatures of this scene; both are from French manuscripts of the popular *Speculum humanae salvationis* series.

10. My comments are based on a non-systematic search, which did turn up enough examples to support these generalizations. Most of the examples I located are woodcuts from Northern Europe, for which an extensive corpus of published catalogs is available. Spanish artists and printers tended to follow similar conventions and sometimes borrowed directly from Netherlandish and German sources. But I have not located examples of these particular scenes from books printed in Spain. None are included in Lyell's study of Spanish book illustration (1976).

11. My examples of hell-mouth representations of the harrowing, in addition to Figure 2, are Beuken and Marrow (1979:51v); Labriola and Smeltz (1990:scene h); Wilson and Wilson (1984:194); and Verdier (1974:fig. 5). "Architectural" renderings, in addition to Figure 3, are illustrated in Falk (1986:vol. 15A, plate 15, vol. 24A, plate 109); Friedländer and Rosenberg (1978:plate 374 by Lucas Cranach); Geisberg (1974:vol. 1, plate G.18b); Hollstein (1954–55:X, 98; XII, 37, 87, 98); Jahn (1972:plate 552); Knappe (1965:plates 64, 193, 279, all by Dürer); Muther (1972:316); Verdier (1976:fig. 6). Stuart (1913) discusses medieval stage settings of the harrowing of hell, which could use either mode of representation or a combination of both: doors enclose Limbo while the dragon mouth represents the deeper hell of the damned, or Christ must first break down the doors and then enter the mouth in order to reach the Holy Fathers.

12. These eight examples are from Falk 1986:vol. 15, plate 13; Geisberg 1974: vol. 1, plate G.13d, vol. 4, plates G.1406, G.1461; Hollstein 1954–55:X, 211; Knappe 1965:plates 242, 261; Muther 1972:plate 173.

13. Álvarez Lopera (1985:16) discusses El Greco's work and mentions that the other four artists also painted the scene. I examined reproductions of the works in Gould (1976); Gudiol (1973); Goldscheider (1938); Friedländer and Rosenberg (1978); Pallucchini and Canova (1973); and Pignatti (1976).

14. Four versions of the painting exist, two of which are probably studio

copies. Gudiol (1973) gives the dates 1587–1597; Goldscheider (1938) places the work in 1580–1590.

Chapter 2

1. On the colonial book trade, see Leonard (1933, 1949, 1992) and Fernández del Castillo (1982). Book registers from the period in question are reproduced in Leonard (1933:263–77) and Fernández del Castillo (1982:263–81).

2. Information on viceroys is from Torquemada (1975–83:II); on Moya de Contreras, from Poole (1987).

3. My estimates for the native, Spanish, and mixed populations are based on the data presented by Gibson (1964:377–81, 460–62). I have attempted to arrive at approximate figures for the period 1585–90. Census data are sketchy at best; these estimates are very rough approximations.

4. There may be some confusion over the terms Mexico, Tlatelolco, and Tenochtitlan. Some early colonial writers identify Mexico with Tenochtitlan and consider Tlatelolco to be separate from Mexico. Also, since Mexico later became the name for the independent republic, there may be confusion between the city and the country. In my usage, Mexico refers to the urban center that included both Tlatelolco and Tenochtitlan.

5. Lockhart (1992:94–96, 114–16) discusses these usages of *macehualli* and *nican titlacah*. See this source also for information on the meaning and functions of the *altepetl* and on native social structure and government.

6. On the San José de los Naturales chapel, see McAndrew (1965:368–98). The Franciscan mission in New Spain left a large corpus of original chronicles, letters, and reports, of which the most important are Motolinia (1979), Mendieta (1980), Torquemada (1975–83), Valadés (1989), Vetancurt (1971), and documents compiled by García Icazbalceta (1971a, 1971b). It has also been studied extensively by later scholars. Much of the literature takes an apologetic, or at least sympathetic, attitude toward the friars. The classic study is Ricard (1966); he discusses the other mendicant orders (mainly Dominicans and Augustinians) as well. Books specifically on the Franciscans include Baudot (1983), Phelan (1970), and Gómez Canedo (1977). The architectural studies of McAndrew (1965) and Kubler (1982) are also useful general sources on the mendicant missions.

7. Gibson (1964:173, 373–76); Torquemada (1975–83:V, 338); Victoria Moreno (1983:292–93). According to Gibson the San Pablo church had been administered by secular clergy for a time before it was turned over to the Augustinians. The principal source on the Augustinians in New Spain is Grijalva (1624); on the Dominicans, Dávila Padilla's chronicle of 1595 (1955) and Franco's of 1645 (1900); on the Jesuits, Pérez de Ribas (1645) and Alegre (1956–60); on the Carmelites, Victoria Moreno (1983).

8. Horcasitas's *Teatro náhuatl* (1974) remains the authoritative treatise. Arróniz (1979) is a good general study; Ravicz (1970) is a useful source in English. Other studies include those of Sten (1982); Rojas Garcidueñas (1935); Pazos (1951);

Garibay K. (1971:II, chapter 5); Bopp (1953); Trexler (1987:chapter 13); Hunter (1961); Cornyn and McAfee (1944); Williams (1990); Ricard (1966:chapter 12); García Icazbalceta (1968); Castañeda (1936). Most recently, Lockhart has included a brief discussion in his lengthy monograph on colonial Nahuas (1992:401–10); he includes some comments on the Holy Wednesday drama. Paso y Troncoso published several scripts in his *Biblioteca Náuatl* series between 1899 and 1907; all of these are republished in Horcasitas (1974). Motolinia (1979) gives the most detailed eyewitness descriptions of early Nahuatl dramas; Ciudad Real (1976) is an important source from the 1580s.

The five known scripts that may be copies or versions of sixteenth-century compositions are "El Juicio Final," "La Adoración de los Reyes," "El Sacrificio de Isaac," and two didactic plays that Cornyn dubbed "Tlacahuapahualiztli (Bringing up Children)" and "Souls and Testamentary Executors." The first three of these are published in Nahuatl and Spanish in Horcasitas (1974). Ravicz's book (1970) includes English translations of these plays, based on Paso y Troncoso's earlier Spanish versions, and of "Souls and Testamentary Executors," based on a translation by Cornyn; she did not publish the Nahuatl texts. Cornyn and McAfee published "Tlacahuapahualiztli" in Nahuatl and English (1944). The "Juicio Final" script, dated 1678, and the undated "Tlacahuapahualiztli" script are housed in the Library of Congress. The other three share a manuscript, dated 1760, that entered the Archivo Histórico of the library of Mexico's Museo Nacional de Antropología in 1945; this manuscript is missing but copies survive. A "Comedia de los Reyes" dating probably to 1607 was published by Paso y Troncoso and is also published in Horcasitas; the original is missing from the Chicago Public Library. Horcasitas and Ravicz also include some later colonial scripts. Hunter (1960) published a 1641 Nahuatl play that is a somewhat abridged and simplified version of Calderón de la Barca's *auto sacramental* "El Gran Teatro del Mundo"; the text is housed at the University of California's Bancroft Library along with Nahuatl translations of two Lope de Vega plays and a comic intermezzo.

Castañeda (1936) published a play written in Spanish about the conversion to Christianity of the Nahua rulers of Tlaxcala. This play may date to the sixteenth century; Castañeda claims that the handwriting is sixteenth century and the piece is older than three other texts bound with it in a volume dated 1619. His attribution of the text to the Franciscan Motolinia is purely imaginative.

9. Cornyn and McAfee (1944:316), followed by Garibay (1971:II, 128), mention an *auto* of the conversion of Saint Paul performed in Nahuatl in 1530 in the patio of the church where the cathedral was later built. They give no source for this information, and Horcasitas could find no substantiation for it (1974:448). The Judgment play was recorded by a native historian for Sahagún (1950–82:VIII, 8) and by Chimalpahin Cuauhtlehuanitzin (1965b:253). Fray Andrés de Olmos is credited with having written a play on this subject, which may or may not have been the one performed at Tlatelolco and San José (see Garibay 1971:II, 131; Horcasitas 1974:563–64; Baudot 1983:142). Victoria Moreno (1983:293) mentions the Carmelites' use of *comedias* for explaining Christian doctrine and morals to the native residents of San Sebastián. Arróniz (1979) includes chapters on Dominican and Jesuit theater. Some of the Jesuit practices are described in Pérez de Ribas

(1645:738, 742). Augustinians sponsored enactments of Mary and Joseph's journey to Bethlehem (Weckmann 1984:I, 256).

10. The preconquest ceremonies performed by the Mexica are described and depicted in colonial sources, which inevitably reflect some selection and reinterpretation. The most important narrative sources are Sahagún (1950–82, especially Book II) and Durán (1967). Nahua concepts of the human being have been most thoroughly explored by López Austin (1980). The principal corpus of Nahuatl ritual songs is the *Cantares mexicanos* (Bierhorst 1985). The construction and dissolution of identity through the manipulation of ritual paraphernalia is an aspect of Nahua religion particularly emphasized by Clendinnen (1990, 1991). Her 1990 article explores postconquest continuities in ritual behavior, especially the use of religious images, vestments, and other paraphernalia.

11. Collections of *huehuehtlahtolli* orations are Bautista (1600, facsimile and Spanish translation 1988), Sahagún (1950–82:VI), Karttunen and Lockhart (1987). On the genre, see also Garibay K. (1971:I, chapter 8), León-Portilla (1969, 1985, 1992), Sullivan (1974, 1986).

12. Horcasitas (1974:73) quotes a passage from a Nahuatl chronicle dating to the mid-sixteenth century. It refers to (one or more) *neixcuitilli* beginning to be performed and states (my translation): "things were not hidden, and the demon (as *tlacatecolotl*) did not mock Christians." Horcasitas reads this as implying that, according to this chronicler, the performance of such plays actually served to protect the community and keep the Devil away. I followed this interpretation earlier (Burkhart 1992a:266), but I now think that the passage refers to the content of the play(s), which showed how Christians should not incite the Devil's mockery by keeping secrets.

13. Trexler states that "the 'signores and principals' who played theatrical roles . . . clearly had a class interest in preserving their hegemony through the new theatre" (1987:608).

14. On these officials and their duties see Borah (1983) and Kellogg (1995). A man named Pero Díaz Agüero was *procurador general* during the 1590s (Kellogg 1995:6, 14, 16–20, 40); it is possible that he was related to this Juan Díaz de Agüero. I do not know what role the manuscript might have played in some legal case.

15. I thank Wayne Ruwet for sending me a copy of this article and calling my attention to its relevance in this context. Mendieta also lists lay brothers, including the great educator and fluent Nahuatl speaker Pedro de Gante, but he does not indicate their language competence.

16. Biographical data on Torquemada are presented by Miguel León-Portilla in Torquemada (1975–83:VII, 21–28). Chimalpahin Cuauhtlehuanitzin (1965a:34) places Torquemada and Gamboa at San José in July of 1590 and April of 1591. Torquemada states that he was at Tlatelolco when Viceroy Velasco instituted the chicken tax in 1592 (1975–83:II, 423).

17. Wayne Ruwet provided me with a copy of this document, dated 1571.

18. David Szewczyk of the Philadelphia Rare Books and Manuscripts Company identified the watermarks in his evaluation of the manuscript in 1986. Szewczyk cites the Reference Department of the Vatican Library for information on the relationship between the dates of Saint Bartholomew's day and the eleventh

Sunday after Pentecost. The only years during the second half of the sixteenth century when this Sunday immediately followed the saint's festival were 1565, 1576, 1585, and 1590.

19. Primary sources on the Colegio include Mendieta (1980:414–18); Sahagún (1950–82:introductory volume, 82–85); documents edited by García Icazbalceta (1947, 1971b:70–73; 1971c:241–71). These include a document called the *Códice Mendieta*, a record of the Colegio's financial accounts intermittently covering the period from 1567 to 1587. This source mentions the four cooks and other employees (García Icazbalceta 1971c:252–53). The description of the boys' living arrangements and daily schedule is in Mendieta. Of secondary studies, Steck (1944) and Kobayashi (1974:292–407) are the most complete; see also Mathes (1985), Osorio Romero (1990:22–45), Ocaranza (1934) and Ricard (1966:218–29).

20. The most important primary sources on the *calmecac* are Sahagún (1950–82, especially Books III and VI) and the *Codex Mendoza* (Berdan and Anawalt 1992).

21. The exclusionary policy applied also to persons of mixed descent. The complicated legal history surrounding the issue of Indian ordination is well explicated by Poole (1981). The policy was never carved in stone and occasional exceptions were made, especially in cases of mestizo offspring of native nobles and in frontier regions. The proceedings of Archbishop Moya de Contreras's 1585 ecclesiastical council also excluded Indians and persons of mixed race. But when the council edicts were finally published and enacted in 1622, the Latin text did not exclude Indians and only urged caution regarding persons of mixed heritage, the word *Indi* 'Indians' having been changed to *Inde* 'whence' in the text but not in the paragraph heading. Poole attributes the change to opposition from the Roman curia, which did not understand Spanish prejudices against the native people and was also concerned about the shortage of priests who spoke native languages. In effect, the edicts as published provided a legal loophole for those ordinations of native men that were performed.

22. On the educated nobility's concern with traditional rank, see also Gruzinski (1991:68–69). On the rhetorical strategy of asserting servitude to Spain in order to claim privileges, see also Klor de Alva (1992:364).

23. The precise dates of the transfers to native control and back to Franciscan control cannot be ascertained. Steck (1944:48) gives 1547 and 1569, but this seems to be based on his own deductions. Kobayashi (1974:348) places the return to Franciscan supervision at 1572 or 1573. Sahagún, the principal source on this matter, contradicts himself. He describes the return to Franciscan supervision as occurring forty years after the Colegio's founding, which would place it in 1576. But he also describes the transfer to native control as occurring "more than ten years" after the 1536 founding, and states that the collegians ran the school for "more than twenty years" (Sahagún 1950–82:introductory volume, 84). This makes for more than thirty years, but not forty. Sahagún writing in 1576 describes the Franciscan takeover as a past event, and one that preceded the 1576 epidemic. Account records from the college state that, as of 1572, it was under the charge of the Franciscans at Tlatelolco, of which Molina was the current guardian; the accounts from 1574 name Sahagún as "the person who is in charge of the administration of said college" (García Icazbalceta 1971c:254, 258). See also Ricard (1966:359n23).

24. On Franciscan utopianism see Phelan (1970), Baudot (1983).

25. The skit is described by Ciudad Real (1976:I, 16–17); I follow Mauricio Mixco's English translation of the quotations (Nicolau D'Olwer 1987:100). The Latin passage, from Psalm 41:1, means "Blessed is he that considereth the poor."

26. The complicated history of the Ponce affair is summarized by Baudot (1974); see also Poole (1987).

27. Dibble's 1974 article on Sahagún's catechistic writings is the first contemporary scholarly study of these Nahuatl texts. My earlier book (Burkhart 1989) is the first monograph to analyze and interpret some of these texts; I have also published several articles on aspects of this literature and particular texts (Burkhart 1986a, 1986b, 1988a, 1988b, 1992b, 1992c, 1995a, 1995b). See also Baudot (1976, 1990), Anderson (1983, 1984, 1990), Sell (1991), Anderson and Ruwet (1993).

28. On Sahagún and his ethnographic project see volumes edited by Edmonson (1974) and by Klor de Alva, Nicholson, and Quiñones Keber (1988); also Nicolau D'Olwer (1987) and essays by Dibble and Anderson in Sahagún (1950–82:introductory volume).

29. Dates are as reconstructed by Nicolau D'Olwer (1987:33, 36).

30. These two scholars from Cuauhtitlan are credited by Velázquez with the authorship of the *Codex Chimalpopoca*, an important source on Nahua mythology written in Cuauhtitlan (Velázquez 1975:x-xi). His only evidence is that the two men happened to be scholars from Cuauhtitlan who helped with Sahagún's research and whose names are recorded. Garibay K. accepts this attribution, and also imagines that Jacobita wrote part of the text (1971:II, 226–27). Gingerich (1986:50) mentions Velázquez's attribution to Vegerano but accepts this as only a possibility. Bierhorst (1992:4) notes that the two scholars were from Cuauhtitlan but takes this as evidence only that that community was involved in the florescence of Nahuatl writing occurring during the period; he prudently treats the *Codex*'s author(s) as anonymous. Jacobita's and Vegerano's employment at the school is noted in García Icazbalceta (1971c: 250–54, 264). Azcapotzalco, Cuauhtitlan, and Xochimilco were major Nahua communities on the mainland near Mexico.

31. I have elsewhere discussed some of the native-style and nativistically oriented materials in the *Psalmodia* (see Burkhart 1992a, 1992b, 1995a; also 1986). Anderson, translator of the entire volume (Sahagún 1993), pays little attention to indigenous input in the text (see also Anderson 1984, 1990).

32. Biographical data are in Zulaica y Gárate (1991:219–21); see also León-Portilla's introduction to Bautista (1988). Bautista apparently died not long before fray Juan de Torquemada finished his chronicle, which was in 1612–13 (Torquemada 1975–83:VI, 124, 395; Beristáin de Souza 1947:I, 230; Zulaica y Gárate 1991:221); León-Portilla considers 1609 a probable date for the friar's death (in Bautista 1988:22).

33. The discussion of the Nahua scholars appears on pages 2 to 5 of the prologue to Bautista 1606. Approval to publish the work was granted in 1597, but Bautista did not write this prologue until 1606; in it he refers to Valeriano's 1605 death as having occurred "last year." The prologue is reprinted in García Icazbalceta (1954:474–78).

34. The financial records from the Colegio, with their notations of Valeriano's wages, are in García Icazbalceta (1971c:250–52, 254). I thank Frances Karttunen

for sharing with me her material on Valeriano, now published in Karttunen 1995. Valeriano's reputation was such that he came to be credited with a version of the foundation legend for the Mexican shrine of the Virgin of Guadalupe, but the evidence linking this story to Valeriano is insubstantial (see Poole 1995, also Burkhart 1993, Karttunen 1995).

35. Bautista gives this date; Torquemada places Oroz's death on June 10, 1597 (1975–83:VI, 388).

36. Bautista's words are *"y por su mano ha scripto, y passado todo quanto he impresso hasta aqui, y podre imprimir en muchos dias."*

37. I have dealt in various works with the friars' treatment of translation and specific problems of translation. Watts provides interesting comments on medieval and Renaissance theories of memory, rhetoric, and signification, including the belief that signs are not arbitrary but are part of what she calls a "theophanic code of the universe" thought to be common to all humanity. Thus, for example, Franciscans could reasonably assume that Egyptian hieroglyphs and the Mesoamerican writing systems were essentially cognate (Watts 1991, see especially 422–23).

38. Beristáin de Souza (1947:I, 231), listing Bautista's works, mentions one entitled: "Spiritual dramas: Dramatizations of the scenes of the Passion of Jesus Christ for the Indians." If such a work indeed existed, it would be a more likely locus for the Holy Wednesday drama than any of the three volumes Bautista mentions. Beristáin de Souza cites Torquemada, who, he says, saw this manuscript and deemed it to be "of much erudition and elegance." What Torquemada in fact says, however, is simply that Bautista made plays "of much elegance and erudition" (Torquemada 1975–83:VI, 395). Torquemada's statement follows a passage describing how another friar, Francisco de Gamboa, had "dramatizations of scenes from the Passion of Christ" performed to accompany his Friday sermons. Gamboa also instituted Sunday afternoon dramatizations of *ejemplos*, or exemplary stories. Torquemada goes on to say that he himself has written such plays, and so had his former teacher, Bautista. Beristáin de Souza's attribution of Passion plays to Bautista is, thus, without foundation.

39. Paso y Troncoso's edition of this play was based on a photostat from the Chicago Public Library. In 1958, when Fernando Horcasitas sought to obtain a copy of the manuscript, it was found to be missing. Paso y Troncoso's transcription omitted passages that he was unable to decipher; also, he transposed the play into his idiosyncratic orthography. Horcasitas republished the text, changing it to a more conventional orthography (Paso y Troncoso 1902; Horcasitas 1974).

As reported by Paso y Troncoso, the manuscript identified Bautista as *Guardia de Santa Teulogia de Santiago Teluco Mexico* and gave the date as *Del y sietecientos y siete años*. The writer appears to have conflated Bautista's position as guardian of the Santiago Tlatelolco friary with his role as teacher of theology. The date poses a more serious problem; 1707 is obviously an impossible date for a text sponsored by Bautista. That 1607 was intended is perhaps the most reasonable guess, but I have no independent evidence that Bautista was back at Tlatelolco as guardian at that time.

40. Mijangos's phrase *todas las demas* could be understood to imply that fray Juan Baustista was responsible for the present work that bears Mijangos's name.

According to Beristáin de Souza (1947:I, 231) and Garibay (1971:II, 186, probably following Beristáin), one of Bautista's works was titled *Teoyotezcatl ó teoyoticatezcatl: Espejo espiritual* and published in Tlatelolco by the printer Diego López Dávalos; the date is not specified. Dávalos, who issued Bautista's other published works as well (with the exception of the 1600 *Huehuetlatolli*) is the publisher of Mijangos's *Espejo divino*, which lists Mexico as the place of publication. No extant copies of this alleged Bautista imprint are known. It may be a figment of Beristáin de Souza's imagination (such are not unknown; see above, note 38) or this may be a garbled reference to Mijangos's book, which bears a note stating that Bautista examined the work in February, 1606. However, if Bautista did write such a work, it is possible that Mijangos borrowed all or part of it. If so, this would help to explain Agustín de la Fuente's association with the Augustinian.

41. Mijangos's next book, issued in 1624, does not mention de la Fuente's name. Garibay (1971:II, 225) states, without offering any evidence, that de la Fuente was born around the time of the Spanish conquest and died by 1610. Yet Mijangos's statement, which Garibay himself cites (1971:II, 195) indicates that the Nahua scholar was alive in 1611 and apparently not quite on his deathbed, for the Augustinian wishes him many more years of life. Garibay seems to have assumed that de la Fuente, like some of Sahagún's other assistants, was one of the Colegio's first students, although Bautista does not specify this. Indeed, Bautista does not even describe de la Fuente as a "son of the Colegio" or as "brought up in the Colegio," as he does for most of the other scholars whom he discusses (all except Gante and Adriano). If de la Fuente had indeed been 10 or 12 years old in 1536, he would have been well into his eighties by 1610. But there is no reason to assume this, for he may have been a younger man and perhaps did not work with Sahagún until that friar's later years. Sahagún does not name him among those who were with him in the 1558–64 period.

42. In recent years scholars have been paying increasing attention to these Nahuatl civil records, publishing original sources and using them as bases for social- and cultural-historical studies. This research provides knowledge of the broader social context in which Nahuas performed their plays and practiced their other religious customs. I cite below some works that deal with the sixteenth to early seventeenth centuries.

A ground-breaking work was the collection of documents published by Anderson, Berdan, and Lockhart (1976). Karttunen and Lockhart produced philological studies of the corpus, focusing on phenomena of language contact between Nahuatl and Spanish (Karttunen and Lockhart 1976; Karttunen 1985; see also Karttunen 1982). Cline and León-Portilla published a collection of Nahuatl wills from the lakeshore town of Culhuacan (1984); these wills were the basis for Cline's 1986 monograph on Culhuacan social history. *Cabildo* proceedings from Tlaxcala are analyzed and excerpted by Lockhart, Berdan, and Anderson (1986). Kellogg has focused on issues of social organization and gender relations, using Nahuatl wills and legal testimony (1984, 1986, 1995, in press). Schroeder's book on the Nahua historian Chimalpahin is the first in-depth analysis of a native chronicler and his work (1991). Haskett's history of colonial native government in Cuernavaca draws heavily on later colonial documents but includes data on the earlier period (1991). Several of Lockhart's articles based on Nahuatl documents are collected in Lockhart (1991); his major work on colonial Nahuas (1992) relies heavily on native writings.

43. Data on tribute and taxation are from Gibson (1964:202–5, 230–31, 251, 360). Torquemada mentions the chicken tax protest, in which he and fray Gerónimo de Zárate participated (1975–83:II, 423).

44. Information on *repartimiento* is from Gibson 1964:224–33.

45. Data on opposition to *repartimiento* and the ecclesiastical council's treatment of the issue are from Poole (1987:179–87). On the council and its treatment of Indian issues, see also Navarro B. (1944) and Vera (1879).

46. Data on the General Indian Court are from Borah (1983:91–120). On Nahua use of the Real Audiencia court, see Kellogg 1995.

47. See my previous works, also Clendinnen (1990).

48. This summary is based mainly on Lockhart's discussion (1992:210–18) and Cline (1986:15). In later colonial times the *fiscal* was typically a high-ranking nobleman second only to the governor as a local authority figure, but Lockhart (1992:211) has found only a few noble *fiscales* mentioned in Nahuatl documents from the sixteenth century, and no *fiscales* at all mentioned prior to 1570. Gruzinski (1991:72–74) also discusses the importance of church offices in providing leadership roles for indigenous persons.

49. Chimalpahin and other native chroniclers also record other religious events from this time period. I was unable to find any references to the Holy Wednesday drama in these sources. In addition to Chimalpahin's works (1889, 1965a, 1965b), I examined the manuscript collection of Nahuatl historical annals in the Biblioteca Nacional de Antropología (*Anales antiguos*) and the chronicles published by Ramírez (1949, 1954).

Prologue to the Translations

1. See especially Hymes (1977, 1981, 1992), Tedlock (1983), Mattina (1987). Hymes has focused on recovering the poetic structure of written texts for which tapes of oral performance are not available. He seeks syntactical indicators of line or larger units, especially particles of speech customarily used to mark poetic structure. Tedlock has focused on oral performance and attempts to suggest on the printed page the performer's pauses and changes in volume and intonation. The differences between the two approaches have, in Hymes's view (1992:84), been overstated by others as a "Tedlock: Hymes = pause: particle" equation. Hymes asserts that there is no basic contradiction between the methods; researchers should look for what counts in a particular text or tradition. With older, written materials, Hymes's strategies are more useful.

2. With regard to songs, which are quite distinct from oratory with respect to style and vocabulary, Karttunen and Lockhart found no consistent evidence of lines but were able to identify larger "verse" units in song texts (1980).

Bierhorst finds evidence of song stanzas composed of verses, refrains, and lita-nies (1985:42–43). See also my discussion of "lines" and stanzas in a song from Sahagún's *Psalmodia christiana* (Burkhart 1992a).

3. Burkhart (1991:155; 1992a:275). I also mistakenly gave the number of speeches in this segment as three.

References Cited

Adorno, Rolena. 1986. *Guaman Poma: Writing and Resistance in Colonial Peru.* Austin: University of Texas Press.

Alegre, Francisco Javier. 1956–60. *Historia de la provincia de la Compañia de Jesus de Nueva España.* Ernest J. Burrus and Felix Zubillaga, eds. 4 vols. Rome: Biblioteca Instituto Historici S.J.

Alvarado Tezozomoc, Fernando. 1975. *Crónica mexicayotl.* Adrián León, trans. Mexico City: Universidad Nacional Autónoma de México.

Álvarez Lopera, José. 1985. *La Pasión de Cristo en la pintura del Greco.* Madrid: Fundación Universitaria Española.

Anales antiguos de México y sus contornos. n.d. Biblioteca del Museo Nacional de Antropología, Archivo Histórico, Col. Antiq. 273–274.

Anderson, Arthur J. O. 1983. Sahagún's "Doctrinal Encyclopedia." *Estudios de Cultura Náhuatl* 16:109–22.

———. 1984. The "San Bernardino" of Sahagún's *Psalmodia. Indiana* 9:107–14.

———. 1990. La Salmodia de Sahagún. *Estudios de Cultura Náhuatl* 20:17–38.

Anderson, Arthur J. O., Frances Berdan, and James Lockhart, trans. and ed. 1976. *Beyond the Codices: The Nahua View of Colonial Mexico.* Berkeley: University of California Press.

Anderson, Arthur J. O., and Wayne Ruwet. 1993. Sahagún's Manual del Christiano: History and Identification. *Estudios de Cultura Náhuatl* 23:17–45.

Andrews, J. Richard. 1975. *Introduction to Classical Nahuatl.* Austin: University of Texas Press.

Anunciación, fray Domingo de la. 1565. *Doctrina Xpiana breue y cõpendiosa.* Mexico City: Pedro Ocharte.

Anunciación, fray Juan de la. 1575. *Doctrina christiana mvy cvmplida.* Mexico City: Pedro Balli.

———. 1577. *Sermonario en lengva mexicana.* Mexico City: Antonio Ricardo.

Arróniz, Othón. 1977. *Teatros y escenarios del siglo de oro.* Madrid: Editorial Gredos.

———. 1979. *Teatro de evangelización en Nueva España.* Mexico City: Universidad Nacional Autónoma de México.

Barlow, Robert H. 1989. *Tlaltelolco: Fuentes e historia. Obras de Robert Barlow,* vol. 2. Jesús Monjarás-Ruiz, Elena Limón, and María de la Cruz Paillés H., eds. Mexico City: Instituto Nacional de Antropología e Historia and Universidad de las Américas.

Barrera y Leirado, Cayetano Alberto de la. 1860. *Catálogo bibliográfico y biográfico del teatro antiguo español desde sus orígenes hasta mediados del siglo XVIII*. Madrid: M. Rivadeneyra.

Baudot, Georges. 1974. The Last Years of Fray Bernardino de Sahagún (1585–90): The Rescue of the Confiscated Works and the Seraphic Conflicts. New Unpublished Documents. In *Sixteenth-Century Mexico: The Work of Sahagún*, ed. Munro S. Edmonson, 165–87. Albuquerque: University of New Mexico Press.

———. 1976. Fray Andrés de Olmos y su tratado de los pecados mortales en lengua náhuatl. *Estudios de Cultura Náhuatl* 12:33–59.

———. 1983. *Utopía e historia en México: Los primeros cronistas de la civilización mexicana (1520–1569)*. Vicente González Loscertales, trans. Madrid: Espasa-Calpe.

———. 1990. Vanidad y ambición en el *Tratado de los siete pecados mortales* en lengua náhuatl de fray Andrés de Olmos. *Estudios de Cultura Náhuatl* 20:39–63.

Bautista, fray Juan. 1600. *Hvehvetlahtolli que contiene las pláticas que los padres y madres hicieron a sus hijos y a sus hijas, y los señores a sus uasallos, todas llenas de doctrina moral y politica*. Mexico City: M. Ocharte.

———. 1606. *Sermonario en lengua mexicana*. Mexico City: Diego López Dávalos.

———. 1988. *Huehuehtlahtolli, que contiene las pláticas que los padres y madres hicieron a sus hijos y a sus hijas, y los señores a sus vasallos, todas llenas de doctrina moral y politica*. Facsimile of 1600 edition, with introduction by Miguel León-Portilla and Spanish translation by Librado Silva Galeana. Mexico City: National Commission of the V Centenary of the Encounter of Two Worlds.

Berdan, Frances F., and Patricia Rieff Anawalt, eds. 1992. *The Codex Mendoza*. 4 vols. Berkeley: University of California Press.

Beristáin de Souza, José Mariano. 1947. *Biblioteca Hispano Americana Septentrional*. 5 vols. Mexico City: Ediciones Fuente Cultural.

Bernard of Clairvaux, and Amadeus of Lausanne. 1979. *Magnificat: Homilies in Praise of the Blessed Virgin Mary*. Marie-Bernard Saïd and Grace Perigo, trans. Kalamazoo, Mich.: Cistercian Publications.

Beuken, W. H., and James H. Marrow. 1979. *Spiegel van den Leven ons Heren (Mirror of the Life of our Lord): Diplomatic Edition of the Text and Facsimile of the 42 Miniatures of a 15th Century Typological Life of Christ in the Pierpont Morgan Library, New York*. Doornspijk, Holland: Editions Davaco.

Bibliotheca Mejicana: A Catalogue of an extraordinary Collection of Books & Manuscripts, almost wholly relating to the History and Literature of North and South America, particularly Mexico. 1968. New York: Burt Franklin.

Bierhorst, John, trans. and ed. 1985. *Cantares Mexicanos: Songs of the Aztecs*. Stanford, Calif.: Stanford University Press.

———. 1992a. *Codex Chimalpopoca: The Text in Nahuatl with a Glossary and Grammatical Notes*. Tucson: University of Arizona Press.

———. 1992b. *History and Mythology of the Aztecs: The Codex Chimalpopoca*. Tucson: University of Arizona Press.

Bohannan, Paul, and Philip Curtin. 1971. *Africa and Africans*. Garden City, N.Y.: Natural History Press.

Bopp, Marianne O. de. 1953. Autos mexicanos del siglo XVI. *Historia Mexicana* 3:113–23.

Borah, Woodrow. 1983. *Justice by Insurance: The General Indian Court of Colonial Mexico and the Legal Aides of the Half-Real*. Berkeley: University of California Press.

Børresen, Kari Elisabeth. 1971. *Anthropologie médiévale et théologie Mariale*. Oslo: Universitetsforlaget.

Bricker, Victoria Reifler. 1981. *The Indian Christ, The Indian King: The Historical Substrate of Maya Myth and Ritual*. Austin: University of Texas Press.

Bright, William. 1993. *A Coyote Reader*. Berkeley: University of California Press.

Brown, Michael F. 1991. Beyond Resistance: A Comparative Study of Utopian Renewal in Amazonia. *Ethnohistory* 38:388–413.

Buck, Vera Helen, ed. 1937. *Four autos sacramentales of 1590*. University of Iowa Studies in Spanish Language and Literature, 7. Iowa City: University of Iowa.

Burkhart, Louise M. 1986a. Moral Deviance in Sixteenth-Century Nahua and Christian Thought: The Rabbit and the Deer. *Journal of Latin American Lore* 12:107–39.

———. 1986b. Sahagún's *Tlauculcuicatl*: A Nahuatl Lament. *Estudios de Cultura Náhuatl* 18:181–218.

———. 1988a. Doctrinal Aspects of Sahagún's *Colloquios*. In *The Work of Bernardino de Sahagún: Pioneer Ethnographer of Sixteenth-Century Aztec Mexico*, ed. J. Jorge Klor de Alva, H. B. Nicholson and Eloise Quiñones Keber, 65–82. Albany: Institute for Mesoamerican Studies, State University of New York.

———. 1988b. The Solar Christ in Nahuatl Doctrinal Texts of Early Colonial Mexico. *Ethnohistory* 35:234–56.

———. 1989. *The Slippery Earth: Nahua-Christian Moral Dialogue in Sixteenth-Century Mexico*. Tucson: University of Arizona Press.

———. 1991. A Nahuatl Religious Drama of c. 1590. *Latin American Indian Literatures Journal* 7:153–71.

———. 1992a. A Nahuatl Religious Drama from Sixteenth-Century Mexico. *Princeton University Library Chronicle* 53:264–86.

———. 1992b. The Amanuenses Have Appropriated the Text: Interpreting a Nahuatl Song of Santiago. In *On the Translation of Native American Literatures*, ed. Brian Swann, 339–55. Washington, D.C.: Smithsonian Institution Press.

———. 1992c. Flowery Heaven: The Aesthetic of Paradise in Nahuatl Devotional Literature. *Res: Anthropology and Aesthetics* 21:89–109.

———. 1993. The Cult of the Virgin of Guadalupe in Mexico. In *World Spirituality: An Encyclopedic History of the Religious Quest*, vol. 4, *South and Meso-American Native Spirituality*, ed. Gary H. Gossen and Miguel León-Portilla, 198–227. New York: Crossroad Press.

———. 1995a. A Doctrine for Dancing: The Prologue to the *Psalmodia christiana*. *Latin American Indian Literatures Journal* 11:21–33.

———. 1995b. The Voyage of Saint Amaro: A Spanish Legend in Nahuatl Literature. *Colonial Latin American Review* 4:29–57.

———. 1996. Pious Performances: Christian Pageantry and Native Identity in Early Colonial Mexico. In *Native Traditions in the Postconquest World*, ed. Elizabeth H. Boone and Tom Cummins. Washington, D.C.: Dumbarton Oaks (in press).

Campbell, R. Joe. 1985. *A Morphological Dictionary of Classical Nahuatl: A Morpheme Index to the* Vocabulario en lengua mexicana y castellana *of Alonso de Molina*. Madison, Wisc.: Hispanic Seminary of Medieval Studies.

Cantares de los mejicanos y otros opúsculos. n.d. MS 1628bis, Fondo Reservado, Biblioteca Nacional de México.

Caro Baroja, Julio. 1978. *Las formas complejas de la vida religiosa: Religión, sociedad y carácter en España de los siglos XVI y XVII*. Madrid: Akal.

Cartas de Indias. 1970. Facsimile of 1877 Madrid edition. Edmundo Aviña Levy, ed. 2 vols. Guadalajara, Mexico.

Castañeda, Carlos E. 1936. The First American Play. *Texas Catholic Historical Society Preliminary Studies* 3:5–39.

Castillo, Hernando del, ed. 1904. *Cancionero general nueuamete añadido*. Toledo: Juan de Villaquiran, 1520. Facsimile printed for Archer M. Huntington from copy in his library. DeVinne Press.

Catalogus Librorum Manuscriptorum in Biblioteca D. Thomae Phillipps, Bart. n.d. Typis Medio-montanis.

Chimalpahin Cuauhtlehuanitzin, Domingo Francisco de San Antón Muñón. 1889. *Annales de Domingo Francisco de San Antón Muñón Chimalpahin Quauhtlehuanitzin, sixième et septième relations (1258–1612)*. Rémi Siméon, ed. and trans. Paris: Maisonneuve et Ch. Leclerc.

———. 1965a. *Die Relationen Chimalpahin's zur Geschichte México's*. Part 2, *Das Jahrhundert nach der Conquista (1522–1615)*. Günter Zimmermann, ed. Hamburg: Cram, De Gruyter & Co.

———. 1965b. *Relaciones originales de Chalco Amaquemecan*. S. Rendón, trans. and ed. Mexico City: Fondo de Cultura Económica.

Christian, William A., Jr. 1981a. *Apparitions in Late Medieval and Renaissance Spain*. Princeton, N.J.: Princeton University Press.

———. 1981b. *Local Religion in Sixteenth-Century Spain*. Princeton, N.J.: Princeton University Press.

Ciudad Real, fray Antonio de. 1976. *Tratado curioso y docto de las grandezas de la Nueva España*. Josefina García Quintana and Victor M. Castillo Farreras, eds. 2 vols. Mexico City: Universidad Nacional Autónoma de México.

Clendinnen, Inga. 1990. Ways to the Sacred: Reconstructing "Religion" in Sixteenth Century Mexico. *History and Anthropology* 5:105–41.

———. 1991. *Aztecs: An Interpretation*. Cambridge: Cambridge University Press.

Clifford, James. 1988. *The Predicament of Culture: Twentieth-Century Ethnography, Literature, and Art*. Cambridge, Mass.: Harvard University Press.

Cline, S. L. 1986. *Colonial Culhuacan, 1580–1600: A Social History of an Aztec Town*. Albuquerque: University of New Mexico Press.

Cline, S. L., and Miguel León-Portilla, trans. and eds. 1984. *The Testaments of Culhuacan*. Nahuatl Studies Series, 1. Los Angeles: UCLA Latin American Center.

Codex Aubin: Histoire de la nation mexicaine depuis le départ d'Aztlan jusqu'à l'arrivée des conquerants espagnols (et au de la 1607). 1893. Paris: Ernest Leroux.

Códice Osuna. 1947. Mexico City: Instituto Indigenista Interamericano.

Comaroff, Jean. 1985. *Body of Power, Spirit of Resistance: The Culture and History of a South African People*. Chicago: University of Chicago Press.

Comaroff, John, and Jean Comaroff. 1992. *Ethnography and the Historical Imagination*. Boulder, Colo.: Westview Press.

Cornyn, John H., and Byron McAfee, eds. and trans. 1944. Tlacahuapahualiztli (Bringing up Children). *Tlalocan* 1:314–51.

Crawford, J. P. Wickersham. 1967. *Spanish Drama Before Lope de Vega*. Philadelphia: University of Pennsylvania Press.

Cruz, Martín de la. 1964. *Libellus de medicinalibus indorum herbis: Manuscrito azteca de 1552*. Mexico City: Instituto Mexicano del Seguro Social.

Dávila Padilla, fray Augustín. 1955. *Historia de la fundacion y discurso de la provincia de Santiago de Mexico, de la orden de predicadores*. Facsimile of 1595 edition. Mexico City: Editorial Academia Literaria.

Díaz de Escovar, Narciso, and Francisco de P. Lasso de la Vega. 1924. *Historia del teatro español*. Volume 1. Barcelona: Montaner y Simón.

Diccionario Porrúa: Historia, Biografía y Geografía de México. 1964. Mexico City: Editorial Porrúa.

Dibble, Charles E. 1974. The Nahuatlization of Christianity. In *Sixteenth-Century Mexico: The Work of Sahagún*. Ed. Munro S. Edmonson, 225–33. Albuquerque: University of New Mexico Press.

Doctrina cristiana en lengua española y mexicana por los religiosos de la orden de Santo Domingo. 1944. Facsimile of 1548 edition. Colección de Incunables Americanos, siglo XVI, vol. 1. Madrid: Ediciones Cultura Hispánica.

Doctrina, evangelios y epistolas en nahuatl. n.d. Codex Indianorum 7. The John Carter Brown Library, Brown University, Providence, R.I.

Durán, fray Diego. 1967. *Historia de las indias de Nueva España e islas de la tierra firme*. Ángel María Garibay K., ed. Mexico City: Editorial Porrúa.

Edmonson, Munro S., ed. 1974. *Sixteenth-Century Mexico: The Work of Sahagún*. Albuquerque: University of New Mexico Press.

Epístolas en mexicano. 1561. MS 1492, Fondo Reservado, Biblioteca Nacional de México.

Escalona, fray Alonso de. 1588. *Sermones en mexicano*. MS 1482, Fondo Reservado, Biblioteca Nacional de México.

Escudero y Perosso, Francisco. 1894. *Tipografía hispalense: Anales bibliográficos de la ciudad de Sevilla*. Madrid: Sucesores de Rivadeneyra.

Falk, Tilman, ed. 1986. *Hollstein's German Engravings, Etchings and Woodcuts 1400–1700*. Volume 24A. Blaricum, Netherlands: A. L. Van Gendt.

Fernández del Castillo, Francisco. 1982. *Libros y libreros en el siglo XVI*. Mexico City: Fondo de Cultura Económica.

Franco, fray Alonso. 1900. *Segunda parte de la historia de la provincia de Santiago de Mexico orden de predicadores en la Nueva España*. Mexico City: Museo Nacional.

Friedländer, Max J., and Jakob Rosenberg. 1978. *The Paintings of Lucas Cranach*. Ithaca, N.Y.: Cornell University Press.

Ferguson, George. 1954. *Signs and Symbols in Christian Art*. New York: Oxford University Press.

Gallardo, Bartolomé José. 1888. *Ensayo de una biblioteca española de libros raros y curiosos*. Volume 3. Madrid: Manuel Tello.

Gante, fray Pedro de. 1981. *Doctrina cristiana en lengua Mexicana (edición facsimilar de la de 1553)*. Ernesto de la Torre Villar, ed. Mexico City: Centro de Estudios Históricos Fray Bernardino de Sahagún.

Gaona, fray Juan de. 1582. *Colloqvios de la paz, y tranquilidad christiana, en lengua mexicana*. Mexico City: Pedro Ocharte.

García Icazbalceta, Joaquín. 1947. *Don fray Juan de Zumárraga, primer obispo y arzobispo de México*. 4 vols. Mexico City: Editorial Porrúa.

——. 1954. *Bibliografía mexicana del siglo XVI*. Agustín Millares Carlo, ed. Mexico City: Fondo de Cultura Económica.

——. 1968. Representaciones religiosas de México en el siglo xvi. In *Obras de D. J. García Icazbalceta*, volume 2. New York: Burt Franklin.

García Icazbalceta, Joaquín, ed. 1971a. *Cartas de religiosos de Nueva España, 1539–1594*. Nendeln, Liechtenstein: Kraus-Thomson.

——. 1971b. *Códice franciscano, siglo XVI*. Nendeln, Liechtenstein: Kraus-Thomson.

——. 1971c. *Códice mendieta: Documentos franciscanos, siglos XVI y XVII*. Nendeln, Liechtenstein: Kraus-Thomson.

García Pimentel, Luis, ed. 1897. *Descripción del arzobispado de México hecha en 1570 y otros documentos*. Mexico City: José Joaquín Terrazas e Hijas.

Gardel, Luis D. 1959. *La cofradía del Santo Despedimiento: Un manuscrito mexicano del siglo XVII*. Rio de Janeiro: published by the author.

Garibay K., Ángel María. 1971. *Historia de la literatura náhuatl*. 2 vols. Mexico City: Editorial Porrúa.

——, ed. 1979. *Teogonía e historia de los mexicanos: Tres opúsculos del siglo XVI*. Mexico City: Editorial Porrúa.

Geisberg, Max. 1974. *The German Single-Leaf Woodcut: 1500–1550*. Revised and edited by Walter L. Strauss. 4 volumes. New York: Hacker Art Books.

Gibson, Charles. 1964. *The Aztecs Under Spanish Rule: A History of the Indians of the Valley of Mexico, 1519–1810*. Stanford, Calif.: Stanford University Press.

Gillet, Joseph E., ed. 1932. Tres pasos de la Pasión y una égloga de la Resurrección (Burgos, 1520). *Publications of the Modern Language Association of America* 47:949–80.

——. 1933. An Easter-Play by Juan de Pedraza (1549). *Revue Hispanique* 81: part 1, 550–607.

Gingerich, Willard. 1986. Quetzalcoatl and the Agon of Time: A Literary Reading of the *Anales de Cuauhtitlan*. *New Scholar* 10:41–60.

——. 1992. Ten Types of Ambiguity in Nahuatl Poetry, or William Empson among the Aztecs. In *On the Translation of Native American Literatures*, ed. Brian Swann, 356–67. Washington, D.C.: Smithsonian Institution Press.

Goldscheider, Ludwig. 1938. *El Greco*. London: George Allen & Unwin.

Gómez Canedo, Lino. 1977. *Evangelización y conquista: Experiencia franciscana en hispanoamerica*. Mexico City: Editorial Porrúa.

Gómez de Cervantes, Gonzalo. 1944. *La vida económica y social de Nueva España al finalizar el siglo XVI*. Alberto María Carreño, ed. Mexico: Antigua Librería Robredo.

Gossen, Gary H. 1986. The Chamula Festival of Games: Native Macroanalysis and Social Commentary in a Maya Carnival. In *Symbol and Meaning Beyond the*

Closed Community: Essays in Mesoamerican Ideas, ed. Gary H. Gossen, 227–54. Albany: Institute for Mesoamerican Studies, State University of New York.

Gould, Cecil. 1976. *The Paintings of Correggio*. London: Faber and Faber.

Grijalva, fray Juan de. 1624. *Crónica de la orden de N. P. S. Augustin en las provincias de la Nueva España*. Mexico City: Juan Ruiz.

Gruzinski, Serge. 1989. Individualization and Acculturation: Confession among the Nahuas of Mexico from the Sixteenth to the Eighteenth Century. In *Sexuality and Marriage in Colonial Latin America*, ed. Asunción Lavrin, 96–117. Lincoln: University of Nebraska Press.

———. 1991. *La colonización de lo imaginario: Sociedades indígenas y occidentalización en el México español, Siglos XVI–XVIII*. Jorge Ferreiro, trans. Mexico City: Fondo de Cultura Económica.

Gudiol, José. 1973. *El Greco*. Kenneth Lyons, trans. New York: The Viking Press.

Hanks, William F. 1986. Authenticity and Ambivalence in the Text: A Colonial Maya Case. *American Ethnologist* 13:721–44.

———. 1988. Grammar, Style, and Meaning in a Maya Manuscript. *International Journal of American Linguistics* 54:331–65.

———. 1989. Text and Textuality. *Annual Review of Anthropology* 18:95–127.

Haskett, Robert. 1991. *Indigenous Rulers: An Ethnohistory of Town Government in Colonial Cuernavaca*. Albuquerque: University of New Mexico Press.

Hollstein, F. W. H. 1954–55. *Dutch and Flemish Etchings, Engravings and Woodcuts ca. 1450–1700*. Volumes 10 and 12. Amsterdam: Menno Hertzberger.

Horcasitas, Fernando. 1974. *El teatro náhuatl: Épocas novohispana y moderna*. Mexico City: Universidad Nacional Autónoma de México.

The Hours of the Divine Office in English and Latin. 1963. 3 vols. Collegeville, Minn.: Liturgical Press.

Hunter, William A. 1960. The Calderonian Auto Sacramental El Gran Teatro del Mundo: An Edition and Translation of a Nahuatl Version. In *The Native Theatre in Middle America*. Middle American Research Institute Publication 27, 105–202. New Orleans: Tulane University.

Hymes, Dell. 1977. Discovering Oral Performance and Measured Verse in American Indian Narrative. *New Literary History* 8:431–57.

———. 1981. *In vain I tried to tell you: Essays in Native American Ethnopoetics*. Philadelphia: University of Pennsylvania Press.

———. 1992. Use All There Is to Use. In *On the Translation of Native American Literatures*, ed. Brian Swann, 83–124. Washington, D.C.: Smithsonian Institution Press.

Jacobsen, Jerome V. 1938. *Educational Foundations of the Jesuits in Sixteenth-Century New Spain*. Berkeley: University of California Press.

Jahn, Johannes. 1972. *1472–1553 Lucas Cranach D. Ä.: Das gesamte graphische Werk*. Munich: Rogner & Bernhard.

James, Montague Rhodes, ed. 1955. *The Apocryphal New Testament*. Oxford: Clarendon Press.

Kan, Sergei. 1991. Shamanism and Christianity: Modern-Day Tlingit Elders Look at the Past. *Ethnohistory* 38:363–87.

Karttunen, Frances. 1982. Nahuatl Literacy. In *The Inca and Aztec States, 1400–*

1800: Anthropology and History, ed. George A. Collier, Renato I. Rosaldo, and John D. Wirth, 395–417. New York: Academic Press.

———. 1983. *An Analytical Dictionary of Nahuatl*. Austin: University of Texas Press.

———. 1985. *Nahuatl and Maya in Contact with Spanish*. Texas Linguistic Forum 26. Austin: Department of Linguistics and Center for Cognitive Studies, University of Texas at Austin.

———. 1995. *Cuicapixqueh:* Antonio Valeriano, Juan Bautista de Pomar, and Nahuatl Poetry. *Latin American Indian Literatures Journal* 11:4–20.

Karttunen, Frances, and James Lockhart. 1976. *Nahuatl in the Middle Years: Language Contact Phenomena in Texts of the Colonial Period*. Berkeley: University of California Press.

———. 1980. La estructura de la poesía náhuatl vista por sus variantes. *Estudios de Cultura Náhuatl* 14:15–64.

———, eds. and trans. 1987. *The Art of Nahuatl Speech: The Bancroft Dialogues*. Nahuatl Studies Series, 2. Los Angeles: UCLA Latin American Center.

Kellogg, Susan. 1984. Aztec Women in Early Colonial Courts: Structure and Strategy in a Legal Context. In *Five Centuries of Law and Politics in Central Mexico*, ed. Ronald Spores and Ross Hassig, 25–38. Vanderbilt University Publications in Anthropology 30. Nashville, Tenn.: Vanderbilt University.

———. 1986. Kinship and Social Organization in Early Colonial Tenochtitlan. In *Supplement to the Handbook of Middle American Indians. Volume IV: Ethnohistory*, ed. Victoria Reifler Bricker and Ronald Spores, 103–21. Austin: University of Texas Press.

———. 1992. Hegemony out of Conquest: The First Two Centuries of Spanish Rule in Central Mexico. *Radical History Review* 53:27–46.

———. 1995. *Law and the Transformation of Aztec Culture, 1500–1700*. Norman: University of Oklahoma Press.

———. In press. From Parallel and Equivalent to Separate but Unequal: Tenochca Mexica Women, 1500–1700. In *Indian Women of Early Mexico: Identity, Ethnicity, and Gender Differentiation*, ed. Susan Schroeder, Stephanie Wood, and Robert Haskett. Norman: University of Oklahoma Press.

Kemp, Alice Bowdoin, ed. 1936. *Three Autos Sacramentales of 1590*. University of Iowa Studies in Spanish Language and Literature 6. Iowa City: University of Iowa.

Klor de Alva, J. Jorge. 1988a. Contar vidas: La autobiografía confesional y la reconstrucción del ser nahua. *Arbor* 131:49–78.

———. 1988b. Sahagún's Misguided Introduction to Ethnography and the Failure of the *Colloquios* Project. In *The Work of Bernardino de Sahagún, Pioneer Ethnographer of Sixteenth-Century Aztec Mexico*, ed. J. Jorge Klor de Alva, H. B. Nicholson, and Eloise Quiñones Keber, 83–92. Albany: Institute for Mesoamerican Studies, State University of New York.

———. 1989. Language, Politics, and Translation: Colonial Discourse and Classic Nahuatl in New Spain. In *The Art of Translation: Voices from the Field*, ed. Rosanna Warren, 143–62. Boston: Northeastern University Press.

———. 1992. El discurso nahua y la apropriación de lo europeo. In *De palabra y obra en el Nuevo Mundo. Vol. 1. Imágenes interétnicas*, ed. Miguel León-Portilla, Manuel Gutiérrez Estévez, Gary H. Gossen, and J. Jorge Klor de Alva, 339–68. Mexico City: Siglo Veintiuno.

———, ed. and trans. 1980. The Aztec-Spanish Dialogues of 1524. *Alcheringa/Ethnopoetics* 4:52–193.

Klor de Alva, J. Jorge, H. B. Nicholson, and Eloise Quiñones Keber, eds. 1988. *The Work of Bernardino de Sahagún, Pioneer Ethnographer of Sixteenth-Century Aztec Mexico*. Albany: Institute for Mesoamerican Studies, State University of New York.

Knappe, Karl-Adolf. 1965. *Dürer: The Complete Engravings, Etchings, and Woodcuts*. Secaucus, N.J.: Wellfleet Press.

Kobayashi, José María. 1974. *La educación como conquista: Empresa franciscana en México*. Mexico City: Colegio de México.

Kubler, George. 1982. *Arquitectura mexicana del siglo XVI*. Roberto de la Torre, Graciela de Garay, and Miguel Ángel de Quevedo, trans. Mexico City: Fondo de Cultura Económica.

Labriola, Albert C., and John W. Smeltz. 1990. *The Bible of the Poor [Biblia Pauperum]: A Facsimile and Edition of the British Library Blockbook C.9 d.2*. Pittsburgh: Duquesne University Press.

Las Casas, fray Bartolomé de. 1967. *Apologética historia sumaria*. 2 vols. Mexico City: Universidad Nacional Autónoma de México.

León, fray Martín de. 1611. *Camino de cielo en lengua mexicana*. Mexico City: Diego López Dávalos.

———. 1614. *Primera Parte del Sermonario del tiempo de todo el año, duplicado, en lengua Mexicana*. Mexico City: Viuda de Diego López Dávalos.

León, Nicolás, trans. and ed. 1982. *Códice Sierra*. Mexico City: Editorial Innovación.

León-Portilla, Miguel. 1969. *Pre-Columbian Literatures of Mexico*. Grace Lobanov and Miguel León-Portilla, trans. Norman: University of Oklahoma Press.

———. 1985. Nahuatl Literature. In *Supplement to the Handbook of Middle American Indians. Volume III: Literatures*, ed. Victoria Reifler Bricker and Munro S. Edmonson, 7–43. Austin: University of Texas Press.

———. 1992. Have We Really Translated the Mesoamerican "Ancient Word"? In *On the Translation of Native American Literatures*, ed. Brian Swann, 313–38. Washington, D.C.: Smithsonian Institution Press.

Leonard, Irving A. 1933. *Romances of Chivalry in the Spanish Indies*. Berkeley: University of California Press.

———. 1949. The Mexican Book Trade, 1576. *Hispanic Review* 17:18–29.

———. 1992. *Books of the Brave: Being an Account of Books and Men in the Spanish Conquest and Settlement of the Sixteenth-Century New World*. Intro. by Rolena Adorno. Berkeley: University of California Press.

Lockhart, James. 1982. Views of Corporate Self and History in Some Valley of Mexico Towns: Late Seventeenth and Eighteenth Centuries. In *The Inca and Aztec States 1400–1800: Anthropology and History*, ed. George A. Collier, Renato Rosaldo, and John D. Wirth, 367–93. New York: Academic Press.

———. 1985. Some Nahua Concepts in Postconquest Guise. *History of European Ideas* 6:465–82.

———. 1991. *Nahuas and Spaniards: Postconquest Central Mexican History and Philology.* UCLA Latin American Studies, vol. 76; Nahuatl Studies Series 3. Stanford, Calif.: Stanford University Press.

———. 1992. *The Nahuas After the Conquest: A Social and Cultural History of the Indians of Central Mexico, Sixteenth through Eighteenth Centuries.* Stanford, Calif.: Stanford University Press.

Lockhart, James, Frances Berdan, and Arthur J. O. Anderson, trans. and eds. 1986. *The Tlaxcalan Actas: A Compendium of the Records of the Cabildo of Tlaxcala (1545–1627).* Salt Lake City: University of Utah Press.

López Austin, Alfredo. 1980. *Cuerpo humano e ideología: Las concepciones de los antiguos nahuas.* 2 vols. Mexico City: Universidad Nacional Autónoma de México.

Lyell, James P. R. 1976. *Early Book Illustration in Spain.* New York: Hacker Art Books.

McAndrew, John. 1965. *The Open-Air Churches of Sixteenth-Century Mexico.* Cambridge, Mass.: Harvard University Press.

McKendrick, Melveena. 1989. *Theatre in Spain 1490–1700.* Cambridge: Cambridge University Press.

Manuale chori secundum usum ordinem Fratrum Minorum. 1586. Salamanca.

Marrow, James H. 1979. *Passion Iconography in Northern European Art of the Middle Ages and Early Renaissance: A Study of the Transformation of Sacred Metaphor into Descriptive Narrative.* Kortrijk, Belgium: Van Ghemmert.

Martí Grajales, Francisco. 1927. *Ensayo de un diccionario biográfico y bibliográfico de los poetas que florecieron en el reino de Valencia hasta el año 1700.* Madrid: Revista de Archivos, Bibliotecas y Museos.

Marx, C. William, and Jeanne F. Drennan, eds. 1987. *The Middle English Prose Complaint of Our Lady and Gospel of Nicodemus.* Heidelberg: C. Winter.

Mathes, W. Michael. 1985. *The America's First Academic Library: Santa Cruz de Tlatelolco.* Sacramento: California State Library Foundation.

Mattina, Anthony. 1987. North American Indian Mythography: Editing Texts for the Printed Page. In *Recovering the Word: Essays on Native American Literature,* ed. Brian Swann and Arnold Krupat, 129–48. Berkeley: University of California Press.

Menchú, Rigoberta. 1987. *Me llamo Rigoberta Menchú y así me nació la conciencia.* Elizabeth Burgos, ed. Mexico City: Siglo Veintiuno.

Méndez Bejarano, Mario. 1922. *Diccionario de escritores, maestros y oradores naturales de Sevilla y su actual provincia.* Volume 1. Seville: Gironés, O'Donnell.

Mendieta, fray Gerónimo de. 1980. *Historia eclesiástica indiana.* Joaquín García Icazbalceta, ed. Mexico City: Editorial Porrúa.

Mexico: Splendors of Thirty Centuries. 1990. New York: Metropolitan Museum of Art.

Mijangos, fray Juan de. 1607. *Espejo Divino en lengua mexicana, en que pueden verse los padres, y tomar documento para acertar a doctrinar bien a sus hijos, y aficionallos alas virtudes.* Mexico City: Diego López Dávalos.

———. 1624. *Primera parte del Sermonario Dominical, y Sanctoral, en lengua mexicana.* Mexico City: Juan de Alcaçar.

Miscelánea sagrada. n.d. MS 1477, Fondo Reservado, Biblioteca Nacional de México.

Missale romanum ordinarium. 1561. Mexico City: Antonio de Espinosa.

Mitchell, Timothy. 1990. *Passional Culture: Emotion, Religion, and Society in Southern Spain.* Philadelphia: University of Pennsylvania Press.

Molina, fray Alonso de. 1565. *Confessionario breue, en lengua Mexicana y Castellana.* Mexico City: Antonio de Espinosa.

———. 1569. *Confessionario mayor, en la lengua Mexicana y Castellana.* Mexico City: Antonio de Espinosa.

———. 1970. *Vocabulario en lengua castellana y mexicana y mexicana y castellana.* Facsimile of 1571 edition. Miguel León-Portilla, ed. Mexico City: Editorial Porrúa.

Montoya Briones, José de Jesús. 1960. *Atla: Etnografía de un pueblo náhuatl.* Mexico City: Instituto Nacional de Antropología e Historia.

Morel, P. Gall. 1866. *Lateinische Hymnen des Mittelalters, Grösstentheils aus Handschriften Schweizerischer Klöster.* Einsiedeln: Gebr. Carl und Nicolaus Benziger.

Moreno, Roberto. 1966. Guía de las obras en lenguas indígenas existentes en la Biblioteca Nacional. *Boletín de la Biblioteca Nacional* 17:21–210.

Motolinia, fray Toribio (de Benavente). 1971. *Memoriales o libro de las cosas de la Nueva España.* Edmundo O'Gorman, ed. Mexico City: Universidad Nacional Autónoma de México.

———. 1979. *Historia de los indios de la Nueva España.* Edmundo O'Gorman, ed. Mexico City: Editorial Porrúa.

Muther, Richard. 1972. *German Book Illustration of the Gothic Period and the Early Renaissance (1460-1530).* Ralph R. Shaw, trans. Metuchen, N.J.: Scarecrow Press.

Nash, June. 1968. The Passion Play in Maya Indian Communities. *Comparative Studies in Society and History* 10:318–27.

Navarro B., Bernabé. 1944. La iglesia y los indios en el III[er.] Concilio Mexicano (1585). *Ábside* 8:391–447.

Nebrija, Elio Antonio de. 1549. *Hymnorvm recognitio per Antonivm Nebrissen, cvm avrea illorvm expositione.* Granada.

Nicolau D'Olwer, Luis. 1987. *Fray Bernardino de Sahagún, 1499-1590.* Mauricio J. Mixco, trans. Salt Lake City: University of Utah Press.

Ocaranza, Fernando. 1934. *El Imperial Colegio de Indios de la Santa Cruz de Santiago Tlaltelolco.* Mexico City: published by the author.

Offner, Jerome A. 1983. *Law and Politics in Aztec Texcoco.* Cambridge: Cambridge University Press.

Olmos, fray Andrés de. 1875. *Arte para aprender la lengua mexicana.* Rémi Siméon, ed. Paris: Imprimerie Nationale.

Ortiz de Montellano, Bernard R. 1990. *Aztec Medicine, Health, and Nutrition.* New Brunswick, N.J.: Rutgers University Press.

Osorio Romero, Ignacio. 1990. *La enseñanza del latín a los indios.* Mexico City: Universidad Nacional Autónoma de México.

Palluchini, Rodolfo, and Giordana Mariani Canova. 1973. *L'opera completa del Lotto.* Milan: Rizzoli.

Pasión en lengua mexicana. n.d. MS, Latin American Library, Tulane University, New Orleans.

Paso y Troncoso, Francisco del, ed. 1902. *Comedia de los Reyes escrita en mexicains á principios del siglo XVII (por Agustín de la Fuente).* Florence: Salvador Landi.

———. 1940. *Epistolario de Nueva España, 1505–1818.* Volume 12. Mexico City: Robredo.

Pazos, Manuel R. 1951. El teatro franciscano en Méjico, durante el siglo XVI. *Archivo Ibero-Americano* 2ª época, 11:129–89.

Peck, George T. 1980. *The Fool of God: Jacopone da Todi.* University: University of Alabama Press.

Pérez, Miguel. 1549. *La vida y excellencias & milagros de la sacratissima virgen Maria nuestra señora.* Toledo: Juan de Ayala.

Pérez de Ribas, Andrés, S.J. 1645. *Historia de los trivmphos de nvestra santa fee entre gentes las mas barbaras, y fieras del nuevo orbe: Conseguidos por los soldados de la milicia de la Compañia de Iesvs en las missiones de la provincia de Nueva España.* Madrid: Alonso de Paredes.

Pérez Gómez, Antonio. 1976–77. El auto llamado «Lucero de nuestra salvación.» In *Homenaje al Prof. Muñoz Cortés,* 491–506. Murcia, Spain: Universidad de Murcia.

Phelan, John Leddy. 1970. *The Millennial Kingdom of the Franciscans in the New World.* Berkeley: University of California Press.

Pignati, Terisio. 1976. *Veronese.* 2 volumes. Venice: Alfieri.

Poole, Stafford, C.M. 1981. Church Law on the Ordination of Indians and *Castas* in New Spain. *Hispanic American Historical Review* 61:637–50.

———. 1987. *Pedro Moya de Contreras: Catholic Reform and Royal Power in New Spain, 1571–1591.* Berkeley: University of California Press.

———. 1989. The Declining Image of the Indian among Churchmen in Sixteenth-Century New Spain. In *Indian-Religious Relations in Colonial Spanish America,* ed. Susan E. Ramírez. Syracuse, N.Y.: Syracuse University.

———. 1995. *Our Lady of Guadalupe: The Origins and Sources of a Mexican National Symbol, 1531–1797.* Tucson: University of Arizona Press.

Psalterivm, An[t]iphonarium Sanctorale, cũ Psalmis, & Hymnis. 1584. Mexico City: Pedro Ocharte.

Quiñones Keber, Eloise, ed. 1995. *Codex Telleriano-Remensis: Ritual, Divination, and History in a Pictorial Aztec Manuscript.* Austin: University of Texas Press.

Rabasa, José. 1993. Writing and Evangelization in Sixteenth-Century Mexico. In *Early Images of the Americas: Transfer and Invention,* ed. Jerry M. Williams and Robert E. Lewis, 65–92. Tucson: University of Arizona Press.

Rafael, Vicente L. 1988. *Contracting Colonialism: Translation and Christian Conversion in Tagalog Society under Early Spanish Rule.* Ithaca, N.Y.: Cornell University Press.

Ragusa, Isa, and Rosalie B. Green, trans. and eds. 1961. *Meditations on the Life of Christ: An Illustrated Manuscript of the Fourteenth Century.* Princeton, N.J.: Princeton University Press.

Ramírez, Fernando, ed. 1949. *Anales Mexicanos: Uno Pedernal—Diez Caña 1605.* Faustino Chimalpopoca, trans. Mexico City: Vargas Rea.

————. 1954. *Anales Mexicanos 1589–1596.* Faustino Chimalpopoca, trans. Mexico City: Vargas Rea.

Rand, Edward Kennard. 1904. Sermo de Confusione Diaboli. *Modern Philology* 2:261–78.

Ravicz, Marilyn Ekdahl. 1970. *Early Colonial Religious Drama in Mexico: From Tzompantli to Golgotha.* Washington, D.C.: Catholic University of America Press.

Rennert, Hugo Albert. 1963. *The Spanish Stage in the Time of Lope de Vega.* New York: Dover.

Las representaciones teatrales de la Pasión. 1934. *Boletín del Archivo General de la Nación* 5:332–56.

Reyes García, Luis. 1960. *Pasión y muerte del Cristo Sol (Carnaval y cuaresma en Ichcatepec).* Xalapa, Mexico: Universidad Veracruzana.

————. 1971. Un nuevo manuscrito de Chimalpahin. *Anales del Instituto Nacional de Antropología e Historia* 7ª época, 2:333–48.

Reyes-Valerio, Constantino. 1978. *Arte indocristiano: Escultura del siglo XVI en México.* Mexico City: Instituto Nacional de Antropología e Historia.

Ricard, Robert. 1966. *The Spiritual Conquest of Mexico.* Lesley Byrd Simpson, trans. Berkeley: University of California Press.

Rivadeneira, Pedro de. 1835. *The Life and Death of the Most Glorious Virgin Mary Mother of our Lord Jesus Christ.* Montreal: T. Maguire.

Rodríguez-Buckingham, Antonio. 1993. English Motifs in Mexican Books: A Case of Sixteenth-Century Information Transfer. In *Early Images of the Americas: Transfer and Invention*, ed. Jerry M. Williams and Robert E. Lewis, 287–304. Tucson: University of Arizona Press.

Rojas Garcidueñas, José J. 1935. *El teatro de nueva españa en el siglo XVI.* Mexico: Luis Álvarez.

Rouanet, Léo, ed. 1979. *Colección de autos, farsas, y coloquios del siglo XVI.* 4 volumes. Hildesheim and New York: Georg Olms.

Sahagún, fray Bernardino de. 1563. *Sermones de dominicas y de sanctos en lengua mexicana.* Ayer MS 1485, Newberry Library, Chicago.

————. 1574. *Exercicio en lengua mexicana sacado del sancto Evanº y distribuido por todos los dias de la semana.* Ayer MS 1484, Newberry Library, Chicago.

————. 1579. *Apendiz desta Postilla.* Ayer MS 1486c and 1486d, Newberry Library, Chicago.

————. 1583. *Psalmodia christiana y sermonario de los sanctos del año en lengua mexicana.* Mexico City: Pedro Ocharte.

————. 1588. *Sermones en mexicano.* MS 1482, Fondo Reservado, Biblioteca Nacional de México.

————. 1950–82. *Florentine Codex, General History of the Things of New Spain.* Arthur J. O. Anderson and Charles E. Dibble, eds. and trans. 12 vols. Santa Fe, N.M.: School of American Research and University of Utah.

————. 1979. *Códice florentino.* Facsimile edition issued by the Biblioteca Medicea Laurenziana and the Archivo General de la Nación. 3 vols. Mexico City: Secretaría de Gobernación.

———. 1986. *Coloquios y doctrina cristiana*. Miguel León-Portilla, trans. and ed. Mexico City: Universidad Nacional Autónoma de México.

———. 1993. *Psalmodia christiana*. Arthur J. O. Anderson, trans. Salt Lake City: University of Utah Press.

Sancha, Justo de, ed. 1872. *Romancero y cancionero sagrados. Colección de poesías cristianas, morales y divinas*. Biblioteca de Autores Españoles 35. Madrid: M. Rivadeneyra.

Sánchez-Arjona, José. 1898. *Noticias referentes á los anales del teatro en Sevilla desde Lope de Rueda hasta fines del siglo XVII*. Seville: E. Rasco.

Santamaría, Francisco J. 1959. *Diccionario de Mejicanismos*. Mexico City: Editorial Porrúa.

Santoral en mexicano. n.d. MS 1476, Fondo Reservado, Biblioteca Nacional de México.

Scarpa, Roque Esteban, ed. 1938. *Poesía religiosa española*. Santiago de Chile: Ediciones Ercilla.

Schechner, Richard. 1985. *Between Theater and Anthropology*. Foreword by Victor Turner. Philadelphia: University of Pennsylvania Press.

Schroeder, Susan. 1991. *Chimalpahin and the Kingdoms of Chalco*. Tucson: University of Arizona Press.

Scott, James C. 1990. *Domination and the Arts of Resistance: Hidden Transcripts*. New Haven, Conn.: Yale University Press.

Sell, Barry D. 1991. "Goliath Was a Very Big Chichimec": Church Texts in Colonial Nahuatl. *UCLA Historical Journal* 2:131–46.

Sempat-Assadourian, Carlos. 1988. Memoriales de fray Gerónimo de Mendieta. *Historia Mexicana* 37:357–422.

Sermones en mexicano. n.d. MS 1487, Fondo Reservado, Biblioteca Nacional de México.

Sermones y ejemplos en mexicano. n.d. MS 1480, Fondo Reservado, Biblioteca Nacional de México.

Shergold, N. D. 1967. *A History of the Spanish Stage from Medieval Times until the end of the Seventeenth Century*. Oxford: Clarendon Press.

Steck, Francis Borgia. 1944. *El primer colegio de América—Santa Cruz de Tlaltelolco. Con un estudio del códice de Tlaltelolco por R. H. Barlow*. Mexico City: Centro de Estudios Franciscanos.

Sten, María. 1982. *Vida y muerte del teatro náhuatl*. Xalapa, Mexico: Biblioteca Universidad Veracruzana.

Stuart, Donald Clive. 1913. The Stage Setting of Hell and the Iconography of the Middle Ages. *Romanic Review* 4:330–42.

Sullivan, Thelma. 1965. A Prayer to Tlaloc. *Estudios de Cultura Náhuatl* 5:39–55.

———. 1966. Pregnancy, Childbirth, and the Deification of the Women Who Died in Childbirth. *Estudios de Cultura Náhuatl* 6:63–95.

———. 1974. The Rhetorical Orations, or *Huehuetlatolli*, Collected by Sahagún. In *Sixteenth-Century Mexico: The Work of Sahagún*, ed. Munro S. Edmonson, 79–109. Albuquerque: University of New Mexico Press.

―――. 1980. "O Precious Necklace, O Quetzal Feather!" Aztec Pregnancy and Childbirth Orations. *Alcheringa/Ethnopoetics* 4:38–52.

―――. 1986 A Scattering of Jades: The Words of Aztec Elders. In *Symbol and Meaning Beyond the Closed Community: Essays in Mesoamerican Ideas*, ed. Gary H. Gossen, 9–17. Albany: Institute for Mesoamerican Studies, State University of New York.

Tedlock, Barbara. 1982. *Time and the Highland Maya*. Albuquerque: University of New Mexico Press.

Tedlock, Dennis. 1983. *The Spoken Word and the Work of Interpretation*. Philadelphia: University of Pennsylvania Press.

―――, trans. and ed. 1985. *Popol Vuh*. New York: Simon & Schuster.

Torquemada, fray Juan de. 1975–83. *Monarquía indiana*. Mexico City: Universidad Nacional Autónoma de México.

Trexler, Richard C. 1987. *Church and Community 1200–1600: Studies in the History of Florence and New Spain*. Raccolta di Studi e Testi 168. Rome: Storia e Letteratura.

Tyre, Carl Allen, ed. 1938. *Religious Plays of 1590*. University of Iowa Studies in Spanish Language and Literature, 8. Iowa City: University of Iowa.

Valadés, fray Diego. 1989. *Retórica cristiana*. Facsimile of 1579 edition, with introduction by Esteban J. Palomera and Spanish translation by Tarsicio Herrera Zapién et al. Mexico City: Fondo de Cultura Económica.

Valdivielso, José de. 1984. *Romancero espiritual*. J. M. Aguirre, ed. Madrid: Espasa-Calpe.

Vargas, fray Melchior. 1576. *Doctrina christiana, muy vtil, y necessaria en Castellano, Mexicano y Otomi*. Mexico City: Pedro Balli.

Velázquez, Primo Feliciano, trans. and ed. 1975. *Códice Chimalpopoca: Anales de Cuauhtitlan y leyenda de los soles*. Mexico City: Universidad Nacional Autónoma de México.

Vera, Fortino Hipólito, ed. 1879. *Compendio histórico del Concilio III Mexicano*. Amecameca, Mexico: Colegio Católico.

Verdier, P. 1974. Descent of Christ into Hell. *New Catholic Encyclopedia* 14:788–93. New York: McGraw-Hill.

Vetancurt, fray Agustín de. 1971. *Teatro mexicano, Crónica de la provincia del Santo Evangelio de México, Menologio franciscano*. Mexico City: Editorial Porrúa.

Victoria Moreno, Dionisio. 1983. *Los Carmelitas Descalzos y la conquista espiritual de México, 1585–1612*. Mexico City: Editorial Porrúa.

Villegas, Alonso. 1760. *Flos sanctorum, y historia general, en que se escrive la vida de la virgen sacratissima madre de Dios, y señora nuestra*. Barcelona: Don Juan de Bezares.

Voragine, Jacobus de. 1900. *The Golden Legend or Lives of the Saints as Englished by William Caxton*. 7 vols. London: J. M. Dent & Sons.

Wagner, Henry R., ed. 1935. *Cartilla para enseñar a leer*. Facsimile of 1569 imprint. San Marino, Calif.: Henry E. Huntington Library.

Wardropper, Bruce W., ed. 1954. *Cancionero espiritual (Valladolid, 1549)*. Valencia: Editorial Castalia.

Warner, Marina. 1976. *Alone of All Her Sex: The Myth and the Cult of the Virgin Mary*. New York: Vintage Books.

Watts, Pauline Moffitt. 1991. Hieroglyphs of Conversion: Alien Discourses in Diego Valadés's *Rhetorica Christiana*. *Memorie Domenicane*, new series no. 22:405–33.

Weckmann, Luis. 1984. *La herencia medieval de México*. 2 vols. Mexico City: Colegio de México.

White, Richard. 1991. *The Middle Ground: Indians, Empires, and Republics in the Great Lakes Region, 1650–1815*. Cambridge: Cambridge University Press.

Williams, Jerry M. 1990. El arte dramático y la iconografía en la trayectoria misionera del siglo xvi. *La palabra y el Hombre* 76:94–124.

Williams, Ronald Boal. 1935. *The Staging of Plays in the Spanish Peninsula Prior to 1555*. University of Iowa Studies in Spanish Language and Literature 5. Iowa City: University of Iowa.

Wilson, Adrian, and Joyce Lancaster Wilson. 1984. *A Medieval Mirror: Speculum humanae salvationis, 1324–1500*. Berkeley: University of California Press.

Wood, Stephanie. 1991. The Cosmic Conquest: Late-Colonial Views of the Sword and Cross in Central Mexican *Títulos*. *Ethnohistory* 38:176–95.

Ximeno, Vicente. 1747. *Escritores del reyno de Valencia, chronologicamente ordenados desde el año MCCXXXVIII de la christiana conquista de la misma ciudad, hasta el de MDCCXLVII*. Volume 1. Valencia: Joseph Estevan Dolz.

Young, Karl. 1909. *The Harrowing of Hell in Liturgical Drama*. Transactions of the Wisconsin Academy of Sciences, Arts, and Letters XVI, part 2. Madison: Wisconsin Academy of Sciences.

Zeitlin, Judith Francis, and Lillian Thomas. 1992. Spanish Justice and the Indian Cacique: Disjunctive Political Systems in Sixteenth-Century Tehuantepec. *Ethnohistory* 39:285–315.

Zulaica y Gárate, Román. 1991. *Los franciscanos y la imprenta en México en el siglo XVI*. Mexico City: Universidad Nacional Autónoma de México.

Index

ORDER FORM

Holy Wednesday
Nahuatl and Spanish Texts

An electronic edition of the Nahuatl-language original of *Holy Wednesday* and of its Spanish model, Ausías Izquierdo Zebrero of Valencia's *Lucero de Nuestra Salvación,* is available as a supplement to the print edition. The texts are available on a 3.5" disk in Adobe Acrobat format, for both IBM and Macintosh platforms.

System requirements for the Adobe Acrobat Reader:

Windows:
- 386 or 486-based personal
  computer (486 recommended)
- Microsoft Windows 3.1 or greater
- 4 MB system RAM
- 2 MB hard disk space

Macintosh:
- 68020- or greater
- MAC O/S 7.0 or greater
- 2 MB application RAM
- 1.5 MB hard disk space

3.5" Mac computer disk, ISBN 0-8122-3367-0, $12.95
3.5" IBM computer disk, ISBN 0-8122-3368-9, $12.95

....

To order duplicate or mail this form to:
University of Pennsylvania Press
P.O. Box 4836
Hampden Station, Baltimore, MD 21211
1-800-445-9880
Check or money order payable in U.S. dollars

		ISBN	Price
Payment enclosed	___ IBM Disk	3368-9	$12.95
Charge my	___ MAC Disk	3367-0	$12.95
___Mastercard	___ Shipping (U.S.)		$ 3.00
___VISA	___ Shipping (outside U.S.)		$ 5.00

Card Number ———————————— Exp. Date ————————

Name (*Please print*)

Address

City   State/Country   Postal Code

Printed in the United States
122315LV00007B/40/A

9 780812 215762